SUBTERFUGE AND SABOTAGE DURING HITLER'S BLITZKRIEG

SUBTERFUGE AND SABOTAGE DURING HITLER'S BLITZKRIEG

Secret British Operations during the German Advance in Holland and Belgium, 1939-40

CLIVE HOLDEN

FRONTLINE
BOOKS

First published in Great Britain in 2026
by Frontline Books
An imprint of
Pen & Sword Books Ltd
Yorkshire - Philadelphia

ISBN 978 1 0361 9 456 7

A CIP catalogue record for this book is available from the British Library

Typeset by Lapiz Digital
Printed and bound in the UK by CPI Group (UK) Ltd,
Croydon, CR0 4YY.

Printed on paper from a sustainable source by
CPI Group (UK) Ltd, Croydon, CR0 4YY

The Publisher's authorised representative in the EU for product safety is Authorised Rep Compliance Ltd., Ground Floor, 71 Lower Baggot Street, Dublin D02 P593, Ireland.
www.arccompliance.com

For a complete list of Pen & Sword titles please contact
PEN & SWORD BOOKS LTD
47 Church Street, Barnsley, South Yorkshire, S70 2AS, England
E-mail: enquiries@pen-and-sword.co.uk
Website: www.pen-and-sword.co.uk
or
PEN & SWORD BOOKS
1950 Lawrence Rd, Havertown, PA 19083, USA
E-mail: uspen-and-sword@casematepublishers.com

TABLE OF CONTENTS

NOTES ON THE TEXT

For some foreign place names, I have used the 'anglicised' versions more commonly used both in official documents and in general at the time, e.g. 'Ymuiden' instead of 'IJmuiden' and 'Flushing' instead of 'Vlissingen'.

For some of the main characters I have included extended biographical details in the main text and for some of the minor, particularly non-British, characters, I have added a very brief 'potted' biography as a footnote on the first page they are mentioned. However, I have not found it possible to include biographical details for every individual mentioned, so the reader must please excuse me for this obvious inconsistency.

I have attempted to be consistent in the way I have referred to military and naval ranks. For first mentions I have used the full rank and with subsequent mentions I have used the generally accepted abbreviated forms. When a character is mentioned multiple times in a chapter, I may omit their rank and use their full name or surname instead. Again, the reader must please excuse another inconsistency.

When quoting from original documents, I have not corrected any spellings, grammar or punctuation and left the text as it was originally written.

Unless quoting from original documents, when abbreviating the unit name of Kent (Fortress) Royal Engineers, I have used 'KFRE', omitting the brackets for the sake of clarity.

INTRODUCTION

It is one of the joys, but also perils, of researching a project that when reading through a file of documents, you come across something totally unexpected and certainly unconnected to the research you are undertaking, but to which your interest is immediately drawn. In such cases it is essential to discipline yourself to avoid such discoveries distracting you from your primary research. This is a situation I found myself facing back in January 2018, when I was at The National Archives in Kew researching a project on the defences of Maidstone in the Second World War – my first major research project since my retirement two years earlier.

During the Second World War, Maidstone was transformed into an officially designated 'Fortress', which involved extensive civil engineering works constructing anti-tank ditches and obstacles, pillboxes, and roadblocks. Much of this work we knew had been carried out either by or under the supervision of the Royal Engineers, but not which specific units were involved. While looking for some clues in the online National Archives catalogue, I found a reference for a War Diary for a unit named 'Kent (Fortress) Royal Engineers', which seemed to me to be a possible candidate for the construction of the Maidstone defences. I made an appointment to visit The National Archives' reading room at Kew and placed a request for the War Diary file, along with some others, for viewing. My normal routine at Kew is to browse through each file and photograph every document enclosed as I go along and then read through them more carefully at home.

While browsing through the Kent (Fortress) Royal Engineers War Diary file, I was disappointed not to come across anything related to Maidstone. However, I continued to photograph every page hoping to find something later. I then came across several handwritten pages in the file. I began to read through these and was fascinated to discover it was an account of an operation to destroy stocks of oil in Rotterdam in May 1940. My time at Kew was limited and I still had many files to go through, so I finished photographing the War Diary documents and then moved on to other files.

When I got home I had over 800 pages to read through from all the files I had seen that day, and my priority was finding information about the Maidstone defences. I had a more careful look through the Kent (Fortress) Royal Engineers War Diary but could still find nothing Maidstone-related. I had ignored reading any more of the handwritten Rotterdam operation account, but I did find accounts of other similar operations that had taken place during the same period. However, with time against me, I opened a folder for the War Diary on my computer and stored everything there, ready to review at some later date.

I completed the Maidstone project in January 2021, and it was published on the Kent Archaeological Society's website under the title 'Fortress Maidstone' a couple of months later, by which time I was already involved in writing another local military history book for which the publisher's deadline was fast approaching. When my work on that was completed, I found myself, for the first time in years, without a history project. It was then that my thoughts turned back to the Kent (Fortress) Royal Engineers and those fascinating operational accounts I had the chance to briefly read through three years previously.

I opened the War Diary folder on my computer and began to study those accounts again, and my fascination with them grew. I had already seen from the War Diary that in the early months of the war, the Kent (Fortress) Royal Engineers (or the KFRE, as I will refer to them from now on) were engaged on manning searchlight batteries along both sides of the Thames Estuary, and on mundane maintenance tasks at various local army barracks. Then in May 1940, we find some of them suddenly being transported across the North Sea to ports in Holland and Belgium, carrying out dramatic operations to deny both, hitherto neutral, country's oil stocks to the invading Germans. I had never previously heard of or read anything about the KFRE or these 'XD' operations (as they were officially designated), and I was determined to find out more. What I discovered convinced me that there was a story there worth telling.

From searching online, I discovered that the KFRE were a part-time volunteer Royal Engineer (RE) unit of the Territorial Army, formed in 1932 from employees at a cement works based alongside the Thames at Northfleet, Kent. When war was declared in 1939, these cement workers suddenly found themselves as full-time soldiers, and within nine months some of them would be in a foreign country facing the enemy at first hand. By now I was certain that there was a fascinating story that needed to be told about these men, and so the seeds of another book had been planted in my mind.

To my initial disappointment, I then discovered that a book had already been written about the KFRE's XD operations, by the unit's commanding officer, and published as recently as 2003.* I bought a copy of the book and read it carefully. Although it provided excellent accounts of the XD operations, it was based mostly on the personal recollections of the KFRE personnel involved and lacked much in the way of official background to the operations themselves.

Numerous searches in The National Archives' online catalogue, using various terms, eventually allowed me to build up a list of files for further research. One of the most important of these was the Cabinet papers of Lord Hankey, who was Minister Without Portfolio in Neville Chamberlain's War Cabinet. He was the minister who, from the early days of the war, had been charged with planning the denial to the enemy of certain economic, industrial and military assets of the, then neutral, Netherlands and Belgium in the event of those countries being invaded by Germany. Amongst Hankey's papers was a file containing over 280 pages of documents relating to these plans. Reading through these documents, it became obvious that the XD operations were just a small part of a much more extensive contingency plan, which ranged beyond the destruction of oil and fuel stocks to include the demolition of port infrastructure and installations, the removal of all shipping from those ports, the securing of gold stocks, and keeping many other assets out of the hands of the Germans.

Also, from reading some of the Chiefs of Staff Committee minutes, it became clear that the KFRE were not the first-choice unit to carry out the XD operations. During the preceding months, two different RE units had, in turn, been detailed to make contingency plans for these missions. It was not until the first unit was deployed to Norway in February 1940, and the second unit joined their division in France a few weeks later, that the KFRE were called on to prepare for these operations.

My research also focussed on the role of the Royal Navy (RN) in the XD operations. It soon became evident that XD was a predominantly naval project, planned by an Admiralty committee chaired by a senior admiral, and that the tasks carried out by the RN demolition teams were of as equal importance and interest as the RE operations, and that the story would not be complete without their inclusion.

The more files I looked at, the more I discovered and the more I understood that the XD operations at the Dutch and Belgian ports were not carried out in complete isolation, but were interwoven with other events happening at the time: the evacuation of civilians, royal families and diplomats, the removal of gold stocks, the arrival of a

* Brazier, C.C.H. & P.H. (Ed), *XD Operations*, (Pen & Sword Books, 2003).

Military Mission together with military and naval reinforcements etc. All of these events and more were part of the story, and I needed to include them in my narrative.

The plans and preparations for the XD operations also needed to be understood in the wider context of the period that became known as 'The Phoney War', those months leading up to the opening of the German offensive on the Western Front, when Belgium and the Netherlands were both defiantly neutral and refusing to cooperate with the Allies. The three covert missions to the ports undertaken by RN captains in October 1939 to reconnoitre some of the XD operations' objectives provided essential intelligence that made a huge contribution to their eventual success.

There were also the unofficial and very sensitive negotiations being conducted during that period with certain Belgian and Dutch officials to ensure the security of both countries' bullion stocks and other financial assets, and to convince their governments to prepare themselves to repel a German invasion that the Allies now deemed inevitable.

My research also involved visits to the Imperial War Museum in London and the Royal Engineers Library and Museum at Brompton Barracks in Gillingham, whose archives contained important documents and photographs not included in the files at Kew. My thanks go to the research room staff at both institutions for their help in making those documents and photographs available for me to view. My thanks, too, to the Netherlands Institute of Military History for permission to use some of the photographs from their excellent and extensive collection. My thanks must also go to Sandra Soder, of the Gravesend Historical Society, for allowing me access to their KFRE archive, which yielded up some fascinating personal narratives and photographs. Finally, I would also like to thank Dilip Sakar for introducing me to Pen & Sword Books, who have made such an excellent job of publishing this book.

It has been eight years since I came across the document that first provided the inspiration for this book. It has certainly been a journey of discovery, and one that has left me full of admiration for all those brave men who took part in these operations, and also a great sadness that Britain will probably never see a generation like theirs again.

Clive Holden
East Malling, Kent

September 2026

Chapter 1

CEMENT SAPPERS

Northfleet is a small town in North Kent. It lays alongside the River Thames to the west of Gravesend. Today it is regarded as a 'commuter town', overshadowed and almost absorbed by its larger neighbour, but in 1939 it was a hive of industrial activity, centred primarily on the cement industry.

This area of Kent was rich in deposits of chalk and alluvial clay, both essential elements of cement production and when, in 1796, James Parker set up kilns on Northfleet Creek to make his Roman cement, it was the beginning of a large complex of cement works along this stretch of the river. The manufacture of Portland cement began in Northfleet in April 1846 when William, son of Joseph Aspdin, its inventor, acquired Parker's works and built new kilns. By 1900, there were nine cement works operating on the Thames between Swanscombe and Gravesend.[1] The largest of these was the Knight, Bevan and Sturge Works at Northfleet, which had been established in 1853 by local landowner Thomas Sturge and chemist John Knight. They were joined in the venture by Thomas Bevan, who had gained experience in languages and exporting while working in the tea industry. Sturge died in 1866, and Knight left ten years later leaving Bevan in sole control. He brought his three sons into the business, and the works became known simply as Bevan's Works. In 1900 Thomas Bevan sold the Northfleet cement business to APCM (Blue Circle Cement), and he and his sons all retired to continue living in comfort from the proceeds of the sale. Despite the change of ownership, the works continued to be known as Bevan's.[2]

During the First World War, many Bevan employees served in the forces, with thirty of them losing their lives. Following the end of the war, the company erected a magnificent memorial to commemorate those thirty employees who had given their lives for their country.

Designed by the sculptor Francis William Doyle-Jones, the memorial features a seated Britannia designed in the Art Deco style, in robes and armour with a crested helmet, her cloak draped over the back of her throne, which stands on a cubed plinth featuring a bronze plaque with the thirty names inscribed upon it.[3]

In the 1920s APCM demolished much of the Northfleet site and rebuilt it, replacing the old kilns with larger models of the latest designs. For two years Bevan's was the largest cement works in the UK until it was overtaken by the nearby Johnson's Works at Greenhithe in 1929.[4]

In the 1930s the general manager of Bevan's was Claude Clifford Brazier. Born in Sussex in 1889, Brazier had trained as an engineer at Manchester University and then with the heavy electro-engineering company, Metropolitan Vickers. In 1910 he went out to work in India.[5] In September 1916 he joined the Indian Army Reserve of Officers (IARO) as an infantry second lieutenant attached to the 3rd Sappers and Miners Regiment of the Indian Army.[6,7] The IARO was mainly made up from men who lived and worked in India and who often had some military background, however the latter was not compulsory. Although not career soldiers, Indian Army Reserve Officers often received high praise from the units that received them and did much valuable work in whichever theatre they found themselves. From a base of just forty-seven officers in 1914, by 1916 the IARO had grown to over 2,600 and, by the end of the war, the numbers stood at over 4,500, with at least 325 known to have lost their lives.[8,9]

Brazier served in Mesopotamia, where British and Indian forces were fighting the Ottoman Turks. In September 1917 he was promoted to the rank of lieutenant.[10] On 7 August 1918, acknowledging his engineering background, he was made Assistant Inspector of Machinery on the HQ staff of the Indian Army's Southern Command at Poona, with the rank of temporary major.[11] He left the army in 1922[12] and following his return to civilian life, he went to work for Blue Circle Cement in South Africa before returning to England to take up a position at their Northfleet works.[13]

In the early 1930s Britain was amid the 'Great Depression' and the War Office was under extreme pressure from the Treasury to make cuts in its budget. The decision was taken to replace the regular army artillery and engineer units manning the country's coastal defences with locally recruited part-time territorials.[14] To encourage recruitment into the Territorial Army, the support of employers was sought. Businesses, local authorities and other public bodies were encouraged to grant employees time off to attend annual training camps, and not to withhold pay from those that did so. Larger employers were encouraged to forge strong links with local units.[15] In 1932, the War Office approached the managing director of the Blue Circle Cement Company, A.C. Davies,* to sponsor a company of Territorial Royal Engineers formed from about 150 employees at their Northfleet works. The works' manager, Clifford Brazier was asked to raise and command the unit which was named Kent (Fortress) Royal Engineers (KFRE),† with A.C. Davies as its honorary colonel.

Brazier managed to raise the unit to full strength within forty-eight hours (a record that still stands to this day),[16] and was gazetted as major in the KFRE on 1 November 1932.[17] In 1938 he was awarded the MBE (Military Division) in recognition of his work in forming the unit,[18] and on 3 January 1939 was gazetted as a brevet lieutenant colonel.[19]

The KFRE was based at Grove House in Grove Road, Northfleet. The house had been built in the early 1800s by Henry Wyatt, a partner in Wyatt & Parker's Cement Works. In the 1930s it came into the ownership of the Kent Territorial Association. The main building was used as offices and stores, with a flat for a caretaker on its upper floors. In 1934 a drill hall was built in the house's extensive grounds, which also contained a grass parade ground and a small-calibre rifle range.[20] The new headquarters was opened by Chief of the Imperial General Staff Archibald Montgomery-Massingberd in November 1934.

Recalling the early days of the KFRE, one of its officers, Captain Bernard Buxton, later wrote: 'Brazier had created an efficient unit, which always enjoyed 99 per cent attendance at all its annual camps, and which also had a good measure of training in Field Works in addition to its Fortress duties. It had a Regimental Band of many instruments and quite good performance.'[21]

In the event of war, the KFRE were designated to man coastal defence searchlights. They trained with the gunners manning the various artillery batteries along the Thames and its estuary. During the 'Munich Crisis' of September 1938, the unit was embodied and dispersed around its various war stations. Although the period of embodiment only lasted a month, it proved a worthwhile rehearsal for the tumultuous events that were to follow just a year later.[22]

---

* Arthur Charles Davies (1878-1950) went on to become Sir Charles Davies, 1st Baronet and Lord Mayor of London 1945-46.

† The history of the Kent Fortress RE dates from 1908 when the Territorial Force was first created. The 1st Sussex Royal Engineers (Volunteers) were split up to provide the Kent and Sussex Fortress Engineers, as well as the field companies of the Home Counties Division. The Kent Fortress Royal Engineers was formed on the basis of K Company of the 1st Sussex based at Tonbridge. The original KFRE saw active service throughout the First World War but was disbanded soon after the end of hostilities.

Chapter 2

TO WAR STATIONS

On 3 September 1939 Prime Minister Neville Chamberlain announced that Britain was now at war with Germany. By 9 September, the first two divisions of the British Expeditionary Force (BEF) had arrived in France, establishing themselves in their pre-arranged positions along the Belgian frontier. By 11 October the Secretary of State for War was able to report that over 158,000 men of the BEF had been transported across the Channel to France without a single casualty being sustained.

The following few months, excepting some confrontations at sea, was a period of relative inactivity and is often described as 'The Phoney War'. The BEF continued to receive reinforcements and dig itself in along its sector of the Belgian border. It also contributed a division to serve alongside its French allies manning the fortifications of the Maginot Line facing Germany. It was accepted that if the Germans were to open a 'Western Front', they would do so by coming through the Low Countries, much as they had done in 1914, but this time also breaching Dutch neutrality to gain use of the port of Rotterdam. In such an event the Allied plan was to advance immediately into Belgium to confront the enemy offensive 'head-on', relying on the Maginot defences to hold off any German attacks from that direction.

Meanwhile, back in England, the KFRE had been preparing for war since August. Their War Diary opens on 22 August, reporting from their Northfleet HQ that duty officers had been detailed; the phone would be manned continuously; and officers on leave recalled. At 16:50 on 24 August, the codeword PLUMER was received, authorising the official embodiment of the unit, and its mobilisation scheme was immediately put into operation. By 17:40 the first officer had arrived at the HQ, followed within the hour by the first of the 'other ranks'. At 21:05 advanced parties left the HQ on buses bound for their War Stations across the Thames at Southend and Canvey Island, and on the Kent side of the river at Sheerness, Grain, and Yantlet. On arrival they took up their duties manning the various Defence Electric Light (DEL)* positions. By 00:10 the next morning all stations were reported 'READY FOR ACTION' to counter any enemy naval units approaching the Thames Estuary.[1]

On 25 August the KFRE closed its HQ at Northfleet† and reopened it at Grain Fort, on the eastern side of the Hoo Peninsula, a land mass separating the Thames and Medway rivers. The Isle of Grain‡ had been a heavily fortified area since Victorian times. In 1849 a gun tower, based on the Napoleonic-era 'Martello Tower' design, was built on the extreme low-water mark of the 'Spit of Grain', a narrow causeway that extends out into the River Medway opposite Sheerness, and is only accessible by foot and at low-tide. The 1860 Royal Commission on defences recommended construction of a large fort at Grain, together with an auxiliary battery further up-river. Further gun batteries were added in later years. Grain Fort was completed in 1868 and was originally intended to mount sixteen heavy guns, but it was not armed until 1874, by which time the plans for the fort had been modified and only seven guns were mounted.[2]

In the early decades of the twentieth century, the range of different military establishments at Grain steadily increased. In 1900 the Admiralty built a new coastguard station to the east of the village and in 1908 they constructed a large oil storage facility at Elphinstone

---

* The term 'Defence Electric Light' (DEL) dates back to the late 1880s with the introduction of the British Defence Electric Light to the British Army. It was designed to be used both to cover sea approaches or a land front. The Royal Engineers adopted the term in its *Manual of Electric Search-Lighting* published in 1890. The manual suggested that: '... the electric light can be used not only to locate the enemy but also to prevent the enemy seeing you by obscuring his vision.' The Royal Engineers controlled all DELs until the end of the First World War (the original KFRE had two Electric Light Companies in 1914). Following the end of the war, the Royal Artillery took over control of the coastal lights and renamed them as Coastal Artillery Search Lights (CASL). However, when they reverted to RE control in the 1930s, the term DEL was re-introduced.

(*British Port Defence – Defence Electric Lights https://pinkroutes.org/research/defended-ports/port-defence/defence-electric-lights/*)

† After Dunkirk, Grove House became the HQ of 17 Bn (Northfleet) Kent Home Guard, whose CO was Lt Col Anwell, general manager of Bevan's Cement Works, a position previously held by KFRE CO Clifford Brazier. (*J. Skellorn - Grove House: Kent Fortress – Northfleet History Group Magazine – Issue 15, Winter 2016*)

‡ The Isle of Grain occupies the eastern extremity of the Hoo Peninsula, separated from the adjoining land mass by Yantlet Creek. Much of the island is marshland, with the main area of settlement being the village of Grain. (*English Heritage – Research Report No. 1-2014: Isle of Grain: Hoo Peninsula, Kent* (2014))

Point, to support naval vessels based at Chatham Dockyard that were in the process of converting from coal to oil fuel.[3] Two Defence Electric Light emplacements were built at Grain in 1911[4] (which were manned by the original KFRE), and then in 1912 a Royal Naval Air Station was established to the south of the village to serve as a seaplane base.[5] By 1914, Grain had become an important and heavily fortified military and naval base and would remain so throughout the First World War.

When the KFRE arrived at Grain Fort to establish their wartime HQ there in 1939, the fort would have already been showing its age and its bleak, remote location would not have helped endear it to its new occupants. Lt Col Brazier graphically described their dismal, new accommodation:

> These forts dating back into history, with their grim masonry walls, miserable little windows, and with the general air of medieval prisons, in themselves gave a background to the mental outlook of the garrison. The living accommodation was mainly old casemates with domed brick roofs covered again by many feet of earth and concrete and through the cracks the water trickled down the walls. With little or no ventilation, two courses remained open – either to have large fires and produce a kind of Turkish bath atmosphere, or alternatively to freeze in one's tomblike surroundings…[6]

However, being typically hardy British 'Tommys', the men settled in and made the best of the spartan conditions, while the important duties of the off-loading of supplies and equipment and the assignment of manning details to their war stations was their immediate main concern.

On 1 September 1939 Germany invaded Poland and war was now inevitable. At 18:55 a telegram was received at the KFRE headquarters. It was from Chatham Area HQ and contained just one word – 'MOBILIZE'. Two days later, at 11:00 on 3 September, the KFRE War Diary records this entry: 'DECLARATION OF WAR AGAINST GERMANY BY BRITISH PRIME MINISTER'. Later that same day, Lt Col Brazier sent a message to all ranks: 'For some years past we have been training for war. Now war has come. I feel confident that I can rely on All Ranks of the Kent Fortress to give of their utmost in the difficult days that lie ahead. I wish you all Good Luck.'

At 03:10 the next morning, the KFRE recorded their first air raid warning of the war.[7]

Despite the declaration of war, nothing much immediately changed in the routine of the KFRE. Throughout the autumn months of the 'Phoney War' they continued manning their DEL stations at night (although now with far more diligence and heightened apprehension), while during the day they performed a long list of mundane but essential maintenance and construction tasks around the many and various defence establishments in their area. In between duties, time was found for recreation: two football teams were raised to play against local sides at Sheerness and Grain; rugby practice was held at Grain, PT performed on Southend pier, and squash played at Sheerness.[8] Results of some of the football matches were even recorded in the unit's War Diary, including a 5-1 win over a team from Bevans Cement Works,[9] a victory which must have seemed bittersweet for the many sappers who were former employees of the firm.

To ensure that all the men kept fit, every company did a route march once a week, with orders to include batmen, cooks and all other ancillary personnel, with every man carrying a rifle and ammunition.[10]

A hint that the KFRE's main role could be changing came on 20 November, when fifty other ranks* from the Royal Artillery reported to 2 Company at Sheerness for instruction in DEL duties.[11]

Two days later, enemy aircraft were reported heading towards the Thames. The KFRE's coastal DEL units were utilised in the anti-aircraft role to track any of the planes flying low over the river. The units based at Yantlet and Southend picked up aircraft in their lights, and their machine gunners opened fire on them. The gunners at Yantlet appeared to have hit one aircraft which was spotted diving low over the river. Meanwhile, over at Southend, another enemy aircraft strafed the pierhead, puncturing the decks with gunfire. Fortunately, no one was injured in the attacks.

Later that night, a mixed armed party of twenty-two sappers and gunners was sent out to capture the crew of the enemy plane thought to have been brought down by the Yantlet unit in an area between Yantlet and Grain. Despite being out for over ninety minutes, no plane or enemy personnel could be found. Further search parties were sent out the following morning but, again, nothing was discovered. Then, at 03:00 on 24 November, reports came in from the local police of an aircraft being spotted in the vicinity of Yantlet Creek. Another search party was immediately raised and sent out. Assisted by the Yantlet DEL, they searched out on the treacherous mud for about a mile in blinding rain, but no wreckage could be found.[12]

With the onset of the first winter of the war approaching, and still no signs of the enemy, except from the occasional seaplane raid, the

---

* The fifty included twenty-eight 'Immatures' (recruits under the age of 19). (*WO 166/3549*)

mood of the KFRE began to darken. They felt that they were stuck in the remotest backwater of what some newspapers were already calling a 'phoney' war. Repeated drill, training, and the manning of the lights on freezing and often wet nights just added to the gloom and boredom.[13] Off-duty, sport offered some occasional light relief for the troops. A novelty event on 13 December was advertised as a 'Shockby Match', where teams of eleven players from 2 Company at Sheerness and 3 Company at Grain played ten minutes each of 'soccer, hockey, and rugger', with the band of the KFRE playing on the field.[14]

Towards the end of December 1939, the KFRE were told that they would be moving their headquarters to Sheerness, which probably came as a welcome relief to the HQ staff. On 27 December a recce party inspected the new office and living accommodation they had been allocated at Sheerness Barracks, and the new headquarters of the KFRE opened there on 1 January 1940.[15,16] As they settled into their new headquarters, none could have guessed the dangers and adventures that the New Year would eventually bring upon their, as yet, mundane military lives.

Chapter 3

MAN OF SECRETS

On 27 September 1939, as the sappers of the KFRE were manning their war stations, a 62-year-old former Royal Marines officer sat anxiously at his desk in his Whitehall office, his brow furrowed with concern. The 1st Baron Hankey had been in the Cabinet Office as the Minister Without Portfolio for less than a month and was already turning his decades of experience in military and political affairs to dealing with a 'particular problem' that had been handed to him by the Prime Minister.

Maurice Hankey was born in Biarritz in 1877, the son of a retired farmer. He spent his early years with his family in Brighton, where he attended a day school. He was later educated at Rugby and then commissioned into the Royal Marine Artillery in 1895. He received his only academic training from the three years he spent at the Royal Naval College, Greenwich, where he was strongly influenced by the teachings of the professor of fortifications, Major General Sir George Aston.*

In 1898 Hankey was appointed subaltern of the Marines on the battleship HMS *Ramillies*, which was then the flagship of the Mediterranean Fleet. A year later he was promoted to captain and became intelligence officer to the Mediterranean Fleet's C-in-C, Admiral Sir Charles Beresford. At the age of 23 he was promoted to captain of Marines (the youngest captain of Marines in the Fleet, at that time) whilst retaining his intelligence post.

* Sir George Grey Aston (1861-1938) was an officer in the Royal Marine Artillery. He was a strong advocate of 'joint' warfare, with the Royal Navy and the British Army co-operating closely together with integrated planning and unified command. (*The British Army, the Royal Navy, and the 'big work' of Sir George Aston, 1904-1914, http://nectar.northampton.ac.uk/5451/*)

In 1902, Hankey was transferred to the Naval Intelligence Department of the Admiralty, where he dealt with the coastal defences of the Empire. In this new post he was heavily involved with the detail of a global system of coastal defences and with considerations regarding policy in the provision of naval bases and coaling stations, and the construction of docks. He was also involved in policy work on the development of the fledgling navies of the British Dominions. These policies were incorporated in a volume of instructions which were later adopted by the Committee of Imperial Defence, whom Hankey himself was soon to be closely associated with.

In 1905 Hankey was appointed to fill a Royal Marines vacancy on a committee, headed by Major General John Owen, charged with reviewing all the land defences of British ports at home and overseas. The Owen Committee's work was vital for the upkeep of imperial defence, which was dependent on the British Fleet and Merchant Navy having access to secure bases and coaling stations around the world. The committee discharged its duties to great effect and Hankey's part in its work marked him out for further advancement.

In 1908, after a spell serving as Chief Intelligence Officer of the Mediterranean Fleet, Hankey was appointed to the post of Naval Assistant Secretary to the Committee of Imperial Defence (CID), the first Royal Marine officer to serve in that role. The CID was the principal advisory body to the government on home and overseas defence matters. It was the start of a long association with the committee, a period which Hankey later described as being the best years of his life. It was also his last appointment as a serving naval officer.[1] From his early days with the CID, Hankey ensured that its records were meticulously organised. Through his long period of involvement with defence planning and coordination, Hankey built up a huge fund of knowledge and experience that was to serve him well.[2] In 1912, Hankey became Secretary of the CID, a post he was to hold until his retirement twenty-six years later. In recognition of his new status, he was also appointed to the Order of the Bath as a Companion (CB) in that year's Birthday Honours List.[3]

Soon after the outbreak of the First World War, Prime Minister Herbert Asquith permitted the CID to lapse and a War Council was formed from senior members of the cabinet, served by the CID secretariat.[4] Hankey was appointed secretary of the Council. He officially retired from the Royal Marines with the rank of lieutenant colonel and from here onwards his new civil service career began to blossom. In February 1916 he was further honoured with a knighthood as a Knight Commander of the Order of the Bath (KCB).[5]

In August 1915, Hankey was sent alone to examine and report back to the government on the situation on the Gallipoli Peninsula, where British and Commonwealth troops had become bogged down in a war of attrition with Turkish forces. His report contributed to the eventual evacuation of the peninsula.

On 7 December 1916 David Lloyd George became Prime Minister. One of his first actions was to insist on a smaller War Cabinet, with just five members. The seed of this idea had been sown a month earlier when, with the war going badly, Hankey and Lloyd George were both attending a conference of the Allied powers in Paris. Lloyd George was then Minister for War in a government beset with problems, and Hankey had suggested that he should 'insist on a small War Committee being set up for the day-to-day conduct of the war, with full power.'[6] On 9 December Lloyd George, now Prime Minister, formed his first War Cabinet and appointed Hankey as secretary.

In his new role, Hankey brought order to the War Cabinet, speeding up its proceedings and coordinating the efforts of the politicians on one side with the military chiefs on the other, something that had been lacking in the early conduct of the war.[7]

In early 1917, Lloyd George invited the leaders of the other Dominions to a meeting in London and on 20 March, the first meeting of the Imperial War Cabinet was held, with Hankey as its secretary.

Hankey played a key part throughout the anxieties of 1917 and 1918. In 1917 there were huge losses of merchant shipping to German submarines, and he argued convincingly for the introduction of a 'convoy' system, an idea that was soon successfully adopted, after which shipping losses declined dramatically.[8] In 1918 he accompanied South African General Jan Smuts on a surveillance visit to the army on the Western Front, where the French were pressing for an extension of the British line.[9]

Hankey became involved in negotiations for the Armistice that was eventually signed in November 1918 and attended the Paris Peace Conference in 1919 as secretary to the British and Commonwealth delegations. The conference signalled the official final end of the First World War, allowing Lloyd George to restore full Cabinet government with Hankey as Cabinet Secretary, a role which saw him initiate the practice of taking the minutes (officially known as 'conclusions') at meetings of the Cabinet.[10] To provide administrative support and ensure good communications across government departments, Hankey developed the Cabinet Secretariat, which eventually evolved into the Cabinet Office, with Hankey at its heart. He drew up the rules of procedure for the Cabinet, prepared agenda, and, as well as taking the minutes, ensured that the decisions were implemented by the departments concerned.[11]

Until his retirement in August 1938, Hankey worked tirelessly in all his roles and became renowned for his efficiency and involvement in the deepest secrets and machinations of government. Sir Robert Vansittart, Permanent Secretary at the Foreign Office in the 1930s, described Hankey as 'A marine of slight stature and tireless industry, he grew into a repository of secrets, a Chief Inspector of Mines of Information. He had an incredible memory…an official brand which could reproduce on call the date, file, substance of every paper that ever flew into a pigeon-hole.'[12]

Following his retirement, Hankey was appointed a British Government director on the board of the Suez Canal Company. In January 1939, he was raised to the peerage as Baron Hankey of The Chart.[13]

When Germany invaded Poland on 1 September 1939, Prime Minister Neville Chamberlain formed a War Cabinet and invited Lord Hankey to join it. Hankey was at first reluctant to end his retirement and surrender his directorships, but eventually, his sense of duty prevailed, and he accepted office as Minister Without Portfolio and was sworn of the Privy Council the same day. His appointment was a mystery to some of his new colleagues and even he seemed unsure himself just what was expected of him. However, the appointment of another 'outsider' to Cabinet may have been giving him some erroneous clues. To his wife, Adeline, Hankey wrote on the morning of 3 September as the clock ticked down towards the expiry of the British Government's ultimatum to Germany:

> I have kept away from No.10 this morning as it is awkward to be constantly running into Cabinet Ministers, who cannot make out what the dickens I am doing.
>
> As far as I can make out my main job is to keep an eye on Winston!* I spent 1½ hours with him yesterday morning. He was brimful [*sic*] of

* Prime Minister Neville Chamberlain had brought Winston Churchill back into government, for the first time in ten years, in the office of First Lord of the Admiralty, the post he had served in at the outbreak of the First World War. Hankey and Churchill had been firm friends and had enjoyed a good working relationship during the First World War. However, the relationship had deteriorated during Churchill's 'wilderness years' when from the backbenches he had been a critic of the Baldwin Government's policy over India and later, disputing the official statements on German air strength. On the latter, Churchill had told Hankey he had 'specially secret information' on which he based his disputes, which had obviously come from a Government official.

> ideas, some good and others not so good, but rather heartening and big. I only wish he didn't give one the impression that he does himself too well! ...He has let it get into the Press that he will be in the War Cabinet – to the great annoyance of many.[14]

As the title of his office inferred, Hankey had no specific government duty. Eventually this was to cause problems, with some MPs querying why a salary was being paid to him. It was left to the Cabinet Secretary Sir Edward Bridges to draft a statement referring to Hankey's 'exceptional experience and qualifications', and his main role being as an advisor to the Prime Minister and to be 'in a position to devote [his] special attention to particular problems which arise from time to time.'[15]

It was one such 'particular problem' that was occupying Hankey's mind as he sat in his Whitehall office that late September morning, writing to his War Cabinet colleague, Minister for Co-ordination of Defence and Admiral of the Fleet, Lord Chatfield.[16]

At a meeting of the War Cabinet four days earlier, Chief of the Imperial General Staff General Sir W. Edmund Ironside had reported that there was just one active German division that had been identified in position near the frontiers with the Netherlands and Belgium (both at that time still neutral) but with elements of a further five just behind, with indications of possible offensive intentions towards the Netherlands.[17] At that meeting, Hankey had warned of 'under-rating' the possibility of an offensive in the West that autumn. He considered that 'The Germans would never get a better chance in the future than they had now ...'[18]

In his letter to Chatfield, Hankey wondered:

> ...whether we ought not to undertake a closer investigation than has taken place hitherto as to the situation in the event of Germany over-running Holland or Belgium or both. You will have noticed that German troops are reported to be concentrating east of the Rhine, which indicates at least the possibility of an attack on Holland.
>
> What disturbs me is the thought that Germany, by occupying these countries, would acquire some loot of a very valuable kind. I suspect that at Belgian and Dutch ports, e.g. Antwerp, Rotterdam and Amsterdam, there are very large stocks of oil fuel and petrol. The Shell Company, for example, has a majority of Dutch Directors, and I should imagine that important depots would exist in Holland. At the outset of the last war, we induced the Belgians to destroy the oil fuel at Antwerp, and a fine old blaze it made covering the whole of the river. The quantity must be enormously larger now.[19]

Hankey went on to suggest other Dutch and Belgian 'loot' that could either be in danger of being seized by the Germans or, conversely, be obtained for Allied use, including warships and merchant vessels, aircraft, machine tools, and even skilled workers such as mechanics and artisans. His view was that:

> ... we should envisage the following aims: -
>
> 1. If circumstances permit, to secure that the most important of the Dutch and/or Belgian assets in the way of fleets, merchant ships (especially tankers), aircraft, oil fuel, skilled labour, machine tools, tugs and barges (which are always useful in war and might be invaluable if the submarine campaign gets bad), should be brought over to this country on the understanding that we would hire it or buy them with a view to return after the war.
> 2. That, if time does not permit us to accomplish this, we should try and secure that some of the items of special value to the enemy, like oil fuel, is destroyed and does not fall into German hands.
> 3. If we cannot induce the Dutch or the Belgians to carry out the necessary destruction themselves, we should have full information as to where such objectives are situated with a view to destroying them ourselves – by air.[20]

Hankey concluded his letter to Chatfield by saying: '…the first thing to do is to get the information, and I wondered if you would be willing to turn the wonderful machine you control on to this as a start. It would be a fine thing if the emergency arose and you were able to suggest at once what ought to be done.'[21]

The following day, Lord Chatfield passed on Hankey's letter to Major General Hastings Ismay, secretary to the Chiefs of Staff Committee.[22] At their meeting on 29 September, the COS agreed to instruct the Joint Intelligence Committee (JIC)* to report on those resources in Holland and Belgium, as indicated by Hankey, that could be denied to the enemy or be obtained for Allied use.[23]

The JIC submitted their report to the Chiefs of Staff on 4 October. The report acknowledged the fact that the Dutch and Belgian governments were anxious to avoid doing anything to provoke Germany and noted that Belgium had even refused Allied proposals for staff negotiations, so it was unlikely that either government would agree to any joint preparations of plans for the destruction or salvage

* The Joint Intelligence Committee (JIC) was founded in 1936 as a sub-committee of the Committee of Imperial Defence to provide co-ordinated intelligence service to policy makers, drawing upon the work of the intelligence agencies and Whitehall departments.

of their assets. However, they suggested that discreet approaches could be made to them via diplomatic channels to draw their attention to the danger of their assets falling into German hands and that they might consider preparing their own plans to remove such assets as may be transportable to the UK or France. HMG would gladly offer all assistance to facilitate removal of the assets or where removal was not possible, the destruction of them.[24] On the latter the report recommended: 'For destruction of stocks and installations on any considerable scale specially trained field engineer units would have to be held in readiness, suitably equipped and arrangements made, all in advance.'[25]

The JIC report went on to list in its appendices the various strategic assets and resources of both countries, covering everything from warships and aircraft to cereals and sugar.

As well as the extensive military, industrial, transport and economic assets there were also substantial financial assets that could not be allowed to fall into enemy hands, including gold bullion, diamonds, bearer bonds and stock securities. The value of the combined bullion stocks of Belgium and the Netherlands was estimated to be about £180 million, while bearer bonds held by both countries were valued at £200 million. The combined weight of the gold bullion was about 1,800 tons and would present serious problems if it had to be hurriedly evacuated in the event of an invasion, when transport facilities would be seriously disrupted. It was thought that most of the bullion stocks were held at banks in Brussels and The Hague, neither of which were well placed for rapid evacuation. It was hoped that both countries could be persuaded to ship these valuable financial assets to the United States.[26]

Oil stocks were another major consideration and concern. Belgium was estimated to have stocks of 200,000-250,000 tons, with similar amounts in the Netherlands.[27] It was thought that little could be done towards destroying or salvaging any of these stocks unless plans were made beforehand, preferably in conjunction with the authorities of both governments.[28]

The Chiefs of Staff prepared a memorandum[29] with proposals for actions based on the JIC report and which was put before a meeting of the War Cabinet on 7 October. At the meeting Chief of the Air Staff, Air Chief Marshal Sir Cyril Newall, presented the JIC report and stated that it would now be for the various departments involved to plan and prepare all the necessary steps to be taken in the event of a German invasion of the Low Countries, with a recommendation that a minister be appointed as a 'prime mover' in the matter. The War Cabinet duly approved the memorandum and invited Lord Hankey to co-ordinate the action of the various departments concerned with preparing the plans and to supervise consultations with the French.[30]

At the same meeting, the Chancellor of the Exchequer Sir John Simon was invited to ask the Bank of England to contact the central banks of the Netherlands and Belgium with a view to securing the removal of their gold stocks to a safe country, preferably the UK.

Hankey went straight to work on his new assignment. Military Assistant-Secretary to the War Cabinet Lieutenant Colonel Ian Jacob, whom Hankey knew well from their time working together at the CID, was seconded to help him.[31] Letters were sent out to the ministers and officials at the various departments involved inviting them to nominate representatives to a meeting at the Cabinet Office in Richmond Terrace two days later.[32] These letters went out to:

Minister of Supply – Leslie Burgin
Secretary of State for War – Leslie Hore-Belisha
Permanent Under-Secretary at the Foreign Office – Sir Alexander Cadogan
President of the Board of Trade – Oliver Stanley
First Lord of the Admiralty – Winston Churchill
Secretary of State for Air – Sir Kingsley Wood
Minister of Economic Warfare – Ronald Cross

In his letter to Churchill, Hankey added: 'I have already seen [Vice] Admiral Binney, who has the Admiralty arrangements in hand, and I think it might be useful if he were present as well as the Admiralty representative.'[33]

Binney headed a committee at the Admiralty that worked on 'special projects', one of which dealt with the arrangements for denying certain oil supplies to the enemy. In this role he also worked closely with Hankey on what became known as the 'Binney Project', the denial of Dutch and Belgian oil assets to Germany.

Thomas Hugh Binney was born in 1883, in Douglas, Isle of Man. He joined the Royal Navy at 14 as a cadet on the training ship HMS *Britannia,* moored up on the River Dart. Binney underwent examinations for several days commencing on 20 July 1897 and gained entrance to *Britannia*'s term of August 1897, his 1540 marks placing him third among the sixty-three candidates accepted as naval cadets.[34] In January 1899, he joined the battleship HMS *Resolution* as a midshipman and was promoted to sub lieutenant in 1902. During the First World War he served as the gunnery officer on the battleship HMS *Queen Elizabeth* during the Dardanelles Campaign of 1914-15 and was promoted to commander in 1916. In 1918 he was appointed to the staff of Admiral Sir David Beatty, C-in-C of the Grand Fleet. He was promoted to captain in 1922 and went on to command the battleship HMS *Nelson,* and the battle-cruiser HMS *Hood* before being promoted to rear admiral in 1934. He was promoted to vice admiral in June 1938 and in January 1939 was appointed commandant of the Imperial Defence College. Following the outbreak of the Second World War, Binney was brought into the Admiralty to undertake committee work on specific problems relating to the war.[35]

On 9 October, Binney attended Lord Hankey's meeting at the Cabinet offices in Richmond Terrace, just off Whitehall. Also present were William Strang, Assistant Under-Secretary at the Foreign Office; Major General Frederick Beaumont-Nesbitt, Director of Military Intelligence; Lieutenant Colonel John Holland RE, from the War Office; Captain D.R. Guinness from the War Office; Wing Commander Lawrence Pendred from the Air Ministry; Desmond Morton, Principal Assistant Secretary at the Ministry for Economic Warfare; Rear Admiral Lumley Lister from the Admiralty; Captain Victor Dankwerts, Director of Plans at the Admiralty; Captain Thomas Troubridge from the Admiralty; Sir Julian Foley, Under-Secretary at the Board of Trade; and C.N. Stirling from the Ministry of Economic Warfare. Hankey's assistant, Lt Col Ian Jacob acted as secretary for the meeting.[36]

Hankey opened the meeting by saying that they would be looking to 'give effect to the recommendations of the Chiefs of Staff' regarding the measures to be taken in the event of a German invasion of the Low Countries.[37] He proceeded to state that he had been in touch with the Treasury and the Governor of the Bank of England (Sir Montagu Norman) regarding the status of gold and other securities held by Dutch and Belgian banks; however, the governor was still awaiting the results of his enquiries. Hankey stressed the importance of knowing the attitude of the Dutch and Belgian governments to the idea of moving their gold elsewhere. William Strang said that the Foreign Office would be prepared to make discreet approaches to both governments on the subject.

The discussions then moved on to the matter of the facilities at the Dutch and Belgian ports. Vice Adm Binney explained the preparations he was putting in motion. He proposed sending three naval captains to Holland and one to Belgium, all in the guise of couriers. After reporting to the Naval Attachés at the embassies, they would each take forty-eight hours 'leave', which would be spent at Amsterdam, Rotterdam, Flushing, and Antwerp respectively looking around the various port and harbour facilities. They would each then be made available at a later period to lead operations against these ports if it proved necessary.

Binney also said that he had been in contact with the War Office who had prepared a draft plan for three field companies of Royal

Engineers to carry out demolitions inland at Amsterdam, Rotterdam and Antwerp, while Royal Navy destroyers carried out as much destruction as they could against coastal facilities.

The Admiralty's other senior representative, Rear Adm Lumley Lyster, said that he had made all preparations for blocking the Belgian ports of Ostend and Zeebrugge and for carrying out certain demolitions in those areas. He also said that the Vice Admiral, Dover, (Vice Admiral Bertram Ramsay) had received a letter from the French admiral in charge at Dunkirk to say that he was also proposing to carry-out demolitions at Belgian ports and so it would be desirable to co-ordinate the actions of the French and British in this respect.

Following further discussions, several points were made, including that without further reconnaissance and the cooperation of the governments concerned, the demolition operations would be extremely hazardous with the possibility of disappointing results. It was also thought that sending the naval captains out in the guise of couriers should not be done until the Foreign Secretary (Lord Halifax) had been consulted.

For the Foreign Office, Strang said they were proposing to ask the British Minister at The Hague (Sir Nevile Bland) whether he thought there was any possibility of the Dutch agreeing to staff conversations and whether he thought anything useful could be achieved by approaching the Dutch Government on the subjects under discussion at this meeting. The latter point might also be put to the British Ambassador at Brussels (Sir Robert Clive), as regards the Belgian Government. If both HM representatives thought that these approaches should be made, then Strang suggested that with both governments' cooperation, more comprehensive plans might be made, although he thought such cooperation unlikely.

The meeting agreed that the Foreign Office would contact HM representatives at The Hague and Brussels, as suggested by Strang, and that until the results of their inquiries were known, the preparation of plans should be confined to the blocking of the ports of Zeebrugge and Ostend, destroying the port facilities at Ghent and Bruges, and the sending of destroyers to Ymuiden,* the Hook of Holland, Flushing, and Antwerp for local demolitions there.

The meeting concluded that all French and British actions should be coordinated through their respective military representatives.

---

* Ymuiden, more commonly known now as IJmuiden, is a port city in the Dutch province of North Holland. It is the main town in the municipality of Velsen, which lies mainly to the south-east. Including its large sea locks, it straddles the mouth of the North Sea Canal to Amsterdam.

Additionally, the Admiralty was instructed to postpone the deployment of the naval captains for their covert reconnaissance missions until the Foreign Secretary's opinion was obtained and approval granted by the First Lord of the Admiralty.

The meeting then went on to discuss the reduction of stocks of important raw materials in Holland and Belgium, the most critical of which being oil. Holland had very large stocks of oil and it was thought that something could be done through the agency of Sir Andrew Agnew. Agnew was a director of Royal Dutch Shell and chairman of the Petroleum Board, which had been set up at the outbreak of the war to control the production and distribution of petroleum products. It was hoped he could persuade the Royal Dutch Petroleum Company to decrease the stocks it held by reducing any future shipments. However, it was thought most unlikely that the Dutch would agree to reducing existing stocks by sending any out of the country.

The meeting concluded that the large quantities of oil being held in Holland and Belgium made it essential for all possible steps to be taken to prevent it falling into the enemy's hands. It was agreed that:

> ... three alternative plans should be prepared for the destruction of the stocks of oil held in Holland and Belgium :-
>
> (a) That it should be done by the Dutch and Belgians themselves. To secure this, it would be desirable that their Governments should be approached, if possible, and urged to prepare the necessary plans. Alternatively if their Governments could not be approached at present, the British Minister should endeavour, in the event of an emergency, to secure that action was taken by the Government concerned to run off or destroy the stocks.
> (b) That it should be done by the Royal Engineers. The War Office to be invited to prepare a plan which could be carried out if circumstances proved favourable.
> (c) That it should be done by aerial bombardment. A plan for this should be prepared by the Air Ministry, from information supplied by the War Office.

The meeting went on to discuss Dutch and Belgian merchant and naval shipping, including tugs and barges, road haulage vehicles, railway locomotives and rolling stock, civil and military aircraft and personnel, machine tools, and power stations, all of which would be invaluable to the Germans but about which little could be done without the cooperation of the governments concerned.

Hankey's meeting, having drawn its conclusions, ended and it was now for the diplomats to begin their work.

Chapter 4

DIPLOMATIC MANOEUVRES

From early 1934, newspapers were reporting on secret German plans to invade the Netherlands in order to reach the North Sea ports and dominate Britain, causing unrest amongst the Dutch public. Germany distanced herself from these rumours, but the damage had been done, and the rumours persisted. In 1935, it was suggested that Hitler himself had ordered his Minister of War, Wenber von Blomberg, to study a fast, motorised attack on the Netherlands.[1]

British ministers then began studying steps to be taken in the event of a German invasion of the Low Countries, an event which would be 'a special menace to British security'. The fate of Holland was a particular concern, and it was deemed necessary that British / Dutch staff contacts should be established to prevent a German dominance of the North Sea coast. However, British diplomats and politicians understood that Dutch neutrality would preclude any joint discussions.[2]

In early 1939, renewed rumours of an imminent German attack on the Low Countries spread quickly and the Dutch Foreign Minister discussed the situation with Lord Halifax, his British counterpart. When Dutch Prime Minister Hendrikus Colijn heard that Britain was considering proclaiming a German attack on Holland as *casus belli*, he refused to discuss the topic and ended the talks.[3]

When war broke out in September 1939, British interest in German military preparations east of the Dutch border increased considerably.

On 28 September 1939, prompted by the concerns raised by Lord Hankey at the War Cabinet four days previously, Orme Sargent, the Deputy Permanent Under-Secretary at the Foreign Office, wrote to the Secretary of the Chiefs of Staff Committee:

> Dear Ismay,
> In view of the accounts which are current about the likelihood of a German attack through Holland, we should be interested to learn what importance the Chiefs of Staff attach to concerting defensive measures in advance with the Netherlands military authorities, if that were possible.
>
> 2. If in the opinion of the Chiefs of Staff such prior consultation should be regarded as a matter of great importance to us, we would consider the possibility of approaching the Netherlands Government, even though there seems little prospect of receiving a favourable reply. The Chiefs of Staff may, however, hold that as we could not help the Dutch anyhow there is no use in trying to concert measures with them.[4]

In Ismay's reply of 30 September, he said that the Chiefs of Staff had discussed the matter in their meeting that morning and that it was their opinion 'that prior consultation with the Dutch should be regarded as a matter of great importance to us.'

Ismay went on to inform Sargent that the Chiefs were:

> ...at present examining the various resources in the Low Countries which it would be desirable, in the event of a German invasion, either to deny to the enemy by destruction or to salve for the use of the Allies. Clearly any plans in this sphere would be far more effective if they could be worked out in close collaboration with the Dutch. We should not be in a position to start the actual conversations until this enquiry had been completed, say next week. But if you think there is any hope of inducing the Netherlands Government to concert defence plans with us, the sooner an approach is made to them the better.[5]

Meanwhile, British discussions with the Belgian Government had already begun, but with little success. On 29 September, the British Ambassador in Brussels, Sir Robert Clive,* reported to the War Cabinet that he had received from Belgian Minister for Foreign Affairs Paul-Henri Spaak an *aide-memoire,* which stated that:

> The Belgian Government is of the opinion that, in the present circumstances, there is little foundation for the hypothesis that Germany will launch an attack through Belgium.

---

* Sir Robert Henry Clive (1877-1948) was distantly related to Lord (Robert) Clive (1725-74), the famous 'Clive of India' who, through his victories against the French, laid the foundations for the British East India Company and, eventually, the British Indian Empire.

The Belgian Government can, on the other hand, affirm that all the requisite military measures have been decided upon, and are being carried out to enable Belgium to offer a strong resistance to any attempt to violate the country by land or air.

[...] The Belgian Government consider in consequence that the opening of Staff Conversations is not called for, such conversations not being in harmony with the situation set out above.[6]

Clive went on to report that Foreign Minister Spaak had told him that their Military Attachés in Berlin had been summoned and told that Germany intended to fully respect the neutrality of Belgium and Holland but had reason to fear Allied attacks through these countries. Clive added that Spaak had summed up the Belgian attitude as 'the political danger – i.e. danger of Germany getting wind of Staff Conversations at a moment when, he was inclined to believe, she genuinely feared that Belgium might allow the Allies right of passage – was greater than the Military danger, in view of the strength of the Belgian defences.'[7]

Clive's telegram was discussed at the following day's War Cabinet. Halifax raised the suggestion made to him by the former Belgian Prime Minister Paul van Zeeland,* that a 'discrete civil intermediary might represent the views of our staff to a similar individual in Belgium who would in turn pass these views on to the Belgian Staff.'[8]

At the War Cabinet held on 1 October, Orme Sargent reported that Halifax had sent a telegram to Ambassador Clive in Brussels:

(i) expressing the hope that it might be possible for him to obtain facilities for the Military Attaché to visit the Belgian defences on the Belgian [/] Netherlands frontier, as suggested in conversation with M. Spaak;

(ii) authorising him, at his discretion, to return to the idea put forward in the course of a recent discussion between the Secretary of State for Foreign Affairs and M. van Zeeland, that it might be possible to find some means of achieving at any rate part of our object through unofficial contacts by the employment of a discrete civil intermediary to represent the views of our Staff to a similar individual in Belgium who would in turn pass these views on to the Belgian Staff.[9]

---

* Paul van Zeeland (1893-1973) had been Prime Minister of Belgium from March 1935 to November 1937 but had been forced to resign in disgrace after it was discovered he had received 330,000 Bfr from the Belgian National Bank. In 1939 he was made president of the, London-based, Committee for Refugees, an agency dedicated to the re-settlement of Jewish refugees from Nazi-occupied Europe.

On 5 October, Churchill, reported to the War Cabinet on a 'most secret' meeting he had had the previous evening with Admiral of the Fleet Sir Roger Keyes MP. By virtue of his heroic exploits in the First World War, when he planned and commanded the famous 1918 raids on Zeebrugge and Ostend,* Keyes enjoyed an 'exceptional confidence' in Belgium, and had brought with him to the meeting a 'M. Stein'† whom Churchill understood to be a former Austrian national but was now a British subject and an economist by profession, who claimed close ties with the Belgian royal family. Stein stated that he was the bearer of a 'special message' from the King of the Belgians‡ saying:

> King Leopold was deeply worried. Whilst he realised that Belgium must be loyal to her neutrality, he foresaw that this neutrality might be violated at any moment. Meanwhile, no preparations were being taken to meet this contingency. For political reasons, which we would understand, the Belgian Government could take no action. The King was therefore seriously considering the possibility of himself taking the matter up secretly with his Generals, excluding all knowledge of his action from his political and diplomatic advisers. The King had, in fact, already consulted General Denis, the Belgian Commander-in-Chief, on the subject, and was now anxious to know whether we would be prepared to accept his personal invitation to enter into military Conversations as to what action we might take in concert with the Belgians in the event of a German invasion of Belgium.[10]

* The raids against Zeebrugge and Ostend in spring 1918 aimed to block access to the North Sea to German submarines sailing through these ports. There were two raids on Ostend (23 April and 9 May) and one against Zeebrugge (23 April) in an attempt to sink blockships at the entrance to the canal to the inland port of Bruges, where the German U-Boats were based. The Ostend raids were failures, while the Zeebrugge operation was only partially successful, and the Germans re-opened the entrance to the Bruges canal within two days. However, the sheer audacity of the raids aided the promotion of the raids as a victory by Allied propaganda and the bravery shown by those taking part was recognised by the awarding of eight Victoria Crosses.

† Walter Johannes Stein (1891-1957) was an Austrian philosopher of Jewish descent. He studied mathematics, physics, and philosophy at Vienna University, before completing a doctorate in philosophy at the end of the First World War. He became a pioneer of anthroposophy, a spiritualist movement which espoused the existence of an intellectually comprehensible spiritual world, accessible to human experience. He moved to London in 1933 and took up studies in economics, geography, and geology. He became involved with King Leopold III of Belgium in 1938 when the king established his 'World Institute' to study international economic problems. (*https://danielhindes.com/blog/2005/06/26/wj-stein-a-biography/*)

‡ Leopold III of Belgium (1901-83)

Stein also claimed to enjoy 'special privileges' with the Belgian king, which would enable him to secretly introduce any emissary the British might choose to send, into the Royal presence. However, Churchill was not convinced of Stein's authenticity. He had, therefore, arranged with the Director General of the Security Service (MI5),* Sir Vernon Kell, to assess the veracity of Stein's claims by sending an envoy to the Belgian king with a message seeking to establish whether he was telling the truth. If the envoy returned with a personal message from the king confirming Stein's *bona fides*, then a valuable contact would have been established that could be followed up by a meeting of military representatives, which Churchill suggested could take place at sea on a Royal Navy ship.[11]

At the following day's War Cabinet, Churchill said that further enquiries had established Stein's identity as being the same man who had met with the Prime Minister the year before, at the request of the Belgian king, in connection with 'certain economic proposals'. Prime Minister Chamberlain recalled Stein saying that although he was normally resident in England, he was employed by King Leopold to study economic plans on his behalf and that he had the use of a private annexe in the grounds of the royal palace at Brussels for this purpose.[12]

The War Cabinet agreed to liaise with the French, without disclosing the involvement of King Leopold, in drawing up a list of questions to put to the Belgian military in the event of contacts being successfully established. Hankey said that the French were well aware of the greater confidence the British Government enjoyed with Belgians and would be happy for this to be taken advantage of in any discussions.[13]

Following Hankey's co-ordination group meeting of 9 October, William Strang drafted a despatch to be sent to HM Ambassador Clive at Brussels, along the lines agreed at the meeting, and sent it to Hankey for his approval, adding that he was preparing a similar draft for Bland at The Hague. Hankey reviewed the draft and made some alterations based on conversations he had with the Governor of the Bank of England, Treasury officials and the Chancellor of the Exchequer regarding Belgian and Dutch financial assets in general and bearer bonds in particular. Hankey returned the amended draft to Strang adding:

> When you come to draft the letter to The Hague, you will perhaps bear in mind that the Governor of the Bank of England [Montagu Norman] is sending over a reliable young official to take soundings with his opposite

---

* MI5 were responsible for the hunting-down of German spies and verifying the credentials of enemy aliens residing in the UK.

number in Holland as to whether they will not take corresponding action. It is believed that the number of bearer securities in Holland is much larger than in Belgium, but it is unlikely that they would be willing to move them until the last moment. Mr. Montagu Norman is not optimistic as to the result of this overture. It may result in a rebuff or Mr. Tripp, the Governor of the Bank of Holland, may at once approach his Government, from whom you may hear more. I think, therefore, that you should let Lord Halifax know what is afoot.[14]

In a further note to Strang the next day, Hankey wrote

> I have again seen the Governor of the Bank of England … The Governor confirmed that he is sending an emissary to Holland but emphasised that his visit is of an informal character. The Governor was not at all hopeful about getting the gold away before the emergency. He said that this could not be done without the fact being known, and he did not believe the Dutch Government would allow the Bank to take action. I then stressed the point that if the gold could not be got away before the emergency, there should at least be an emergency plan so that, even if only a few hours were available, the gold could be moved. That at least would be a second best arrangement. We all urged, however, that it would be much better if they could get the gold away before the emergency arises. It was clear by the way that, as in the case of Belgium, securities which are private property would be harder to deal with than gold which is Government property.[15]

The final approved despatches were sent to the embassies in Brussels and The Hague on 12 October, signed by Sir Alexander Cadogan. (See Appendix I) The despatches stressed to the British representatives the importance of impressing on both governments that, in the event of an invasion by Germany, it would be in their interests to 'leave behind as little as possible in the way of military and economic resources which would be of value to Germany in the conduct of the war.' The offer of British assistance in the removal or destruction of these resources would be made to both governments.

Both documents go on to detail those resources which included raw materials, oil, gold and securities, shipping, aircraft, military assets and key personnel.[16]

It was believed that the Belgian Government had already removed some of their gold bullion stocks to a 'place of safety' but that a substantial amount could remain in the vaults of their banks. Cadogan prompted Sir Robert Clive that he should suggest to the Belgians 'the desirability, as a measure of precaution, of getting the gold away in good time.' If the Belgians were receptive to the suggestion about their gold, then Clive should raise the question of their negotiable securities, particularly bearer bonds and stocks, stressing the importance that they too should not fall into German hands.

Cadogan also stressed the importance of not allowing stocks of oil in Belgium to be captured by the Germans and asking Clive if he knew if the Belgians had any plans to avoid this. If not, then Clive should make an approach to them to suggest they prepared the necessary steps and adding that if they failed to do so, then Britain would take action themselves, the plans for which were already being formed.

As a result of Cadogan's letter, Clive met with the Governor of the Belgian National Bank, who told him the greater part of the Belgian gold reserve was already in London, with some held in New York, leaving just a small portion in Belgium. Further enquiries made with the Governor of the Société Générale de Belgique (SGB)* established that the proportion of the reserve held in New York was a third of the total, with the 'greater part' in London representing just a half, leaving a sixth still in Belgium. The Governor of the Belgian National Bank was reluctant to confirm precise details, but Clive pressed him to reveal that the gold left in Belgium was not held either in Brussels or Antwerp but 'at some place not very far from the coast', which Clive took to mean either Bruges or Ostend.[17]

As far as negotiable securities were concerned, the SGB governor told Clive the securities in their possession had all been photographed and copies lodged in Bradford (England), New York, and Saumur (France). These copies would constitute proof that the securities were held by the SGB in case the originals had to be destroyed. The Governor of the National Bank told Clive no special precautions had yet been taken to safeguard negotiable securities in their possession, although he was fully aware of the necessity of preventing them falling into German hands.

Cadogan's letter to Sir Nevil Bland at The Hague contained very similar views and suggestions adding the information that the Bank of England's governor was sending an official over on an informal visit to 'take soundings with his opposite number in Holland as to whether the Dutch will not take the necessary action' in respect of moving their gold and negotiable securities out of the country.[18]

* The *Société Générale de Belgique* was founded by King William I of the Netherlands in 1822 to administer the Belgian ducal estates. When Belgium became independent in 1830 it became a Belgian company and served as the National Bank of Belgium until 1850. It then became a major source of capital for Belgian industry and infrastructure, with close ties to the Belgian Government. Its governor in 1939 was Alexandre Galopin (1879-1944).

The Bank of England's overtures to the Dutch were feared to have possibly resulted in some serious diplomatic consequences. On 12 October Strang wrote to Hankey informing him that he had received a visit from Baron Michiels van Verduynen, the Dutch Minister in London, that morning. The minister told him that he had just heard from a Dutchman 'of the highest repute in London' informing him that the latter had received information from 'a person of authority in London, who would be in a position to know what he is talking about' claiming the British Government had strong reasons to believe that Germany was about to invade the Netherlands within the next few days. Although he was not free to reveal the names of his source and the British informant, the minister felt bound to come immediately to the Foreign Office to seek assurances that if the British Government did indeed have such information about German intentions, then they would not have failed to warn the Dutch Government, either through himself or through Bland at The Hague. Strang had asked the minister if the British informant held an official position. He did not receive a direct answer to his question but had received the impression that it was not an official, but someone who had close connections with official quarters. The inference from Strang was that it was someone from or with connections to the Bank of England.[19]

Hankey responded the same day saying:

> I do not think somehow that the Minister's impressions can have resulted from my conversations with the Governor [of the Bank of England], though the description of the person with whom he talked would rather fit. The point is, however, that on every occasion I have been at pains to say that the emergency we were discussing is one for which no one could foresee the date. It might be six months hence, or it might be in one week's time, or never. In fact, I have repeatedly declared my personal opinion that an attack on Holland is much less likely than one on Belgium owing to the fact that it would be an advantage to Germany for the same reasons as in the last war to keep Holland neutral…[20]

Nothing more appears to have come of the matter and the identities of the Dutchman 'of the highest repute' and his British informant remain a mystery. However, the nervousness of the Foreign Office over the matter was apparent.

On 20 October, Hankey updated the War Cabinet on the progress of the preparations and actions of the various Government departments dealing with the Dutch and Belgian situation. In neither country did the British representatives think it advisable to take up, on a diplomatic footing, the matter of preventing assets falling into German hands with the governments concerned, as both were terrified of taking any action which the Germans might construe as a pretext for breaching their neutrality. However, the British Naval, Military, and Commercial Attachés in both countries would endeavour to exert some influence in their respective fields.

Hankey was also able to report that the Bank of England's emissary to *De Nederlandsche Bank* (DNB, the Dutch Central Bank) had now returned from his visit. He had seen the bank's governor who informed him that 60 per cent of DNB's gold had been held outside the Netherlands since February that year.* In Sterling terms this equated to approximately £110 million out of a total holding of £185 million. The DNB governor was anxious to export a further £40 million, shipping it to London for onward shipment to the United States. Although the governor himself was fully aware of the urgency of the situation, he did not expect a final decision from his government for a week or two. He was also anxious that the Bank of England emissary's visit should not be made known to the Dutch Government through diplomatic channels. The DNB governor went on to say that major Dutch companies had already made their own arrangements about safeguarding their holdings of foreign securities, but the Dutch Government had so far avoided taking any emergency measures to safeguard their own holdings, fearing they would undermine public confidence.

As far as oil stocks were concerned, Hankey reported that there were over 600,000 tons in Holland, with little chance of removing any before an invasion. However, experts at the Royal Dutch Shell Company in London considered that all the stocks could be destroyed at short notice. The company's managing director, Guus Kessler, was on his way to Holland to try to discover if the Dutch Government had any plans to destroy the oil in an emergency. British diplomatic representatives in Holland and Belgium would also impress upon the governments the urgent need of action to destroy their oil stocks if an invasion occurred, or failing that, to cooperate with the British in demolition plans currently being worked out with the War Office and Admiralty.[21]

On 23 October, the chairman of Royal Dutch Shell wrote to Permanent Secretary at the Ministry of Economic Warfare Sir George Mounsey, to say that he had ascertained on 'unimpeachable authority' that the Belgian Government had made plans for the prompt destruction of all their oil stocks in the event of an invasion. He also reported that Guus Kessler had returned from his consultations with the Dutch

---

* This date would coincide with the first fears of a possible German invasion of the Netherlands, as mentioned at the beginning of this chapter.

Government and that they, too, had made plans for the destruction of stocks of all petroleum products and that this could be completed 'in a question of hours'.[22]

The proposals to send naval captains to Holland and Belgium, on reconnaissance missions in the guise of couriers, had not been well received by the Foreign Office. Back on 10 October, William Strang had written to Vice Adm Binney, expressing Lord Halifax's concerns over the proposals. Halifax doubted the propriety of such missions in view of the 'delicacy of the question of military collaboration between His Majesty's Government and the Belgian and Netherlands governments in advance of hostilities.' Strang went on to say that the Foreign Secretary's preference was for the suspension of the proposals, although he was prepared to reconsider if the Admiralty considered that there were strong military reasons to pursue them and would provide him with the relevant military details of the proposals and the results they hoped to gain from them.[23]

Halifax's reservations appear to have been satisfied as, on 17 October, Strang wrote again to Binney to inform him that he had contacted Sir Robert Clive at Brussels and Sir Nevile Bland at The Hague to request their views on sending the naval officers on reconnaissance in the guise of couriers to the ports in their respective domains

Clive responded to say he had no objection and was prepared to pass the naval officer off as his cousin and put him up as such at his residence if that would be of help. He could then arrange for the officer to visit Antwerp the next day and arrange for the British Consul General to put him up there to avoid him using a hotel.

Bland had also responded positively, saying that he thought the visits to the Dutch ports could be arranged without arousing suspicion. However, as the British Vice Consul at Flushing was a Dutch subject, Bland thought it inadvisable that the officer should stay overnight there, but instead he could make a brief visit as a courier with the naval attaché and return to England direct from that port.

Strang said that the officers would need new passports, in their own names, but with no mention of their naval rank. They would also need to be supplied with the necessary courier's passports. The Foreign Office would arrange issue of all these documents.[24]

By 19 October, Binney was able to inform Lord Hankey that First Lord of the Admiralty Churchill and the Foreign Office had given their final agreement for the visits of the Naval Captains to go ahead, the only stipulation being that those going to Holland should do so at weekly intervals, and that they were all to travel on courier passports without any naval rank. The first two were to leave for Rotterdam and Antwerp as soon as their passports were available.[25]

Chapter 5

SECRET MISSIONS

On the morning of 21 October, Captain Clement Moody RN was at Victoria Station in London. Born in 1891, he had been in the Royal Navy since he was 13. A veteran of the First World War, Moody had been promoted to captain in 1933 and commanded the aircraft carrier HMS *Eagle* from 1937 until its return from China in June 1939. The Commander-in-Chief of the China Station, Admiral Percy Noble, described Moody as 'An officer possessing the highest virtues and qualities ... Excellent influence – good judgement – can take any responsibility and is quick in action'. On 9 October 1939, Moody was posted to the Admiralty for 'special service' with Vice Adm Binney's committee.[1]

At Victoria, Moody boarded the 09:28 train to Brighton. From there he went to Shoreham Airport. Travelling on his Foreign Office courier passport, he caught the KLM flight to Amsterdam. Some of his fellow passengers were travelling on to Copenhagen via Amsterdam, but those whose final destination was Holland had to sign statements that they were not 'actively employed in any military capacity by any of the belligerents' and that 'they have not been ordered to take passage by any civil Government department'. During the flight, Moody noted that all the windows had been 'frosted' over, and the cabin height indicators disconnected so at no time during the two-hour flight, apart from take-off and landing, did he have any idea of the height or course of the aircraft or even whether they were flying over land or sea.

On arrival at Amsterdam airport, he was met and driven by car to the British Legation at The Hague, where he would be staying during his visit. At the legation, Moody had a brief meeting with the Minister, Sir Nevile Bland, and his Service Attachés. Bland told Moody that Holland was '100 per cent neutral' and that her politicians and senior military officers were determined not to engage in any staff talks with either the British, French or Belgians. Nor would the military answer any questions put to them by the attachés which might involve them in any way in the war.

After the meeting, Moody and the Naval Attaché, Captain Schofield, travelled by car to Rotterdam, where they spent three hours looking around the port and its facilities.

According to his report, on the following day, 22 October, Moody, accompanied by Schofield, paid a visit by train to Amsterdam. The reason for this visit remains a mystery as Moody's report makes no further mention of it, but they appear to have spent the day there. (I have speculated on one possible reason for this visit, in Appendix II.)

On the next day, Moody spent the morning back at Rotterdam (it is not clear from Moody's notes if Schofield accompanied him, but it is safe to assume that he did). Moody had gained considerable detailed information about the port and its facilities from a guidebook about Rotterdam and its waterways, which he had purchased earlier. From reading the book, Moody was struck by its vastness, with 16 miles of berths for shipping and sixteen floating docks and considered it to be bigger than the Port of London. He also personally counted over 200 oil tanks to which he thought 'it might be possible to do serious damage in the daylight hours of one day.'

The oil tanks were grouped into four main installations, two of which belonged to Shell and one to Esso (the owner of the fourth was not recorded). Moody also counted four further subsidiary installations which he thought may be partially used for the storage of asphalt. At the Shell installations the oil tanks were built into pits, four tanks to a pit, all of which were sunk about 6 feet below ground level and surrounded by a barrier. The pumps appeared to Moody to be situated about 8 feet below ground level. The tanks at the Esso installation were built at ground level, as were the pumps, and were surrounded by a 4-foot-high barrier. The tanks and pumps at the remaining installations were mostly built at ground-level with no barriers around them. Moody surmised that most tanks and pumps had been constructed with sufficient arrangements for catching any oil that might escape if they were holed. So, to deny the oil to the Germans it would be necessary not only to puncture them, but to burn their discharged contents as well.

Rotterdam was also a major shipbuilding centre. Moody took note of the ships under completion on the various slipways and dry docks. These included three submarines being completed for the Dutch navy. However, the slipways for these had been boarded up to keep the work from sight, so Moody was unable to tell at what stage the work on them was at.

From Rotterdam, Moody travelled by tug along the Nieuwe Waterweg (New Waterway)* to the Hook of Holland. Here Moody took note of all the port's defences (unfortunately, the plan of these is missing from the file copy of his report), which included four 4-inch guns on dunes to the north of the waterway. He concluded that there was 'almost certainly' a minefield laid off the entrance to the Hook. Local officials alleged that the mines were of Vickers manufacture and with rotten moorings which had caused some to break free and drift ashore. He also saw a Dutch destroyer patrolling the entrance to the Hook from the North Sea. He was told (presumably by Schofield) that there was always at least one patrolling there.

On entering the waterway from the sea, Moody searched for the London and North Eastern Railway (LNER) jetty. The jetty had handled the LNER boat service from Harwich before the war and would be the logical landing point for any military demolition party, but it was difficult to find. He eventually located it next to the offices of the local Senior Dutch Naval Officer and Harbour Master. Also, alongside the jetty he found the Dutch Naval Mine and Torpedo Station. He could not locate the office of the local senior military officer but presumed it would be somewhere amongst the extensive temporary military barracks that had been built there since the outbreak of the war in Europe.

From his observations and conversations, Moody considered that it would be easy to block the entrance to the New Waterway by sinking blockships there. Failing that he was told that if the northern breakwater could be breached then the entrance would rapidly silt-up and render it unusable.

The only road from the Hook to Rotterdam ran along the northern side of the waterway and at varying distances, up to 5 miles, from it. There was no bridge across the waterway from the road until it reached Rotterdam. The road was very narrow in most parts and Moody thought that it could easily be blocked if the Dutch wanted it to be. In the event of a German attack on Holland, it would also likely be crammed with refugees and military vehicles, making any speedy communication along it exceedingly difficult, if not impossible. Because of this, Moody concluded that the only way to move a military demolition party from the Hook to Rotterdam, in an emergency, would be by boat along the waterway.

---

* The Nieuwe Waterweg is a ship canal, built in 1872, running from het Scheur (a branch of the Rhine-Meuse-Scheldt delta) west of the town of Maassluis to the North Sea at the Hook of Holland. It is the artificial mouth of the river Rhine.

During his time in Rotterdam, Moody also met up with the officers of the British Naval Control Service* based at the port. In discussions with the NCSOs Moody was told that if the Naval Attaché informed them a RN destroyer was to be arriving at the Hook, they could arrange to send a tug or tugs from Rotterdam to meet her. The NCSOs often hired tugs to inspect merchant ships so it would not be unusual to have one sent to the Hook.

Moody left the Hook on the evening of 23 October and returned by car to The Hague. He left the next morning to return to England, arriving in London at 15:00.

In his report to Binney, Moody gave his general, and somewhat unfavourable, impressions on the Dutch situation and the attitude of their government, as gained from his short visit.

> ... (b) The Dutch are very keen on making money and their principal idea at present is to continue to do so despite of the war. Mobilisation of about 300,000 men is costing them a lot and for this reason alone it is considered essential to take every opportunity to make more money.
> (c) Holland is about 50/50 in its feelings for or against Germany or the Allies. German propaganda is very intense and highly organised by a very large, well trained and expert staff in comparison with which the British staff is minute.
> Note: An often recurring form of German propaganda is the warning that the British are about to land on the Dutch coast.
> (d) The general feeling appears to be that the Germans might quite likely attack Belgium through the Limburg appendix† but if they did Holland would merely sit back and carry on trading etc. with the remainder of their country and not make war.
> (e) I found it very difficult to form any clear idea as to how prepared Holland is to prevent Germany over-running her country, except as in (d). There is no doubt that parts have been effectively "wetted" (as opposed to "flooded") but I did not see or hear of any organisation for systematic demolition etc.
> (f) I formed a very definite conclusion that it would be quite impracticable and most unwise to attempt to send parties (Naval or Military) to Holland's aid without the previous concurrence of the Dutch Government. H.B.M.'s [His Britannic Majesty's] Minister was very definite on this point. I personally doubt if they would ever give

* The Naval Control Service Officers (NCSOs) were based at those major ports throughout the world not controlled by the Axis. They monitored and controlled British and Allied merchant shipping calling at those ports.

† Limburg is the southernmost province of the Netherlands. Its long eastern boundary forms the international border with the state of North Rhine-Westphalia, in Germany, while its western boundary borders Belgium, thus forming an obvious 'invasion route' for Germany into Belgium.

> their permission in time as I feel that neutrality and money making are so prominent in their minds and would occupy their whole attention until the last minute.[2]

The same day Moody left London for Holland, another Royal Navy captain flew to Brussels.

Captain Harold Hickling was 47 years old. He joined the Royal Navy at 13 and was made a lieutenant just before the outbreak of the First World War. He was promoted to captain in 1935 and went on to be the commander of the destroyer HMS *Duncan* and captain (D) of the 8th Destroyer Flotilla on the China Station from 1937 to August 1939. On his return home from China, he was granted a month's leave before being appointed to Vice Adm Binney's committee in October 1939.[3]

Like Moody, Hickling was travelling as a civilian on a Foreign Office courier passport. The object of his mission was for him to make a reconnaissance of the port of Antwerp and its approaches, and by personal contact, obtain detailed information about the port. He was to gauge the extent to which, in the event of a German invasion of Belgium, the port's facilities could be destroyed in the space of twelve hours by the actions of small RN demolition parties.

Hickling arrived in Brussels in the late afternoon and went straight to the British Embassy where he first met Colonel Edward Calthrop, the embassy's Passport Control Officer (PCO). At first this seems an odd first meeting for Hickling to have however the office of PCO was one invented in 1919 by Mansfield Cumming, the then head of Britain's Secret Intelligence Service (MI6) as a cover for his agents working in overseas embassies, and Colonel Calthrop was, in reality, an MI6 agent and SIS Chief of Station at Brussels.[4] Although Hickling recorded no details of his meeting with Calthrop, this would go some way to explain the reasons behind it.

Hickling then discussed his mission with the ambassador, Sir Robert Clive. During their two-hour discussion, Clive told Hickling that the chances of Germany violating Belgian neutrality were '100 to 1 against'. He thought that the situation in Belgium now was very different to that in 1914; Belgium was fully mobilised with 400,000 men under arms and was determined to fight any invasion. Belgium's outer lines of defences, along the Albert Canal in the north and the line Liege – Namur to the south, were very strong. There was also a second line of defences around Brussels and the Scheldt and a third based along the line Bruges – Ghent – Ypres.

Clive also thought there was no foundation for the belief in some British Government circles that the Belgians were not taking adequate steps to delay a German advance. Hickling reported 'On the contrary, nothing is being left to chance, at any rate on the frontier. All bridges, railway crossings, roads, etc., are mined and can be destroyed at the touch of the key ...' However, so confident was the Belgian Government of delaying any advance that no active steps appeared to have been taken to prepare any demolitions deeper behind the frontier; this included at the port of Antwerp. It seemed the Belgian Government believed they would have ample time to conduct such demolitions if the situation demanded.

Clive summed up the Belgian Government's official attitude as being strictly neutral, with no intention of giving either side cause for complaint. With this in mind, Hickling was strongly advised not to get himself 'locked-up', as the Belgian police had been instructed to be 'unsympathetic in that respect'.

Despite their government's official line, the upper classes in Belgium were believed to be strongly pro-British, as were the Walloons (the French-speaking Belgians). However, the Flemish majority were said to be strongly pro-German.

Hickling stayed at the embassy that night. The following afternoon he left the embassy and travelled to Antwerp, where he was put-up overnight at the residence of the British Consul General, Godfrey Fisher, with whom he discussed his mission. Fisher informed him that, with Belgium being practically on a war-footing, business at the port was almost at a standstill and the docks were 'dead'. There was also some irritation as the result of Belgian shipping being held up for contraband examination by the Royal Navy. However, there were strong indications of pro-British sympathies among certain companies based at the port. Some of the companies that had supplied barges for the Allies in the last war had volunteered their services again, and the Flandria Steamship Company had put their fleet of ferry ships at Britain's disposal and also would collect and re-condition several smaller craft that had been dispersed at the end of the last war, should they be required.

The following morning, 23 October, Hickling visited the various oil installations at Antwerp. He reported that the total oil storage capacity was just under 1 million metric tons, with the bulk of it at a multi-national facility about 3 miles upriver from the port at Hoboken. A second installation, the British-owned Antwerp Oil Wharves Ltd., with a capacity of 70,000 tons was situated at Hemixen, about 6 miles upriver from Antwerp. A third installation with a capacity of 108,000 tons, owned by Raffineries Belge de Pétroles S.A., was located within the docks itself.

Hickling was able to ascertain that the stocks held in Antwerp as of 14 October were:

Benzine –	92,094 [metric] tons
Kerosine –	9,400
Gas oil –	45,000 " "
Fuel oil –	26.000 " "
Marine diesel –	20,000 " "
Lubricating oil –	38,000 " "
Crude oil –	31,000 " "

In his report, Hickling noted that:

> ... By [Belgian] law all fuel tanks must be inside bunds and saucers sufficient to take a quarter of the capacity of the tanks.
>
> The majority of the saucers have a rain water drain (controlled), which would allow oil to be run off into the river if desired.
>
> ... As light and heavy oil tanks are mixed up indiscriminately there should be little difficulty of setting fire to any installation.
>
> ... All installations have wharves alongside which ships up to 18,000 tons can berth.

After visiting the oil installations, Hickling went on to tour the docks, locks and various other port facilities. He took particular interest in the lock gates at the four entrances to the River Scheldt, noting that their destruction 'should present no difficulties'.

The next day he visited some of Antwerp's barge depots and commercial wharves. He also took the opportunity to contact the British Naval Control Staff based at the port, who were able to provide him with valuable navigational information regarding the approaches to the port via the Scheldt, and the oil facilities further up-river. From this he reported that:

> ... In clear weather the navigation of the Scheldt should present no difficulties to a British warship provided the various aids to navigation are functioning.
>
> In low visibility the services of a pilot are strongly recommended.
>
> If a Scheldt pilot cannot be obtained the Captains of the L.N.E.R steamers SSs – *Malines* – *Antwerp* would be competent to carry out this duty. The Captain of the *Bruges* is the first choice.

> Mr. Horace Vine – a one-time Eng. Lt. Cdr. now believed to be at Harwich who was until recently berthing officer for tankers at Antwerp – also has considerable local knowledge.
>
> … The depth of water in the Scheldt is ample at all states of the tide for a destroyer to reach points well above Antwerp. The river is wide enough for her to turn.
>
> There are numerous quays between the Docks and Hoboken […] alongside which a destroyer and in most cases a 10,000-ton cruiser could berth. Ships up to 18,000 tons have discharged cargo at Hemixen – six miles above Antwerp.

Hickling also made contact with Reginald 'Rex' Newman, an English resident of Antwerp engaged in the maritime business. He was a member of the Maritime Federation of Antwerp, chairman of the British Chamber of Commerce in Brussels and chairman of the British Community in Antwerp. He was also manager of the Antwerp Aviation Club, and an officer in the RAF Reserve.[5] Newman's business had two motor cruisers and two speedboats up for sale, all of which he was prepared to make available for the use of demolition parties, if required.

Hickling then went to visit the British Vice Consul at Ghent, William Whipp.* Whipp had a fleet of lorries at his disposal, which he could make available for the transportation of troops. In addition to these vehicles, Hickling reported that there were about a dozen private cars belonging to the Consul General, the Naval Control Staff and others that could be used if required.

Hickling returned to the Embassy in Brussels to spend the night there before returning to London the next morning.[6]

On Wednesday, 1 November, Captain Edward Aylmer RN was at Victoria Station, waiting for the Brighton train. Aylmer was 47 years old and had been in the Royal Navy since he was 13. He served in the First World War as a sub lieutenant on board the destroyer HMS *Unity*, where he was promoted to lieutenant on the recommendation his CO and the captain (D) of his destroyer flotilla. The latter's recommendation stated: 'I should like to bring to favourable notice the coolness displayed by S.L. Aylmer both on sighting the enemy and while under fire he brought the foremost gun into action quickly and took every opportunity to damage the enemy under difficult

---

* Unfortunately, I have been unable to find any further information on William Whipp

circumstances.' He was promoted to commander in 1927, and captain in 1935. In September 1939 Aylmer was assigned for 'Special Service inside Admiralty' with Binney's committee.[7]

From Brighton, Aylmer went on to Shoreham Airport and boarded a KLM flight to Amsterdam, where he was met by car and driven to the British Legation at The Hague. He was first received by the Minister, Sir Nevile Bland, and then proceeded to the Chancery where he met with the Naval Attaché, Captain Schofield, to discuss the programme for his visit. That evening Aylmer attended a dinner party held at the legation where he also spent the night.

The next morning Schofield made arrangements for himself and Aylmer to visit the British Vice Consul at Flushing [Vlissingen],* on Friday, 3 November. The vice consul was a Dutch national, businessman Pieter de Bruyne.† That same morning the Dutch Government had proclaimed a state of siege‡ in the frontier municipalities and other strategic locations, which included the whole of Walcheren Island.§ This situation had threatened to put paid to Aylmer's plans for the day. Fortunately, Schofield was on very good terms with the head of Dutch military intelligence at The Hague, General van Oorschot, from whom

* Vlissingen, historically known in English as Flushing, is a municipality and city in the southwestern Netherlands on the former island of Walcheren. With its strategic location between the Scheldt River and the North Sea, Vlissingen has been an important harbour for centuries. It was granted city rights in 1315.

† Pieter de Bruyne (1884-1981) was born in Middelburg, the son of Pieter Louis de Bruyne. In 1904 he joined his father's brokerage firm, a firm in which his grandfather Pieter and great-grandfather Gerard had already been active since 1801 as bankers, cashiers, commission agents and insurance brokers. They also managed the petroleum storage facility at the Vlissingen harbour for Pakhuismeesteren and the American Petroleum Company in Rotterdam. In 1905 he became a partner in the company that was then named 'PL de Bruyne & Son'. In Vlissingen this firm was, as 'De Bruyne & Co.'s Scheepsagenten en Rapportagebedrijf', working in ship chartering and reporting of passing ships on their way to or from the ports on the Western Scheldt. The company was also an agent for the British Lloyd's Register of Shipping. De Bruyne held the position of British vice consul in Vlissingen from 1908-40, succeeding his father, who had held this position since 1871. (*Archives.nl - 2. Pieter de Bruyne (1884-1981) (Zeeuws Archief).html*)

‡ The state of siege was a reaction to reports from the Dutch Military Attaché in Berlin, who had obtained intelligence forewarning of an imminent German invasion of Holland.

§ Walcheren is a region and former island in the Dutch province of Zeeland, at the mouth of the Scheldt estuary. It lies between the Eastern Scheldt in the north and the Western Scheldt in the south and is roughly the shape of a rhombus. The two sides facing the North Sea consist of dunes and the rest of its coastline is made up of dykes.

he was able to obtain special passes to allow them to visit Flushing and the surrounding district.

Aylmer and Schofield travelled to Flushing by train where they were met on arrival by de Bruyne, who then drove them in his open car to his offices in Middelburg.* Aylmer noted that the office building had a Lloyd's signal station on the roof and the Port Pilot's office next door had a good view of the ships entering and leaving the Scheldt.

After having lunch at his house, de Bruyne drove Aylmer and Schofield around the Flushing / Walcheren Island district. To minimise any interference from the military authorities, he had already informed the colonel commanding the district, who was an old friend, that he would be driving around the island with two other friends. This seemed to have the desired effect as, despite the whole island being under martial law, their passes were never asked for throughout the day.

De Bruyne drove Aylmer and Schofield around the area slowly, allowing them ample time to view everything of interest, only pausing to put the car's hood up when approaching any sentries or guard posts.

At Flushing, Aylmer counted thirty main oil tanks of various sizes, most he which, he was informed, contained crude oil and were run by commercial firms, not the government. There were also four other large oil tanks sited in the naval base.

Some of the oil tanks were sunk in pits, like those seen by Moody at Rotterdam, with others built at ground level with a low barrier around them. They were all contained in a compound surrounded by an iron and barbed wire fence, which prevented any close-up viewing.

In the docks, Aylmer took note of the nearby power station, a recently completed new, large dry dock, and a cruiser under construction on the stocks. There was a submarine afloat in the basin and an old training ship moored up alongside the naval base in the Inner Haven. The base itself covered an extensive area, surrounded by a high iron and barbed wire fence. It included a hutted barracks and a mine depot. Aylmer noted two warships, possibly minelayers, moored up alongside the depot. He was also informed that the Deurloo Channel, in the mouth of the Western Scheldt, had been mined by the Dutch. The mines, like those Moody had reported off the Hook, were said to be of Vickers production and were constantly breaking free from their rotting moorings.

---

* Middelburg is a city and municipality in the south-western Netherlands, serving as the capital of the province of Zeeland. Situated on the central peninsula of the Zeeland province, Midden-Zeeland (consisting of former islands Walcheren, Noord-Beveland and Zuid-Beveland). The first mention of Middelburg was as one of three fortified towns (borgs) erected on Walcheren (then an island) to guard against Viking raids.

Regarding possible berthing points in the harbour, Aylmer considered the berth at the railway jetty used by cross-channel passenger steamers, as the easiest one to use. Since the outbreak of the war, the Harwich to Flushing steamer service had been reduced from twice daily to just three trips per fortnight. This was indicative of the greatly reduced trade at the port in due to the war situation.

From Flushing they went on to visit Middelburg, which was connected to the former by the Walcheren Canal. They visited the town hall, guildhall, cathedral, and the East India Docks. They also saw the barracks with numerous army personnel walking around the town. Aylmer also noted that many of the town's citizens were clothed in traditional Dutch national dress and clogs.

The canal ran though the centre of Middelburg and then onto Veere, which was their next destination. Veere was a small town with a harbour and a naval seaplane base. It had been heavily fortified while under Napoleon's occupation and many of the fortifications and moats he built were still standing.

From their drive around the island, Aylmer gained the impression that it was all heavily garrisoned with large numbers of military and naval personnel. De Bruyne also told him that any house found empty was quickly taken over by the military. He had some personal experience of this when he and his family had vacated their own house whilst it was undergoing some expensive repairs. They were forced to return and camp in the roofless building to avoid it being forfeited to the military, who had already taken possession of some of the outlying farm buildings he had recently sold.

Aylmer considered that overall, Walcheren was strongly defended and that any landing and demolition of military objectives attempted without the cooperation of the Dutch authorities would be both 'suicidal and impracticable'.

Aylmer returned to England the next morning, travelling by boat from Flushing to Tilbury having slept the night on board, arriving back in London in the late afternoon.

Included in his report to Binney, Aylmer gave some general impressions of his visit:

> During this short visit the main opinion I formed was the strong endeavour of Holland to remain neutral.
>
> Officers of Dutch armed forces have been ordered to hold no conversations with our Naval, Military or Air Force Attachés.
>
> Talking with the Netherlanders one feels that though outwardly they are 100% neutral, in their heart of hearts they are 100% (or nearly) pro-Allies, though they dare not show this openly.

(a) The towns and even villages have their "dug-out" shelters. "Dug-out" is perhaps the wrong term as if you dig three feet down anywhere in this country you come to water, these therefore take the form of erections cobbled and grassed over.

(b) British newspapers arrive regularly – usually one day late, though some papers do arrive by air mail on the day of issue.

German newspapers and periodicals flood the news agencies and bookstalls and I was able to get a number of these and bring back with me.

[...]

The Naval Attaché told me that he would be able to send these regularly by Foreign Office bag, to this country if required, so getting up-to-date press information. I suggest they would be well worth obtaining, the illustrated papers in particular give much more information, particularly photographically, than was the case in the last war.

The German papers are at present enhancing the "U" boat campaign by making public heroes of its personnel. Army and Air Force matter is relegated to a minor setting in all these papers.

(c) **Press**. British propaganda at The Hague suffers from working with a minute staff when compared with the large and efficient staff provided at the German Legation – I was told this latter numbers over 40, many of whom are professional pressmen.

I was told that the reason given for proclaiming a state of siege was due to the public and press clamouring for more news on the subject of the country's defence scheme. There has been a good deal of individual spying going on and the Army has now lost patience and taken this action to stop further trouble.*

(d) **Wishful thinking.** There appears to be a strong body of opinion in the country that if Holland were invaded Britain would come to their help. On someone suggesting unkindly that it might take the same form as help given to Poland, they had really no answer, but there is no doubt they have great faith in England.

Other Minor Points of Interest Connected with my Visit.

(a) **Shops at The Hague**. All the shop keepers I spoke to talked good English and seemed pleased to do so, a large percentage of goods in these shops were English.

The stationers' shops in particular had all the latest English books and magazines. German newspapers and books were much in evidence too.

---

* This would appear to be just a 'cover story' to hide the real Dutch Government fears of an imminent German invasion, based on the information it was receiving from its intelligence sources in Berlin.

The cost of living generally, at The Hague, appeared to be high in comparison to England.

(b) **The Military.** Large numbers of the Netherlands Army were seen throughout the country. A large percentage mounted on bicycles. I was given to understand there is nothing the soldiers cannot do on bicycles.

(c) **Trade.** The Dutch Government will apparently not sign any trade agreement with the Allies for fear of repercussions. It is extremely difficult therefore to control the passage of foodstuffs and war materiel destined for the enemy. I was given many instances of this. It was suggested as a partial solution of this problem that foreign firms and combines would be prepared to have a working agreement with Great Britain, not bringing the Dutch or Belgian Governments into the scheme.

Ymuiden

I consider that it would be definitely unwise for a visit to be made to Ymuiden at present for the following reasons:-

(a) It is one of the areas declared to be in a state of siege.

(b) There is no real excuse for a visit there.

[...]

Binney copied Aylmer's full report, together with those of Captain Moody and Captain Hickling, to Lord Hankey as well as to the Director of Plans at the Admiralty and the Director of Naval Intelligence.[8]

Chapter 6

PLANS AND PREPARATIONS

Weeks before his captains had departed on their secret missions, Vice Adm Binney had been busy preparing his plans for possible operations in the Low Countries. On 9 October he had informed Lord Hankey's meeting that he was in contact with the War Office regarding draft plans to deploy Royal Engineers on demolition missions and Royal Navy destroyers to Dutch and Belgian ports. Three days later, on 12 October, in response to a verbal order from the Chief of the Naval Staff and First Sea Lord, Admiral of the Fleet Sir Dudley Pound, he produced a minute for the Director of Plans at the Admiralty (Captain Victor Danckwerts), the Director of Naval Intelligence (Rear Admiral John Godfrey), the Director of Operations Division (Captain Cecil Harcourt) and Rear Adm Lyster on his proposals for naval operations in the event of Germany invading Holland and / or Belgium:

(i) 4 destroyers to be sent, one to each of the following ports – Ymuiden, Hook of Holland, Flushing and Antwerp.

(ii) Each ship to have on board a trained party of about 20 men under an officer, with explosives for demolition purposes.

(iii) Each destroyer to be accompanied by a Captain member of my Committee. The duties of the Captains and the destroyers would be as follows:

  (a) To induce all neutral shipping to leave the port.

  (b) By their presence to induce the Dutch and / or Belgians to destroy as much as possible of certain of the harbour facilities, to prevent their falling into the hands of the enemy.

  (c) To carry out as much demolition as possible in the immediate vicinity of the ships themselves.

  (d) In the event of R.E. demolition parties being sent, to escort them overseas and generally assist them in the achievement of their object.

2. With regard to the above the following action has been taken :-
(i) The Captains on my Committee are studying the relevant intelligence reports.
(ii) C.in.C. Nore* and C.in.C. Portsmouth† have detailed a party of four officers and eighty men, who are now in the VERNON‡ being trained in demolition work. They require two weeks training, but could be used at any time after one week, say after 18 October, provided that the gear is assembled by that time.

3. Additional Action Required by Admiralty.
(i) It is requested that 4 destroyers may be earmarked for this duty. They should be ready to proceed to Chatham to embark demolition parties at short notice.
(ii) If and when the War Office has authorised the despatch of R.E. demolition detachments, to take up the requisite shipping (probably two or three cross channel steamers) to transport the personnel to Amsterdam, Rotterdam and possibly Antwerp respectively.

Appreciation of the Situation at the moment when it will be necessary to decide to send these destroyers.
4. Germany will have invaded Holland and it may be assumed that her land forces will reach the coast in anything from 2-7 days.
5. There may be bombing activity in the neighbourhood of the ports. It is unlikely that the Germans will wish to destroy anything that might be of value to them later, but it is pretty certain that British destroyers (if identified) in Dutch or Belgian ports would be attacked. For this reason it is possible that the destroyers would be unable to remain in harbour more than one period of daylight. It would be best if they arrived before daylight one day and left before daylight the next. In view of the value of these vessels I consider that their Captains should not unduly hazard them and consequently should be authorised to leave when they considered it right to do so.
6. One of the Dutch ports mentioned above (Hook of Holland) must be approached through the Dutch protective minefield. There are no

---

* Admiral Sir Studholme Brownrigg.

† Admiral Sir William James.

‡ HMS *Vernon* was a shore establishment or 'stone frigate' of the Royal Navy in Portsmouth. Vernon was established on 26 April 1876 as the Royal Navy's Torpedo Branch, also known as the Torpedo School, named after the ship HMS *Vernon* which served as part of its floating base. In the Second World War, and following on from the increasing use of mines, Vernon took on responsibility for mine disposal and developing mine countermeasures.

similar minefields off Ymuiden or Flushing.* It is possible that in the event of an invasion the Germans would also lay minefields backed up by submarines off all the Dutch ports. I propose, however, to ignore this threat, though an air reconnaissance off the Dutch coast to give warning of the approach of German surface forces from the Northward would be desirable. This should be established immediately our destroyers arrived off the ports and continued until they retired.

7. If it is agreed I principle that the destroyers should not remain in several ports more than 24 hours, I would propose that the Captains of my Committee, whom I hope will be able to exert influence on the shipping to clear out, should be flown over so as to be at their ports before the arrival of the destroyers.

8. If circumstances and particularly time permits, I propose to proceed to Holland in person to get in touch with the C.in.C. of the Dutch Navy and endeavour to persuade him of the necessity of prompt action if valuable material is not to be allowed to fall into the hands of the enemy.

9. I consider that the N.A. [Naval Attaché] at The Hague should be acquainted with the foregoing.[1]

In reviewing Binney's minutes, the Director of Operations Division (Home), Captain Harcourt, questioned the use of destroyers, considering them too large and too valuable to risk on the demolition missions. As an alternative, he suggested using MTBs (Motor Torpedo Boats), which would offer greater speed, greater security (being smaller craft they would present smaller targets for air or surface attack), less risk of grounding on the sandbanks off the Dutch and Belgian coasts, and little risk of being identified as RN vessels. Harcourt also considered MTBs to be immune from submarine attack and mines, with an additional advantage of being far more manoeuvrable than destroyers in confined waters such as ports, rivers and canals.

Harcourt admitted that a major disadvantage of employing MTBs on the missions was that they could be hampered by bad weather, although he had also been assured that only a full gale would prevent them being able to make the passage.

Another possible restriction would be the actual availability, at such short notice, of four suitable MTBs. Harcourt advised that, if MTBs were to be used then early action should be taken to secure them.[2]

Despite Harcourt's reservations, Binney insisted that destroyers should be used. Following the completion of his captains' secret

* Captain Aylmer, from his visit to the port, later reported that there was a minefield off Flushing.

missions to Belgium and Holland and their subsequent reporting, Binney got his way. He suggested that 'S' Class vessels would be suitable to convey the small RE demolition parties for the Ymuiden and Antwerp missions, but a larger 'V' or 'W' Class ship would be needed for the Hook of Holland mission with its additional ninety men and 4½ tons of explosives.[3]

Meanwhile, the War Office had been busy drafting plans and objectives for the Royal Engineers' land demolition parties. On 15 October the Director of Military Intelligence, Major General Beaumont-Nesbitt, forwarded the draft plans to the Military Attachés at The Hague and Brussels. The plans took the heading: 'Measures to be taken in the event of an invasion by Germany – Draft plan for Land Demolition Parties'.

In the draft plan for Holland the stated objectives were to destroy all existing oil stocks at Rotterdam, Amsterdam, Flushing, and The Hague. In addition, the facilities for the handling of iron ore at Rotterdam were also to be destroyed.

Most of the Dutch oil stocks were held at Rotterdam (est. 435,000 tons). A further 65,000 tons were held at Amsterdam; 40,000 tons at Flushing; and 35,000 tons at The Hague.

It was estimated that fifty-four men would be required to destroy the oil tanks, with a further twenty needed to destroy the iron ore handling facilities. The demolition parties would need to disembark at the Hook of Holland for Rotterdam and The Hague, and Ymuiden for Amsterdam. With both ports being some distance from their objectives, it would be necessary to pre-arrange transport to take the demolition parties and their stores onto their final destinations.

For Belgium the plan was to destroy all oil stocks held at Antwerp (est. 150,000 tons), Ghent (20,000 tons), Zeebrugge (4,000 tons), and Bruges (3,000 tons).[4]

The plans also set out the suggested method for the destruction of the oil stocks:

<u>Demolition of Oil Storage Tanks</u>

1. The method suggested is to puncture the tank and fire the oil or petrol gushing out.

   3lbs of high explosive is sufficient to make a hole in any tank.

2. <u>Method of laying charge</u>.

   Gelignite, Blasting Gelatine, Dynamite or Gun Cotton is recommended. Tie together three slabs of gun-cotton, or the requisite number of sticks of explosive. Cut a two-foot length of safety fuse (this will give a delay of one minute) and insert it in the detonator. Make a hole in one stick of explosive with a pencil and insert the detonator. (In the case of gun cotton a primer must be used.) Place the charge close against the side of the tank at ground level. Soak half a blanket in paraffin and place down-wind of the explosive in such a position that, when lit, the flames will not touch the explosive, but with the oil gushing out will eventually reach it. The full stream of oil should not fall on the blanket, or in the case of heavy oil, it will probably put it out.

3. Method of Firing.

Prepare twice as many tanks as the number of men employed. Allot two tanks to each man. On the given signal, each man lights first the fuse and then the blanket of the two tanks allotted to him. All men then run to a prearranged position of safety (50 yards should be sufficient).

Start work on the down-wind end of the area.

Stores Required.

A tank 30 feet in diameter and 20 feet high will hold 100,000 gallons, or 400 tons, of petrol or oil.

Allow the following stores for 300 tons of oil: -

3 lbs explosive.
1 detonator.
2 feet of safety fuze.
½ blanket.
¼ gallon paraffin.
Each man requires a two gallon tin, a knife and matches.
Two charges may be placed against the larger tanks.

Time.

Allow half an hour per man, per pair of tanks.[5]

The 'go-ahead' to prepare the Royal Engineers demolition parties for their missions was given by the Director of Military Operations and Plans (DMO), Major General Richard Dewing, on 16 October. The unit allocated for the missions was 55 Field Company, Royal Engineers, a 5th Infantry Division unit then based at Bordon Camp in Aldershot, which had been on notice since September for possible service overseas. Instructions would be given for its commanding officer to visit the Directorate (MO4) at the War Office on 21 October, when he would be given full details of his task and put in touch with Military Intelligence, and the naval officers who would be responsible for transporting his parties.[6]

On 21 October, Major Sir John Forbes, a baronet and Officer Commanding 55 Field Company RE, attended the War Office, as ordered,[7] where he met the DMO who informed him that his unit had been selected to provide the RE demolition teams for the 'Binney' operation. He received his written orders instructing him to hold his unit in readiness to move at four hours' notice, with an attached list of the stores that would be required for the missions:

Boys A.T. rifle	8
A.T. Rifle Ammunition	3,600 rounds
Blankets old	360
Stretchers	9
Guncotton Slabs	126
Primers	126
Detonators (No.27)	126
Safety fuse, feet	252
Axes, felling, 7lbs	18
Hammers, sledge, 7lbs	18
Torches Large Mariel	27
Torches, small, with positive switch	63
Verey Light Pistols	9
" " Cartridges red	27
" " " green	27
" " " white	27
Revolvers .38	18
Holsters Revolver	18
Pouches, ammunition revolver	18
Ammunition, revolver .38	1,000
Fuzees boxes	90
Emergency Rations	270
Kerosine gallons	360
2 gallon containers (for Kerosine)	180[8]

The DMO also enclosed a copy of an outline plan of the operation, now officially codenamed Operation *XD*:

<u>Object</u>

1. In the event of a German invasion of Holland and / or Belgium to ensure, in cooperation with the authorities in these countries, the destruction of certain defences, oil stocks and other facilities.

<u>Composition of the Force.</u>

2. The Force will be divided into four parties, carried in H.M. Ships, each headed by a Captain R.N. and destined for the following ports:

Party A. Ymuiden.
" B. Hook.
" C. Flushing.
" D. Antwerp.

Each of these parties consists of twenty naval ratings with demolition gear and in the case of A, B, and D, the following Royal Engineer detachments which will be under the command of the respective Captains R.N.

A. 12 R.E. for the destruction of oil stocks at Amsterdam.
B. 66 R.E. for the destruction of oil stocks at Rotterdam.
C. 24 R.E. for the destruction of oil stocks at Antwerp.

<u>Method.</u>

3. On invasion of either or both countries –
(a) The force will be assembled at Chatham under the orders of the Admiralty and War Office as detailed in Appendix 1.
(b) H.M. Diplomatic Representatives at The Hague and in Brussels have instructions to approach the Dutch and / or Belgian Governments as to their willingness to receive the expedition and will wire the result of their conversations to the Foreign Office, who will inform the Admiralty and War Office.
(c) In the event of the Governments of Holland and / or Belgium agreeing to receive the forces, the Naval Attaché in Holland and the Military Attaché in Belgium will arrange with the local Naval and Military authorities to meet and pilot H.M. Ships to their destination and, on arrival, to provide accommodation, if required, and the transport, guides and interpreters as detailed in Appendix II.
(d) On receipt of the reply of the Dutch and / or Belgian Government the First Lord of the Admiralty and the Secretary of State for War will raise in the Cabinet the question of the despatch of the force or part of the force, and will communicate the Cabinet decision to the Admiralty and the War Office respectively. The executive order for the force to sail will be issues by the Admiralty.
4. On arrival overseas the Captains R.N. at each port will keep in close touch with the Dutch and / or Belgian Naval and Military authorities. They will be responsible, with the consent of such authorities, for the operations in their areas, including the time at which the military demolition parties should be despatched to their tasks.
5. The final executive order to carry out the demolitions must initiate with the Dutch and / or Belgian authorities.

The naval captain in charge of each party will be responsible for laying down the channels by which the executive order to effect the demolitions will be conveyed to the personnel concerned.*

6. No fixed timings and plan for the withdrawal can be made. If possible, demolition parties will be re-embarked in H.M. Ships.

> Should this method not be feasible they will withdraw in hired land or sea transport as circumstances may dictate.
>
> *Note If necessary, the British Consul Generals at Rotterdam, Amsterdam and Antwerp could provide a useful communication link between the Naval Captain or the local authorities and the R.E. demolition parties. They should be warned by the attaches accordingly.[9]

There followed a more detailed plan of the operation set out in three appendices covering the assembly and despatch of the force, the composition of the four parties and their individual objectives, and the administration arrangements for the force.[10]

Back at Bordon Camp, the next day Forbes and his second-in-command, Captain Wilson, worked on the Binney Plan producing a draft of their own appreciation of the operation.[11] The detailed plan had envisaged the demolition parties being transported from their respective ports of arrival by water to their final destinations, but with a back-up option of using road transport. Forbes and Wilson considered the advantages and disadvantages of both options. By using the water route, they could preserve secrecy; avoid the possibility of taking the wrong road or having to deal with roads that were either congested with refugees and military vehicles or blocked by hostile action. Also, all their objectives were situated on waterfronts so they could berth right next to them. The main disadvantage with using water transport was speed, or rather, lack of it. Any form of water transport would be slower than road transport, but if they could maintain 6 knots using motor launches, they would still have enough time to carry-out their tasks.

Apart from being faster, road transport would offer an alternative means of withdrawal over land in the event of the parties being unable to re-join their destroyers for any reason. However, using road would also involve extra handling of stores and more complicated routes. They would also be more vulnerable to air attacks; they would require more local guides; and there would be greater dispersal of personnel amongst the various vehicles required.

Forbes and Wilson expressed doubts on the methods proposed for the puncturing of the oil storage tanks. The War Office plan was to use 3 pounds of guncotton as an explosive charge to rupture the tanks at ground level. However, during the 1936-39 Arab Revolt in Palestine, Arab terrorists had made several attempts to sabotage the Iraq – Haifa oil pipeline using high explosives. No demolitions of the pressurised steel pipe were successful using this method, the charges merely blowing away from the pipe. Forbes and Wilson thought the same may happen with the pressurised steel oil tanks, which presented similar conditions. However, successful punctures of the pipeline had been made using rifle bullets fired at close range; the escaping oil then being ignited by firing cotton waste soaked in kerosene. Forbes and Wilson considered that a better alternative would be to use the four Boys anti-tank rifles that the unit was to be equipped with. It was thought that these could puncture any thickness of steel plate likely to be encountered, although this needed to be confirmed by tests as soon as suitable specimen plates were available to use.

Another concern was that to ensure the complete destruction of all the oil in the tanks in the time allowed, it was essential that the protective earth bund surrounding them should also be destroyed. Extra explosives would therefore be required for this task, together with smaller quantities for dealing with any locked buildings and gates.

In their appreciation of the plan, Forbes and Wilson went onto determine the number of launches required to take the demolition parties on to their final objectives; the distribution of stores to the those parties; the amounts of foreign currency that would be needed for each party to cover the costs of hiring land or sea transport, supplies, bribes etc.; the motor transport that would be required for each party in the event of delay or obstruction in returning to the destroyers by launch; and the allocation of time allowed for each stage of the demolition work.[12]

The following day Forbes went back to the War Office to present their appreciation of the Binney Plan, while Wilson went around collecting up the various stores required for the operation. Both officers were then present at the War Office on 24 October for further consultations and again the following day after first visiting the Nore Command HQ at Chatham to co-ordinate plans for the operation with the Royal Navy.[13]

Meanwhile, Lord Hankey ensured the War Cabinet were kept updated with the progress of all the plans and preparations for the military and naval operations, as well as the various diplomatic manoeuvres and Allied consultations. The latter included the agreement to hand over full responsibility for the operations at Ghent and Bruges to the French, leaving Antwerp as the only Belgian objective for British land forces, while the destruction of port facilities and the sinking of blockships at Zeebrugge and Ostend would be a naval operation in cooperation with the HQ of the French army's 16th Corps, behind whose sector of operations the two ports lay.[14] Radio communications for these latter operations would be handled by the Royal Signals, who would have two wireless sets at the French HQ in direct contact with the RN ships at each port, and with the GHQ of the British Expeditionary Force in France, which would relay messages from the French to the War Office to pass onto the Admiralty. The executive order for the blowing of the demolition charges and sinking of the blockships would be issued by the HQ French 16th Corps, via this route.[15] The Zeebrugge and Ostend operation would be known as 'LYSTER', after Rear Adm Lyster, who would be commanding the naval operation.[16]

In a briefing on the proposed operations, prepared for the War Cabinet being held on 26 October, the DMO suggested that:

> ... the Naval and Army plans, when co-ordinated, should be submitted for approval to the Chiefs of Staff, and possibly to the War Cabinet. They involve important decisions which may have political as well as military repercussions, ...
>
> ... For military as well as for political reasons, it is essential that demolitions and similar measures in Holland and at ANTWERP should not be taken prematurely, or in such a manner to antagonise the Dutch and Belgians.
>
> I suggest that H.M. Representatives in BRUSSELS and at THE HAGUE might be made responsible for giving the Naval and Military Commanders on the spot executive instructions to put the plans into operation, if possible by agreement with the Belgians and Dutch.
>
> Alternatively, the Naval and Military Commanders might be instructed not to execute the plans, except in the last resort, without the agreement of H.M. Representatives.[17]

At the meeting of the War Cabinet on 26 October, Hankey presented a memorandum reporting on the steps taken to give effect to the recommendations of the Chiefs of Staff Committee, made earlier in the month, in the event of a German invasion of the Low Countries. As well as the military preparations, the memorandum included details of the progress measures to prevent Dutch and Belgian economic and financial assets, including gold and other financial securities, from falling into the hands of the Germans. Hankey explained:

> ... The objects aimed at were, first, to ensure the reduction of the assets which might fall into the hands of the Germans: secondly, to try and induce the Dutch and Belgian Governments to make plans to meet the emergency: thirdly, to have our own plans ready to assist the Dutch and Belgians: and, finally, to place ourselves in a position to secure our vital interests by our own exertions.
>
> The only decision required at the present time was whether or not the contents of the Memorandum should be communicated to the French.[18]

As the French had undertaken to take responsibility for the demolitions at Bruges and Ghent and to give the executive order for the sinking of the blockships at Zeebrugge and Ostend, Hankey thought it only right they should be made aware of the progress that had been made in the British plans. The War Cabinet agreed, authorising the communication of the Memorandum to the French with the proviso that no mention should be made of the arrangements concerning gold and securities, or of any of the enquiries on that subject.[19]

That same day, Hankey's assistant, Ian Jacob visited Binney to discuss the proposed operations in Holland and Belgium. Binney told Jacob that ideally, he would like to sail his ships directly into the Dutch ports, informing the Dutch Government that they were there to cooperate and hoping that would stir them into action. However, he realised it would not be practicable to sail into the Dutch ports without the prior agreement of the Dutch Government. Dutch pilots would be required to guide the ships through the minefields and the ports' defences warned not to open fire on them. Jacob and Binney agreed that it was out of the question for the RN ships to set sail until the Dutch Government had been approached and given its consent. The same applied to the Belgian Government.

Binney told Jacob that he would need twenty-four hours to collect the destroyers and prepare them for departure. He hoped that this would be sufficient time to gain the agreement of the Dutch and Belgian governments before the expeditions sailed.

Providing these agreements had been made, Binney would arrange for naval captains from his committee to fly out to each port to control the expeditions' arrivals. It should also then be possible for the respective naval and military attachés to get in touch with the Dutch and Belgian naval and military authorities to arrange for the ships to be met at the ports and brought into harbour.

The military parties would come under the command of Binney from the time they embarked. On arrival at the ports, they would come under the control of the RN captains, who would inform each commanding officer that it was thought unlikely the destroyers would be able to stay at the ports longer than twenty-four hours. The captains would despatch the military parties under their command, informing the parties COs of the time their respective destroyers would be expecting to leave. It would be then the responsibility of the military commanding officers to carry out their tasks and return to the ships, if possible, by the appointed time.

The military parties would proceed to their destinations under arrangements made with the authorities by the Military Attachés.

Once they had left their ships the parties would no longer be under the control of Binney's naval captains, and would therefore act on their own, subject to the general direction of the Dutch and Belgians. They would be out of radio contact and so would be unable to receive any orders. The only method by which they could be given the word to blow their charges would be for them to be authorised to do so by the Dutch and Belgian authorities. In the last resort, with the enemy approaching and no orders having been received from the Dutch or Belgians, the demolition parties would have to take the responsibility themselves for blowing their charges.

Binney informed Jacob that he was preparing a joint military and naval plan which would be sent to each Attaché so they could make all preparations their end.[20]

Meanwhile, back at Bordon Camp, the sappers of 55 Field Company were experimenting with methods for destroying a pressurised steel tank. Tests were made using shots from Boys anti-tank rifles to penetrate the tanks, which appeared to be successful, allowing the oil to flow out and be ignited using kerosene-soaked blankets or exploding kerosene cans.[21]

By 30 October, Forbes had finalised his plans and submitted to the War Office his 'Operations Order No. 1' for 55 Field Company to provide a detachment to be ready to move from Bordon Camp at four hours' notice, to deploy in six demolition parties to area objectives in Belgium and Holland. The detachment would be prepared ready with all the necessary stores and equipment required to fulfil their missions.[22]

The next day, Forbes issued 'Operation Order No. 2' with further details: from Bordon, the detachment would be transported by road to the RN base at Chatham where the demolition parties would board, with their stores, on destroyers for shipping to their respective ports of disembarkation.[23]

This order was followed by 'Operation Order No. 3', which updated the number of RE demolition parties now required to just three, to be deployed as: Party A (12 REs) to Ymuiden for objectives in Amsterdam; Party B (66 REs) to the Hook for objectives in Rotterdam; and Party D (24 REs) to Antwerp for the objectives there. Demolition Party C would be made up entirely from RN personnel and would deploy to Flushing. It would be the intention of the RE parties to destroy all oil stocks at objectives A, B, and D. From the ports, the demolition parties would travel by launch to their final objectives.

The cooperation of the Dutch and Belgian governments would be sought by HM Diplomatic Representatives in those countries. If they agreed to receive the force, the Naval and Military Attachés would arrange with the local naval and military authorities for assistance with guides, transport and interpreters.

On arrival at the ports the demolition parties would wait for instructions from their respective RN captains (who would be liaising with the local authorities) as to whether they could proceed on by launch to their final objectives and, if so, when. Also, whether demolitions could commence without further orders and if not, from whom these orders were to be received. It was noted that if no orders were received then the RE officer in charge of each party would take responsibility for blowing the charges on close approach of enemy forces.[24]

The order for the sappers to move from Bordon would come from the M.O. 4 duty officer at the War Office. If any reports came in of German action against the Low Countries, the duty officer would, after first telephoning his superiors, telephone the Operations Division at the Admiralty with reference to the implementation of the BINNEY and LYSTER Plans and ask them to inform him as soon as possible the time and date at which the RE demolition parties should report at Chatham.

The duty officer would then telephone 55 Field Company at Bordon, instructing them to be prepared to move to Chatham at short notice. Once he had heard back from the Admiralty confirming the time the sappers should arrive at Chatham, he would then instruct 55 Field Company accordingly, telling them to report to the Commodore RN Barracks on their arrival.[25]

Binney prepared an *aide-memoire* to assist the Admiralty when the time came to decide whether to despatch the destroyers with their demolition parties. In it Binney re-iterated that the force should only be sent with the permission of the Dutch and Belgian authorities and, given the small demolition parties it was intended to send, it would be impossible to destroy anything without the cooperation of the governments concerned. Binney hoped that sending the destroyers would stimulate the Dutch and Belgian governments into acting themselves to destroy assets to prevent them falling into enemy hands. To save some time in the event of a German invasion of the Netherlands, Binney was personally in favour of, rather than asking their permission, simply informing the Dutch Government that on the presumption they would welcome British assistance, that the destroyers were on their way. But of course, consideration would need to be given that they would need a Dutch pilot to guide them through the minefields and that Dutch defences may open fire on the destroyers arriving 'unheralded', so it would certainly be best to obtain Dutch permission before despatching the force.[26]

Binney was also acutely aware of the importance of the time factor. As far as he was concerned the operations should be of a 'tip and run' nature to avoid being caught by German air and naval forces.

Meanwhile, in Brussels, the British Military Attaché, Lieut. Colonel Francis Blake,* reported to the Deputy Director of Military Intelligence, Brigadier William van Custem, that he had been entertaining Commandant Georges Goor, from the Belgian Board of Admiralty to dinner. During their conversation, Goor disclosed that all preparations had been made for dealing with the shipping at Antwerp in the event of hostile action by Germany. He said their arrangements included the getting away to safety of all Belgian shipping, and arrangements for blocking the channel of the River Scheldt at short notice. Goor also told Blake that the Belgians were making their own arrangements for blocking Zeebrugge and Ostend. Blake doubted he would be able to obtain any information of such interest out of any of the Belgian General Staff as his French counterpart had already been warned off approaching them.[27]

The British Naval Attaché at Brussels, Captain Brian Schofield, had also been present at Blake's dinner with Commandant Goor. In his report of the evening to the Director of Naval Intelligence, Rear Admiral John Godfrey, Schofield confirmed Blake's recollections of the conversations with Goor, with the important addition that Goor had said plans were in hand for the Belgians to destroy stocks of fuel and other stores at Antwerp themselves. Schofield also reported that Goor had told them it was not the intention of the Belgian authorities to commence the destruction of their property until it was clearly evident that the country, or a substantial part of it, was about to fall into German hands, and it was considered that any efforts on behalf of Britain to do so prematurely would be met with considerable opposition. However, on the naval side, Schofield was confident of the whole-hearted support of Commandant Goor, when the time came, his sympathies being entirely pro-British.[28]

The reports found their way to Hankey who told Ian Jacob that although the reports were interesting, he saw no reason to change any of the plans that had been made regarding Belgium. He would, however, refer to it the next time he reported to the War Cabinet.[29]

---

* Francis Arthur Alexander Blake (1897-1966). Commissioned as a 2nd lieutenant in the Royal Artillery in 1916 and promoted to lieutenant in 1917. He was appointed as an Interpreter to Inter Allied Commission of Control at Koenigsberg in 1920, then promoted to captain in 1929 and major in 1938. In 1939 he was appointed Military Attaché Brussels with the local rank of Lieutenant colonel. (*https://www.bloodysunday.co.uk/castle-intelligence/blake-faa/faa-blake.html*).

Sir Nevile Bland, at The Hague, had also been busy socialising. In a letter to Sir Alec Cadogan written on 29 October, Bland said that he had dined with Snouck Hurgronje,* from the Dutch Foreign Ministry the previous evening. After their second glass of port, conversation had become 'free and unrestricted'. Bland took the opportunity of asking the Dutchman what he thought they would do with all the oil at Rotterdam if the Germans invaded. The response he received was that they would 'just set a match to it'. Bland responded saying, 'Surely it would take more than that?' to which the Dutchman replied, 'Oh no, it's quite easy to destroy it, and anyhow I don't think there's much there'. Bland's information was that if fired on a rising tide, there was enough oil at Rotterdam to set the city ablaze.[30]

In a second letter sent to Cadogan that same day, Bland informed him that the Legation Secretary, Adrian Holman, had lunched with the Director General of the Dutch Ministry of Economic Affairs, Dr Hans Hirschfeld.† During the lunch Holman raised the question of the Dutch gold reserves. Hirschfeld told him that 'although it might have been kept secret from the Bank of England, it was a fact that two-thirds of the Dutch gold reserve was at present in the United States of America and South Africa, most of it being in the former.' Holman then attempted to draw information from him about the security of the remaining third in Holland if the Germans invaded, implying that the remainder should also be moved to safety, but Hirschfeld gave the impression to him that the Germans 'would not pay particular attention to Dutch gold.' However, Holman thought that Hirschfeld had taken the hint and that measures would be taken by the Dutch to prevent any gold falling into German hands, but the equally important question of Dutch bearer securities had not been raised.[31]

By the end of October 1939, indications from various diplomatic and intelligence sources pointed towards an imminent German invasion of the Netherlands and Belgium. The British Government's Chief

* Jonkheer Aarnout Marinus Snouck Hurgronje (1882-1951) was Secretary General of the Netherlands Ministry for Foreign Affairs. (*https://www.thepeerage.com/p63294.htm*)

† Heinz Max Hirschfeld (1899-1961) was a Dutch economist of German-Jewish descent. He was a controversial character because he stayed on after the Germans occupied the Netherlands in 1940 to work with the Nazi administration. The Germans put great trust in him. They were well aware of the fact that Hirschfeld was of great importance to them as a mediator between Dutch and German interests. They even went so far as to acquit him of his Jewish descent. (*John Rhijnsburger: 'The Political Biography as a Vehicle for the Political Scientist: Dr. H.M. Hirschfeld and the Dutch National Interest, 1931-1952', Journal of Political Science, Nov 1992.*)

Diplomatic Advisor, Sir Robert Vansittart,* had his own personal intelligence source in the form of Group Captain (Malcolm) Grahame Christie, a retired former British Air Attaché and intelligence agent in Germany. Christie, now a private citizen, lived in a house close to the German – Dutch border and was still in touch with some of his contacts inside Germany, the most important of which was Hans Ritter, a former German air force pilot and Air Attaché who was then working as an advisor to the Junkers aircraft company. Ritter sent regular reports to Christie on the situation inside Germany, which Christie then sent on to Vansittart. One such report sent on 25 October warned of a 'big air offensive against Great Britain'. However, the Luftwaffe only had one suitable type of bomber (the Heinkel He.111) that could transport large bombloads to Britain from airfields in Germany. Ritter explained that the situation had now become 'acute' in that Luftwaffe chief Herman Goering was saying he had insufficient numbers of He.111s for launching heavy massed attacks and that he was urging for an occupation of Belgium and its airfields so that the Luftwaffe could utilise all types of its shorter-range bombers for its offensive. Hitler had agreed and had ordered preparations to be made for a surprise attack on Belgium. This had met with opposition from the German General Staff and its Chief, General Halder had threatened to resign. Ritter then updated Christie on 3 November saying that Goering had insisted that if an air offensive against Britain was considered essential for a German victory in the war and if an invasion of Belgium was ruled out, then the German army must occupy Holland instead.[32]

On 2 November, Clive had written from Brussels to Cadogan at the Foreign Office to inform him that the Belgians would resist a German invasion to the utmost of their ability and, in such event, would not hesitate in invoking the British guarantee of their independence. Nevertheless, the Belgian king and government were determined not to take any steps in advance of an invasion that might compromise

---

* Robert Gilbert Vansittart (1881-1957) was a senior diplomatist. He was appointed to the Paris embassy, where he was promoted third secretary in March 1905. In April 1907 he was transferred to Tehran. He was promoted second secretary in December 1908 and transferred to Cairo in January 1909. In August 1911 ill health brought him back to the Foreign Office, where he was to spend the remainder of his career. In February 1928 he was promoted to Assistant Under-Secretary and joined the staff at 10 Downing Street, where he acted as Private Secretary to prime ministers Stanley Baldwin and Ramsay MacDonald. Two years later he was appointed Permanent Under-Secretary at the Foreign Office. In January 1938 he was appointed Chief Diplomatic Adviser to the government. (*Oxford Dictionary of National Biography: https://www.oxforddnb.com/display/10.1093/ref:odnb/9780198614128.001.0001/odnb-9780198614128-e-36630*).

Belgium's neutrality, including cooperating with Britain in facilitating the removal or the destruction of assets that may prove useful to the Germans. However, they were preparing plans of their own to deny to the Germans the use of their principal ports, and for the destruction of fuel and other stores at Antwerp. Clive was also able to reassure Cadogan that the concerns regarding gold and negotiable securities were already receiving the attention of the governors of the Belgian National Bank and Société Générale.[33]

Meanwhile, all the British plans for action in the event of a German invasion of the Netherlands and Belgium had been finalised and Hankey was able to present to the War Cabinet a summary of the measures to be taken by each government department concerned.[34] The plans were also sent to Clive in Brussels and Bland at The Hague, with instructions as to their responsibilities in seeking the cooperation of the Belgian and Dutch governments.[35]

On 4 November, following the warnings that had been received, Cadogan sent an urgent telegram to Bland at The Hague:

> We have some evidence to show that a German attack on Holland may be imminent; though it seems that Hitler has not finally made up his mind as yet. Object of attack, if made, would be to secure advanced air bases for operations against Great Britain.
>
> If you think it desirable I have no objection to you passing on the above information to the Dutch Govt.[36]

Chapter 7

TENSIONS RISE AND FALL

Following receipt of Cadogan's telegram of 4 November, Sir Nevile Bland called on the Dutch Minister for Foreign Affairs, Eelco van Kleffens, to inform him of its contents warning of a German attack. Van Kleffens admitted that he had received similar warnings but had also received categorical assurances from Berlin that Germany 'entertained no intentions against Holland'. He also told Bland that he had his own high-placed, secret source of information within Germany from which he had learned that the Luftwaffe command were 'of the opinion that no material advantage which [the] German air force could possibly acquire in Holland could conceivably outweigh the devastating political losses which would ensue from an invasion, and that there was no intention to put matters to the test.'[1]

On 7 November, the Belgian news agency *Belga* published a communiqué from Berlin stating that the same German 'shock troops' that had fought in Poland were now stationed on the Dutch frontier and a considerable number of armoured units were also stationed in border villages. The German explanation for these deployments was that lack of accommodation made it impossible for the troops to take up their planned defensive positions among their own Siegfried Line fortifications.[2] The Belgian Government itself was now becoming worried about German intentions regarding their neutrality. That evening, Spaak, the Minister for Foreign Affairs, asked Sir Robert Clive to call on him. Spaak told Clive that he was very disturbed at the recent massing of German troops on the Belgian frontier and Luftwaffe reconnaissance flights that had been detected in Belgian airspace. They had protested to the Germans but had simply received denials in response. Spaak also said that the Dutch were even more disturbed and hence the king had gone to Holland yesterday at the invitation of the Dutch queen to discuss the situation.[3] As a result, in what many perceived to be a 'last ditch' attempt to forestall German aggression, Queen Wilhelmina of the Netherlands, in conjunction with King Leopold of the Belgians, in letters addressed to the leaders of France, Britain, and Germany, appealed for them 'to find a reasonable, sound basis for peace', and, as 'heads of neutral States', offering their services as mediators.[4]

Despite official denials on both sides, the general mood in Holland was still one of resignation that a German invasion was imminent. On 9 November, Captain Schofield, who combined his role as the British Naval Attaché at The Hague with the same at Brussels, dined at the home of Lieutenant Commander Cornelis Moolenburgh, the head of Dutch Naval Intelligence. Also present was another Dutch naval intelligence officer, Lieutenant Commander de Booy, who happened to be the brother of the Dutch Naval Attaché in London.

In his report to the Director of Naval Intelligence, Admiral John Godfrey, Schofield said that after dinner, the three men began discussing the current situation in the Netherlands. The Dutchmen said that their Naval Staff expect the country to be invaded within a week. The reasons they gave included the internal situation in Germany, with Hitler needing a military success to quell frustration and unrest with the war; the necessity of obtaining airfields nearer Britain to allow fighter escort of bomber missions; and the gaining of several submarine bases.

Counting against the prospect of a German invasion was the lateness of the season, now heading into winter, which would make the use of mechanised units impossible, especially with the recent flooding operations that had been carried out. However, the Dutchmen understood that Hitler was insisting on the campaign against the advice of his General Staff. Dutch intelligence had identified German forces concentrating on the border; the construction of pontoon bridges on the Rhine in the vicinity of Emmerik, just 4 kilometres from the border; and had received reports of large numbers of flat-bottomed lighters being assembled at Hamburg, Bremen, and Emden that could be used to capture the Dutch Frisian Islands.*

The Dutchmen told Schofield that several approaches had been made to the German Naval Attaché at The Hague in recent days to ask him what all these measures could portend and why the German

* The Frisian Islands, also known as the Wadden Islands or the Wadden Sea Islands, form an archipelago at the eastern edge of the North Sea in northwestern Europe, stretching from the northwest of the Netherlands through Germany to the west of Denmark.

press had suddenly become so hostile regarding the Netherlands. All he could do was either plead ignorance or provide evasive answers.

The Dutch officers assured Schofield that if the Netherlands were attacked then they would resist with all the force at their disposal. They also said that it was a definite intention to evacuate all ships, stores and aircraft to the UK and to destroy all stocks of oil and other materiel that could prove useful to the Germans, although Schofield doubted that the quantity of explosives required to do this would be available to the Dutch at such short notice.

At the end of the discussion, Moolenburgh told Scofield 'Well, if the Germans do attack us they will get nothing but a swamp, because we shall cut every dike [*sic*] in Holland and flood the whole country.'[5]

On 9 November, Sir Robert Clive informed the Foreign Office of a report he had received from a German socialist exile, now living in Belgium close to the border with Germany and who maintained close contacts inside Germany. The report contained current German views regarding Holland. It was thought that Holland had been playing a 'double game', with the allegation that the German-born, former SS officer, Prince Bernhardt of the Netherlands* had revealed the existence of a secret agreement between Great Britain and the Netherlands. In view of this Germany considered herself released from her obligations to respect Dutch neutrality and hence, that a German invasion was now expected either on 12 November or, failing that, before the end of the following week at the latest.[6] Although the allegation regarding Prince Bernhardt and the 'secret agreement' was dismissed by Foreign Office officials as 'undiluted nonsense', they agreed about the claimed time frame for the German invasion.[7]

Hankey now prepared an extensive update of the plans for the measures to be taken in the event of a German invasion of Belgium and the Netherlands, ready to present to the War Cabinet.[8] He also wrote to Churchill regarding the naval side of the plans and informed him of the intelligence coming from the Service Attachés at The Hague and Brussels regarding the preparations the Dutch

---

* Prince Bernhard of Lippe-Biesterfeld (1911-2004) was the son of Prince Bernhard Casimir and nephew of Leopold IV, the last reigning prince of Lippe-Biesterfeld. He was educated at the universities of Lausanne, Munich, and Berlin, where he studied law. Following the majority of German princelings after 1933, he joined the Nazi party and the Reiter SS Corps. In 1936, while working for the German chemical concern IG Farben in Paris, he met Crown Princess (later Queen) Juliana of the Netherlands, and on January 7, 1937, they were married and Bernhardt took Dutch citizenship and received the title of prince of the Netherlands, (*https://www.britannica.com/biography/Bernhard-prince-of-the-Netherlands-prince-of-Lippe-Biesterfeld*)

and Belgians were making for denying to the enemy the use of their ports and for the destruction of fuel stocks held there. However, Hankey told Churchill that he still saw no reason to change any of the British naval plans, but he did suggest that the RN captains who would oversee XD operations at the ports, be kept informed of the latest intelligence so as to avoid the risk of any clash with the Dutch or Belgian authorities when they arrived. Once the diplomats had agreed with their respective host governments that the cooperation of British forces would be welcomed, the Service Attachés would play their part by making all necessary arrangements to ensure the safe arrival of those forces. The main difficulty, as Hankey saw it, was the timing of the despatch of the expeditions. He hoped that the twenty-four-hour period required to gather and prepare the destroyers for their operations would be sufficient time to gain the agreement of the Dutch and Belgian governments to the expeditions.[9]

The War Cabinet held on Saturday, 11 November, saw Hankey present his updated plans. He informed the meeting that:

(i) A short 'War Book' had been drawn up defining and assigning the responsibility for the action required of Departments.

(ii) The Foreign Office had on the 1st November communicated a summary of the measures to our Ambassador at Brussels and our Minister at The Hague, with a letter explaining to them exactly what their responsibilities were.

(iii) The Naval arrangements for sending destroyers to Dutch Ports and to Antwerp, and the Military arrangements for sending Demolition Detachments in those destroyers had been tuned up and coordinated. The military party was ready to move at twelve hours' notice, and the Destroyers at twenty-four hours' notice. The Naval Captains who would be in charge of this work had visited the ports at which they would have to operate.

[…]

(iv) A summary of the plan, excepting only the arrangements with regard to gold, had been communicated to the French Military Authorities.[10]

Hankey went on to present further details of the updated plans and then, to summarise, he said:

… that it would be seen that the most important changes, since [I] had last reported to the War Cabinet were as follows: -

(i) A tuning-up of the readiness and completion of our own arrangements.

(ii) The receipt of information indicating that the Dutch and especially the Belgian arrangements, were probably more complete than we had anticipated.[11]

The evidence of greater preparedness on the part of the Dutch and Belgians did not, in Hankey's opinion, justify any alteration in the British plans and claimed that it was 'impossible to foresee' how they would react to a sudden invasion, and therefore to know whether they would carry out their plans or not.[12]

With 55 Field Company RE now on just 12 hours' notice to move to Chatham to board their destroyers,[13] concern was being raised in military circles that the French authorities were not being kept up to date with the latest plans. The Deputy Director of Military Operations, Brigadier Lund, wrote to Ian Jacob, seeking assurance that the XD operations were going to be coordinated with any plans the French military were making along similar lines. He was concerned that, thus far, the French had only been informed about the operations in general terms but had not been given the locations. He made the point that both Flushing and Antwerp were in areas that would be assigned to French military operations if the Germans attacked.[14] Jacob responded on 12 November, saying that the French would be told at the meeting of the Anglo-French Liaison Committee, to be held that morning, about the plans for the expeditions to Flushing and Antwerp and to inquire if they too planned similar operations at those ports, if so, stressing the necessity to coordinate plans. Jacob went on to say that once the French intentions were known, it would be up to the War Office and the Admiralty to decide whether to continue with the expeditions to Flushing and Antwerp, balancing the 'considerable risk of misunderstanding or worse' between British, French, Dutch and Belgian forces, with the danger that the French forces might fail to get to their destinations and the demolitions then would not be carried out.[15]

Following the meeting of the Liaison Committee, Jacob reported that the planned action of the British demolition parties at Antwerp and Flushing was discussed, emphasising the importance of coordinating these plans with those of the French.[16]

Meanwhile, Captain Schofield at The Hague had sensed a slight relaxation in fears coming from the Dutch naval authorities of a German invasion, although they still had concerns about the defences of one of the ports that were included in the British plans. In a message to Adm Godfrey, Schofield wrote:

[…] although situation at the present time appears to have eased, Dutch Naval Staff are very concerned with the defences of the West Frisian

> Islands against attack from shallow draught troop transport which is considered will be part of[the] plan of attack. Since they have not sufficient means to deal with such attack it is considered that they will call on our Navy and Air Force to assist with this.
>
> Ymuiden is a stronghold of Dutch Nazis and a coup to seize [the] port coincident with German attack is possible. ...[17]

Schofield now turned his attention to the reasons behind the recent invasion scare. On 15 November he again wrote to Godfrey:

> An interesting feature of the recent crisis has been the refusal of the Dutch Government to disclose the reason which prompted them to take all the precautionary measures which they did last week. It is generally considered by most Dutch people that the mere presence of an albeit fairly large body of German cavalry on their frontier was not in itself a sufficient threat to cause the large scale flooding operations which were carried out (despite the denials of the Dutch Military Intelligence section) and the [Dutch] Prime Minister's speech* is generally regarded as 'eyewash' and has not deceived thoughtful people. As reported in my last letter, the Dutch Naval authorities made little attempt to hide their anxiety, but even they could not or would not give any inkling as to the reasons for their apprehension. The presence of a large body of heavily armed police in all the large towns has given a rise to the belief that a Nazi Putsch was planned, and it is certainly difficult to account for their presence unless some internal disorder was expected. Dutch Naval and Military circles talk freely of the 'stab in the back' which they expect the Nazis to give them and the fact that the Government does little or nothing to curb their activities, undoubtedly out of fear of Germany, increases apprehension on this score.
>
> Why the Putsch, if one was intended, misfired is hard to say, but it is not unlikely that the Government got wind of it and took sufficient measures to render its success unlikely, and the German plan may hinge on a successful internal uprising.
>
> As long as both the Dutch and German Nazis are allowed free rein the danger of such a coup will remain and it is difficult to see what the Government can do, other than take precautionary measures. I have been told that there are 1,300 Nazi sympathisers in the Dutch Army and I know of one Captain of a Dutch Minesweeper who is out and

* On 13 November the Dutch Prime Minister, Dirk Jan de Geer, broadcast a statement to the effect that his government had no immediate reason to fear a breach of its neutrality, and that the precautionary measures recently taken by them had been necessary to keep pace with the increased tension in Western Europe. (*Hansard -. HC Deb 16 November 1939 vol 353 cc873 – 'The War Situation', statement by Chancellor of the Exchequer, Sir John Simon*)

> out pro-German (there is another who is equally pro-English) and it will be interesting to see what headway the Germans make with their propaganda during the coming months. One of the themes which is being played on with particular emphasis at the moment, is the rise in the cost of living which is attributed to our holding up of Dutch ships. Pamphlets are distributed attempting to prove that since we are buying butter from Holland, the poor Dutch soldier has to go without, and so on. It is doubtful that this sort of propaganda is making much headway, but it is still being assiduously pursued all the same.
>
> My French colleague told me last night that they had reliable information that the Dutch shipped another £10 million of gold to the USA yesterday and I have been told by two fairly reasonable sources that practically the whole of South Beveland* was flooded on Monday for the defence of Flushing and that it will take 5 years to get this land back into condition for pasture.
>
> Since writing the above the Military Attaché† has just told me that the [Dutch] Military Intelligence section admitted to him this morning that they had definite evidence of an internal Nazi coup for the 8th or 9th November, and that it was true that 30 to 40 arrests had been made. This after they had strenuously denied that there was anything of the sort!
>
> As far as the Naval side is concerned, some of the precautionary measures which were taken were being relaxed, such as the re-opening of Ijmuiden [Ymuiden] and the Hook to shipping at night …[18]

The easing in Dutch–German tensions mentioned by Schofield was acknowledged in Britain. Speaking for the government in the House of Commons on 16 November, Chancellor of the Exchequer Sir John Simon said: 'The relaxation in tension […] is a satisfaction to His Majesty's Government who, I need hardly say, have every intention, in accordance with the consistent policy of this country, of continuing to respect the neutrality of the Netherlands and of Belgium.'[19]

The cause for optimism was reflected in Rome, where the Counsellor at the British Embassy, Sir Noel Charles, in conversation with the Italian Foreign Minister, Count Ciano, asked the question whether he had any news of a German offensive in the West. Ciano answered that 'he thought it probable that there would not now be an attack this year.'[20]

Despite the easing in tensions, preparations for the XD operations stayed in place, with the 'Special Squads' of 55 Field Company,

---

* Zuid-Beveland ("South Beveland") is part of the province of Zeeland in the Netherlands north of the Western Scheldt and south of the Eastern Scheldt. (*https://en.wikipedia.org/wiki/Zuid-Beveland*).Military Intelligence section

† Lt Col W.L. Gibson

remaining on twelve-hours' standby at Bordon to implement the 'Binney Plan'.[21] However, there were now questions being raised as to whether Binney's plan needed to be implemented in full.

The Belgian Government had now adopted a more robust attitude towards the possibility of a German invasion, indicating that they would put up very strong resistance and were preparing their defences accordingly. Antwerp would act as the final redoubt of the Belgian Army, and demolitions of the oil stocks and docks there would be undertaken by the Belgians themselves. In addition, in the event of a German invasion of the Low Countries, the French Army would make its move into Belgium placing troops around Antwerp, helping to forestall the German advance on the port and allowing more time for the Belgians to prepare their demolitions. If the Belgians failed to complete the demolitions, the French would be close at hand to take over responsibility. The French also intended to occupy Walcheren and South Beveland in Holland and would then be in a strong position to undertake demolitions at Flushing.[22]

Following a meeting with Captain Troubridge, who was now acting as Binney's Staff Officer, Jacob wrote to Hankey on 21 November, saying:

> [...] It would seem, therefore, that the best plan would be to hand over responsibility for Antwerp, in so far as the demolitions will not be completely accomplished by the Belgians, to the French, who can deal with Antwerp in the same way as they are dealing with Bruges and Ghent. The Admiralty would be greatly relieved at the thought of not having to send a destroyer up the Schelde [*sic*], and the War Office would have similar feelings regarding their 20 Sappers, who would be playing a lonely game in Antwerp.[23]

As far as Flushing was concerned, Jacob wrote:

> [...] There seems to be no reason why Flushing should not also be handed over to the French, in any rate in all circumstances in which they would be sending their forces to the island. If the French troops arrive, and disembark according to plan, they can be trusted to look after the demolitions when the time came for them to leave again. If they fail to get ashore, it will be because they have been forestalled by the Germans; in which case it seems hardly likely that our destroyer would meet with better success.[24]

Two days later, after consulting with Binney, the Director of Plans at the Admiralty, Captain Dankwerts proposed, in view of the changed situation, cancelling plans to send a destroyer and demolition party to Antwerp, and retaining a destroyer on standby for Flushing, but cancelling it immediately if news was received that the French had successfully landed at Walcheren. In the unlikely event of the Netherlands being invaded but Belgium remaining neutral, Dankwerts proposed that RN destroyers should be sent with demolition parties to Ymuiden, the Hook of Holland, and Flushing.[25]

Hankey, it appeared, disagreed with the above proposals, and forwarded them on to Ismay to obtain the views of the Chiefs of Staff Committee. The COS in turn referred the matter on for discussion to the Deputy Chiefs of Staff Committee, which met on 28 November. The DCOS agreed with Hankey's wish to keep the arrangements in place for the destroyers and demolition parties to be sent to Antwerp and Flushing, but suggested that the French should still be asked to take on the commitment at Antwerp, thus providing a 'second-string to our bow'. The French had already undertaken to carry out the demolitions at Flushing but this would depend on their successful occupation of Walcheren, so the despatch of British parties to both Flushing and Antwerp would be for a decision at the time dependent on the progress of the French forces.[26] Hankey approved the DCOS recommendations and his War Cabinet sub-committee submitted its revised plans to the full War Cabinet on 20 December.[27]

That same day Binney was appointed Flag Officer Orkney and Shetland and was already on his way to Scapa Flow.[28] His Admiralty Committee had also been disbanded but its plans and preparations would live on into a new year.

Chapter 8

NEW YEAR, NEW THREATS

The new year began with the attention of the Allies turning northwards to the Baltic Sea and the frozen lands of Scandinavia. The Soviet Union had declared war on Finland on 30 November 1939, and the two countries were now engaged in a bloody conflict, with the Finns fighting for their very survival as an independent state. Allied sympathies were, quite naturally, with the gallant Finns and they indicated their willingness to offer military support. However, the real Allied goal was economic warfare: to cut off shipments of Swedish iron ore to Germany. Most German iron ore imports, deemed vital for their war industries, now came from neutral Sweden via the Norwegian, ice-free port of Narvik. The Norwegian and Swedish governments were to be urged to help the Finns, or at least to help others to help them, by allowing aid to pass through their territory. At the same time, British troops were being prepared for direct action in the area, under the guise of assisting the Finns, which would involve disembarking at Narvik and occupying the Swedish iron ore fields at Gallivare together with their lines of communication. On 6 January General Massy, the Deputy Chief of the Imperial General Staff, wrote to the Commanders of British Home Forces announcing:

> ...measures are being taken to hold certain troops in readiness for the possibility of immediate operations in Scandinavia. [. . .] The force will be known as 'Stratforce', and it is thought that the earliest time and date of embarkation will be noon on 17th January. It is possible, however, that the units earmarked for this operation may have to be kept at short notice for an indefinite period.[1]

One of those units earmarked for STRATFORCE was 55 Field Company, RE and two days later, their CO, Major Sir John Forbes, was summoned to the War Office to attend a conference on the operation.[2] The allocation of this new task meant that the unit would no longer be available on standby for the Binney / XD operations so responsibility for the latter was handed over to the Commander, Royal Engineers of the 12th Infantry Division, a territorial division then dispersed around Kent completing training and preparation for its eventual deployment with the BEF in France. The Director of Military Operations at the War Office wrote to the 12th Division CRE on 12 January with instructions to provide demolition parties for the XD operations and informing him that all plans and supplies for the operations would be delivered to him by Lt Stevens of 55 Field Company, who, along with two other 55 Field Company officers, would be posted to his unit.[3] The 12th Division Royal Engineers were based at Milton Barracks in Gravesend and in its War Diary for 14 January, the CRE noted: 'A "Special Party" consisting of 8 Officers and approximately 100 men has been detailed for special duty on direct instructions from the War Office.'[4]

Meanwhile at Bordon, 55 Field Company had received their orders to hand over all plans and supplies for the XD operations to the 12th Division RE and to transfer Lt Stevens and the two other officers, who had been due to take part in the operations, to Gravesend for duties with the Special Party. However, on 14 January, with preparations for joining STRATFORCE '90 per cent complete', 55 Field Company received an urgent telegram from the War Office with the order to suspend those preparations and revert to 'Stand to' at two hours' notice for the Binney plan.[5] With all their supplies for the operations already transferred to Gravesend, should they be called upon they would now need to collect these supplies from Gravesend before proceeding to Chatham to board their destroyers.[6]

To understand the reasons for this sudden reversion, it is necessary to go back a few days to the morning of 10 January, when a German Messerschmitt Bf 108 *Taifun,* a reconnaissance and liaison aircraft flown by Luftwaffe Major Eric Hoenmanns, crash-landed inside neutral Belgium, resulting in what became known as 'The Mechelen Affair'. Hoenmanns had been flying from Loddenheide in Germany to Cologne when he lost his way in fog. While searching for the River Rhine, which he hoped would enable him to regain his bearings, he flew too far west and ended up circling Vucht, near the River Meuse in Belgium. At that point he appears to have inadvertently cut off the fuel supply to the plane's engine, which then soon stopped, and Hoenmanns quickly decided that his only viable option was to land in a nearby field at Mechelen-sur-Meuse. Also on board the aircraft was Major Helmuth Reinberger, another Luftwaffe officer who had been assigned to the planning staff of General Kurt Student's Seventh Air Division. In breach of all regulations, and unknown to Hoenmanns, in the yellow pigskin briefcase that Reinberger clutched tightly on his lap were the top-secret plans for Hitler's invasion of the Low Countries, which was due to take place just a week later, on 17 January. Hoenmanns only discovered that Reinberger was carrying secret documents when, after they had landed, they asked a farmer where they were. When the man replied that they were in Belgium, Reinberger turned white as a sheet. Borrowing matches from the farmer, he rushed back to the plane after exclaiming that he had secret documents that must be destroyed immediately. Hoenmanns moved away from the plane, acting as a decoy. However, before they could destroy all the documents, Belgian soldiers arrived and arrested them. Two hours later, officers from the Belgian intelligence service, the *Sureté d'Etat*, arrived, bringing the documents to the attention of their superiors in the late afternoon.[7] Belgian Intelligence translated and assessed the documents and, at noon on 11 January, their results were handed to King Leopold, who immediately informed his Minister of Defence, General Denis, at the same time ordering that the Allied C-in-C General Gamelin and the British and Dutch Military Attachés also be informed at once. The king's military advisor, General Van Overstraeten, summoned the British Military Attaché Colonel Blake and gave him a copy of a summary derived from the information recovered from the charred German documents.[8] Blake then returned to his Embassy to update the new British Ambassador, Sir Lancelot Oliphant.

Another copy of the summary was handed to Colonel Hautcoeur, a French officer acting as Leopold's secret liaison officer with the Allied C-in-C. Van Overstraeten asked Hautcoeur to take the summary to Gamelin and ask him how soon Belgium could expect assistance in the event of a German attack. Hautcoeur left for Paris that night and met with Gamelin and his Staff the following morning. Although the French Staff suspected that the whole episode could be a German hoax, the information in the summary, together with warnings they had already received elsewhere, convinced them to issue a 'top priority alert' to their army and to prepare to send a French Military Mission to Belgium. Acting on the same information, the BEF were also ordered to 'Stand To'.[9]

The head of the Belgian *Sureté d'Etat*, Baron Fernand Lepage, also passed on copies of some of the captured documents to SIS Head of Station at Brussels, Colonel Calthrop. Calthrop immediately sent them on to MI6 headquarters at Broadway, in London, in the care of his deputy, Captain John Bygott. However, experts at Broadway dismissed them, ridiculing them as 'obvious forgeries'.[10]

Leopold's concerns were heightened when he received a message from his Military Attaché in Berlin stating that he had received intelligence that the Germans now assumed the Reinberger documents had been captured and, to forestall Belgian countermeasures, they would bring their attack forward to the following day (14 January). With his own General Staff and some of his ministers still reluctant to involve the Allies, Leopold decided to take it upon himself to communicate directly with the British and French governments to seek undertakings regarding his nation's future should she be involved in a war with Germany. Rather than use official channels, Leopold would employ the offices of one of his oldest friends to assist him with this urgent task.[11]

Meanwhile, back in Britain, on Saturday, 13 January a War Cabinet meeting was in progress. Being the weekend, some members were away in their constituencies or at their country estates, including Prime Minister Chamberlain and the Foreign Secretary Lord Halifax, so the meeting was chaired by Lord Chatfield, with Jacob acting as Military Secretary in the absence of Ismay. Item five on the agenda was 'The Western Front – Possible German attack on Belgium and Holland'. The Secretary of State for War designate,* Oliver Stanley, informed his colleagues of 'certain information received from the Military Attaché at Brussels indicating the possibility of an attack by Germany, from the North Sea to the Moselle, being launched during the next few days.'[12] Stanley went on to say that the War Office had no information to confirm this German plan, but they considered that the Germans had sufficient divisions in place to launch a surprise attack.

As some in the War Office had raised doubts regarding the authenticity of the report, the Military Attaché in Brussels had been asked if his informant had any original documentary evidence to support his claims. The Military Attache's reply stated:

> … that the information was derived from an aircraft which had crashed at Hasselt in Belgium with two German Staff Officers on board. These officers were believed to have been carrying out a reconnaissance over Belgium. Papers found in the aircraft contained an alleged plan for an attack on Belgium – papers which the German Staff Officers had endeavoured, but had failed to destroy, and which were now in the possession of the Belgian Staff. The Belgians had asked that the strictest

---

* Following an acrimonious dispute with the senior Command of the BEF, Leslie Hore-Belisha had resigned as Secretary of State for War on 5 January. Chamberlain had appointed Oliver Stanley to replace him, but the latter had yet to receive his Seals of Office from the King.

> secrecy should be observed. Meanwhile, it was stated that the German Embassy in Brussels was in a state of panic.[13]

Chief of the Imperial General Staff, General Sir W. Edmund Ironside thought the plan was feasible. He had sent a warning to the Commander of the BEF Lord Gort and had also informed Gamelin, French Commander of all the Allied land forces in the area. Ironside assured the War Cabinet that the plans for meeting such an attack, in cooperation with the French, 'were ready to be put into operation immediately the need arose'. Hankey also confirmed that the demolition plans he had been responsible for drawing up 'were likewise ready to be put into immediate operation'.

Before the meeting ended, a brief reference was made to the fact that the King of the Belgians had sent an urgent message to Admiral of the Fleet, Sir Roger Keyes, asking to see him. The necessary arrangements had been made for Keyes to arrive in Brussels that afternoon. [14]

Following the War Cabinet meeting and in response to the information received, the First Secretary at the Foreign Office, Roger Makins, sent a telegram to Oliphant at Brussels saying: 'In view of certain disquieting reports you should be prepared to act at short notice. Similar message sent to The Hague.'[15]

That same evening, Makins and Jacob met with a Belgian official, Monsieur de Samblanx, who claimed to be the personal representative Antoine Delfosse,* the Minister of Transport and Communications in the Belgian Government. Samblanx said that he had been charged by Delfosse with the handling of the possible evacuation of Belgian civilians, and of certain stores and equipment. He had already been to Paris and met with government and military officials there with whom he had discussed plans for the evacuation of Belgian refugees into France in the event of a German invasion of his country. Whilst there, he had also met the British Military Attaché, Colonel Redman, who had suggested he visit London to discuss aspects of the evacuations the British Government may be interested in. Samblanx agreed with the suggestion and obtained the authority of his minister for the visit. The object of his meeting with Makins and Jacob appeared to

---

* Antoine Delfosse (1895-1980) was a Belgian Catholic politician. He was the only minister present in 1940 in occupied Belgium. In June 1940, he went to France to look for personnel and equipment for Belgian radio. Active in the resistance, Delfosse fled to London during 1942. There he received the portfolios of Justice, National Information and Propaganda in the Belgian government in exile. (*https://www.belgiumwwii.be/belgique-en-guerre/personnalites/delfosse-antoine.html*).

be to try to obtain some idea of what the British would do to help the Belgians evacuate shipping, goods and personnel. Still being unsure of Samblanx's credentials, Jacob and Makins refused to discuss the British plans, but did not rule out the possibility of using him to provide the opportunity of starting correspondence with the Belgians. Samblanx proposed a channel of communication using the British and French Military Attachés in Brussels. Samblanx claimed to be in close touch with the latter, who was fully acquainted with the whole matter and was already acting as an intermediary between the Belgian authorities and the French GHQ. Jacob thought that this channel of communications would be rapid and effective but inquired if it would be acceptable to the Belgian military authorities. In response, Samblanx explained that as Belgium was not yet on a war footing, the matter could only be handled on a civilian plane, and that it was just a matter of preparing for rapid action should the need arise. He went on to say that his minister was, at this stage, responsible for the evacuation plans but was adamant that the utmost secrecy should be maintained, hence that was why Delfosse had sent him on a personal mission rather than communicate through the usual diplomatic channels.

Jacob said that he would put the matter before the appropriate authorities and would respond through the channels discussed. Samblanx said that he was fully satisfied with Jacob's proposals and that he would now be returning to Paris to continue discussions there, before his return to Brussels on Monday, 15 January.[16]

The following day, Jacob sent a report and full transcript of the meeting to Hankey, having first contacted Colonel Redman in Paris and established that Samblanx had no connection to the Belgian Military Staff and that the Belgian Military Attaché in Paris had no knowledge of his visit there. However, Jacob thought that if the Belgian military were still reluctant to engage in Staff conversations with the Allies, despite the present alarm, then the channel Samblanx had suggested could prove useful and that such communications should take the form of a note saying:

> We realise that, in the event of a German invasion of Belgium, there will be a great number of assets which should not be allowed to fall intact into the hands of the Germans. In particular, the following should be dealt with:-
>
> Oil, and other raw materials;
> Dock and harbour facilities;
> Shipping, including barges, tugs, etc;

Aircraft and aerodrome facilities;
Machine tools;
Power stations; and
Skilled labour.

> These could be prevented from falling into the hands of the Germans by evacuation, where possible, or otherwise by demolition. If you agree that this is so, would you tell us what plans you have made to deal with the various problems, and, as we would be willing to cooperate to the best of our ability, would you be willing for us to send personnel to assist?
>
> As it is essential for real success that plans should be made beforehand, by what means can the appropriate authorities get into touch for the purpose?[17]

Jacob thought that such a communication 'would set the ball rolling, without giving away any dangerous information.'[18]

The following day, on Hankey's instructions, Jacob visited the Principal Assistant Secretary at the Ministry of Transport, Robert Tolerton* to discuss the problems that would be confronted in evacuating Belgian shipping in the event of a German invasion of that country. Tolerton invited Jacob to attend that morning's meeting of the ministry's Port and Transit Committee, where he was shown the working of the 'machinery' for the control of all incoming shipping. Tolerton explained that they would have no problem in dealing with the Belgian ships at short notice if required, but that it would still be of great assistance to get a representative of Belgian shipping interests to attend the daily meetings of the committee. This representative could then act as a channel of communication about shipping with the Belgian Government and provide information about the ships themselves and their cargoes.[19]

Hankey and Jacob realised that the question of how to open communications with the Belgians about their shipping was just one which Samblanx could provide the answer to. On 18 January Jacob

---

* Sir Roberrt Hill Tolerton, (1887-1956) he was a civil servant who joined the Board of Trade in 1910. He served with 1/23rd (County of London) Battalion, The London Regiment, in the First World War and obtained the rank of lieutenant colonel. After the First World War, in 1919 he transferred to the Ministry of Transport, where he became Principal Private Secretary to Sir Eric Geddes and other ministers. Sir Robert enjoyed a distinguished career, holding the posts of Secretary to the Royal Commission on Transport 1928-30; Assistant Secretary (1929), Principal Assistant Secretary (1934) and Under-Secretary (1946) at the Ministry of Transport and Assistant Director-General, Ministry of War Transport 1942-6. (*https://discovery.nationalarchives.gov.uk/details/r/64f2b6b8-b25c-49a1-8a6f-fa1a7a41a25f*).

wrote a message for Samblanx to be handed to him, while the latter was in Paris, by the Military Attaché, Colonel Redman, confirming the questions that needed to be addressed regarding the assistance of Britain in the prevention of certain Belgian assets falling into German hands and the opening up of communications between their respective authorities to deal with them. Jacob included Tolerton's suggestion for a Belgian representative to attend the British Port and Transit Committee. An offer was also made to provide British assistance with any plans, preparations, and the provision of personnel for the demolition of port and harbour facilities 'if, in the last resort, such action became necessary.'[20] Jacob instructed Redman that the message was not to be handed to Samblanx until the Foreign Office had received information from Ambassador Oliphant in Brussels establishing the Belgian's *bona fides*. Oliphant replied the following day advising caution and Redman was telephoned and ordered not to hand the message to Samblanx. By the end of the month, the Foreign Office had still been unable to confirm Samblanx's credentials, so Hankey and Jacob decided not to commit to any further communication with the Belgian,[21] who was eventually disowned by the Belgian Government[22] and who remains a mysterious figure to this day.

Meanwhile, another, unofficial, channel of communication had already been opened between Belgium and Britain. On the morning of 13 January, King Leopold asked Keyes to come to Belgium to see him. Keyes arrived at the Royal Palace at Laeken on the evening of the 13th. He was invited into the king's study, where Leopold asked him to obtain the following guarantees from the British Government in the event of Belgium being invaded by Germany:

1. No opening of peace negotiations [with Germany] without Belgium's participation.
2. Guarantees for the total restoration of the political and territorial status of Belgium and of the [Belgian] Congo.
3. Help in the economic restoration of Belgium.

Keyes said that an official request along these lines from the Belgium Government might be favourably received in London, but he was unable to give any assurance on this without consulting the Cabinet. He then left Laeken to travel to the British GHQ in Arras, where he intended to take a plane to London that night. Unfortunately, when he arrived in Arras the airfield was enveloped in thick fog, thus preventing any possibility of a flight that night. Instead, Keyes slept at the British HQ. The following morning, he used the telephone to contact Winston Churchill at the Admiralty. Keyes gave a report of his conversation with Leopold to Churchill, reading out the king's guarantee proposals.[23] Unfortunately, no official transcript of the telephone conversation seems to exist, but Keyes appears to have added a rider of his own when speaking to Churchill, giving the impression that if the guarantees were forthcoming, then Leopold would be able to convince his government to invite the Allies into Belgium at once, even if the Germans did not attack.[24]

When the War Cabinet met next, on the Sunday lunchtime of 14 January, Churchill relayed the Belgian king's message to his colleagues, adding that he had discussed the proposals on the telephone with the Prime Minister, who had 'strongly disliked' the suggestion that the Belgians should attach conditions to receiving Allied help at this late stage. Chamberlain's view was that this was not the time to give guarantees other than those implicit in a military alliance. Churchill said that he had instructed Keyes to take this line with Leopold, whilst also expressing sympathy with Belgium at such an anxious time and saying that the most useful step the Belgians could take was to immediately establish Staff conversations with the Allies. Keyes was now on his way back to Brussels to relay the Prime Minister's response to Leopold.[25]

Those ministers that were present were unanimous in their anxiety that the opportunity for British forces to enter Belgium before the Germans made their move should not be missed, and Churchill was emphatic that the Prime Minister should return to London that afternoon.[26]

Chamberlain did return and chaired a further meeting of the War Cabinet that evening. Chancellor of the Exchequer Sir John Simon and Lord Hankey also returned to London for the meeting, as did 'Pug' Ismay, who took over as Secretary. The only item under discussion was the possible German attack on the Western Front.[27]

Chamberlain brought the War Cabinet up to date with developments since their earlier meeting that day:

(a) Sir Alexander Cadogan had visited the French Embassy, and communicated to the French Ambassador* the message received from King Leopold through Sir Roger Keyes. He had told him

* André Charles Corbin, (1881-1970) was a French diplomat. After the First World War, Corbin served in the press bureau of the French Foreign Ministry at the Quai d'Orsay, in Paris. He made many British friends; he spoke English fluently and had a profound sympathy for Britain and British ways. Corbin served as the French Ambassador to Spain (1929-31) and to Belgium (1931-33) before being appointed French Ambassador to the Court of St. James. He resigned his position on 26 June 1940, following France's armistice with Germany.

that a temporizing reply had been sent through the same channel, and invited him to inform M. Daladier* immediately of what had occurred, and to ask for his reactions as early as possible. A reply from the French Government had been received, which was as follows: -

(i) they agreed that we could give the assurances asked for, and

(ii) that if King Leopold would invite our armies to enter Belgium, that would be of great military advantage. But in order to have the full benefit of that advantage, we must be ready to move immediately the King issued his invitation.

Pending a decision by His Majesty's Government, the French Government, who had received no suggestion from Brussels about these assurances, or the invitation to enter Belgium, would make no move.

(b) […] a message had been sent to Sir Roger Keyes asking him to tell King Leopold that the matter was under consideration, and that a reply would be sent as soon as possible.

(c) A telegram had been received from The Hague, […], the gist of which was as follows: -

The Dutch Minister for Foreign Affairs, in an interview with Sir N. Bland, said that, although he thought something might be brewing, he had nothing to show what it was. Such indications as were available pointed rather to next Wednesday than today. Certain extra defensive precautions were being taken in Holland.

The Minister for Foreign Affairs was outwardly calm, and thought that the invasion of Holland would be an act of such folly that even the Germans would hesitate to embark upon it. From the military point of view, he thought that the present moment was particularly unfavourable, as the break-up of thick ice on the rivers made pontoon building impossible.[28]

After some discussion on the military aspects of the situation, the War Cabinet, agreed with Chamberlain's view that 'nothing short of dire peril would convince the Belgian Government of the wisdom of inviting [the Allies] into their country; …'.[29] Chamberlain went on to read a draft of the reply which he proposed to send to Leopold via telegram to Keyes. After some discussion and amendments, the reply was finalised to read:

* Édouard Daladier, (1884-1970) was a French socialist politician, and the Prime Minister of France who signed the Munich Agreement in 1938. He resigned as Prime Minister on 21 March 1940 following France's failure to aid Finland in her conflict with the Soviet Union.

> We are ready to accept invitation to British troops to enter Belgium and understand French attitude is the same.
>
> We are asked to give guarantees to Belgium which go further than anything we have promised to France and which we might not be in a position to carry out at the end of the war.
>
> Subject to the above we are ready to promise as follows if such an invitation were given at once –
>
> (1) If Belgium thereupon becomes involved with the Allies in hostilities against Germany, we will not open peace negotiations without informing Belgium and we should expect them to do the same with us.
>
> (2) We will do our utmost to maintain the political and territorial integrity of Belgium and her colonies.
>
> (3) If after the war Belgium is in need of financial and economic assistance, we will include her in any assistance we may be able in conjunction with our Allies to render in these respects.
>
> The King will realise that the value of the invitation will be seriously discounted from the point of view of Belgium as well as ourselves unless the invitation is given in sufficient time to enable the British and French troops to secure a strategical advantage of position before any German attack begins.[30]

Hankey suggested to the meeting that it would be undesirable to make any mention to the Belgians about the plans made for the demolitions at their ports. He went on to inform the War Cabinet of 'an indirect channel of communication' [Samblanx] with the Belgian Minister of Transport, which might prove suitable for communications on the demolition schemes at a later date. Chamberlain agreed that no mention of the demolitions should be made at present, and Ironside emphasised that no action should be taken on the demolitions once the Allies had advanced into Belgium. However, he considered it may still be desirable to carry out the Dutch demolitions and the occupation of Walcheren.[31]

The meeting ended with the War Cabinet authorising the despatch of their response to the Belgian king's questions and agreeing that no action was to be taken at present regarding the Belgian demolition schemes.[32]

When King Leopold received the War Cabinet's response the following morning, 15 January, he was appalled at the assumption contained in it that he would invite the Allied armies into Belgium even before the Germans attacked. In fact, the king had given no such undertaking nor invitation, as this would have fallen outside his constitutional powers. Keyes claimed that, in his telephone conversation to Churchill, he only expressed his purely, personal opinion of the *possibility* of the Belgians admitting Allied troops at once, and that somehow Churchill had misconstrued this as a firm intention on behalf of the king.[33]

Meanwhile overnight, working on the assumption that Leopold had received a satisfactory response from the British Government regarding the guarantees requested, Gamelin had ordered the Allied forces under his command to advance to the Belgian frontier so they would be ready to enter the country immediately the signal was given.[34]

As the Allied armies lay poised to enter Belgium, Leopold summoned his military advisor, Van Overstraeten, and showed him the British two-page response just handed to him by Keyes. The general agreed that it was unacceptable, and to invite British and French forces in now would plunge Belgium into an immediate war with Germany. Leopold turned back to Keyes and told him that the British response would have a very bad effect on his government if he was to pass it on to them, adding that any advantage to be gained by allowing the Allies to take up positions in his country would be out of all proportion to the sufferings inflicted on his people if they became involved in a war fought on Belgian soil. He was also annoyed that the British Government had not granted him the specific guarantees he had requested, let alone making them conditional on terms that were unacceptable. After unsuccessfully attempting to persuade the king that the evidence of the captured German documents alone provided sufficient justification for inviting the Allies in, Keyes took his leave and returned to the British Embassy. From the embassy that night, Keyes sent a telegram to the Foreign Office summarising Leopold's angry reaction to the British response.[35]

Earlier, at the meeting of the War Cabinet held that afternoon, War Secretary Oliver Stanley had informed his colleagues that the BEF was being held at four hours' notice, with seven of its mechanised regiments ready to start 'at a moment's notice' to move into Belgium once an invitation was received. Ironside said that he had received a telegram from Gamelin expressing his concern that the dispositions his forces had taken up on the Belgian frontier the previous night might soon become known to the enemy and could not be maintained indefinitely because of the bad weather. Gamelin was 'evidently extremely disappointed'.[36]

French frustrations were echoed by Halifax, who drew the Cabinet's attention to two telegrams he had received from the British Embassy in Paris. According to these telegrams, the French Prime Minister, Daladier, had summoned the Belgian Ambassador and told him that

French forces could not be left for more than another four hours in their current positions on the French side of the frontier. They must be either permitted to enter Belgium or be withdrawn. Daladier had demanded an answer from the Belgians by 20:00. Halifax went on to say that the French Ambassador in London had informed Cadogan at the Foreign Office that although they had agreed with the War Cabinet's response to Leopold's request for guarantees, they thought that '[the British] might have taken up a somewhat less reserved attitude in connection with the discussion of possible peace terms'.[37]

Reviewing the Belgium situation, Chamberlain told the meeting that he was now even more convinced '(a) that the whole affair of the discovery of the German plan sounded fishy, and (b) that there was not the slightest chance of Belgium inviting us into their country until they were absolutely certain of invasion …'[38]

Chamberlain's scepticism was reinforced later that evening when he saw Keyes' telegram from Brussels summarising Leopold's reaction to the British proposals. After Halifax had read out the telegram at the following day's War Cabinet meeting, Chamberlain made his feelings clear saying that 'the telegram made a deplorable impression on him, since it appeared that the Belgians had never intended to invite us to cross their frontier before the Germans invaded Belgium.[39] […] and all the talk about guarantees was merely an attempt to get something more out of us while the going was good.'[40]

With the failure to obtain the 'invitation' from the Belgian Government, Gamelin was left with no choice but to order his forces back to their original defensive positions away from the frontier.

Meanwhile, unbeknown to the Allies, Hitler had called off his invasion. Although the German forces remained ready to strike at short notice, as soon as it was realised that the Belgians were in possession of the invasion plans and had consequently strengthened their defensive positions on their northeast frontier, Hitler decided to change the direction of the assault and move the Panzer divisions further south. This would obviously delay the invasion until new plans could be drawn up.[41]

Although the German invasion threat seemed to be subsiding, the Belgians appeared at last to be taking measures to safeguard their oil stocks. The British Military Attache in Brussels, Colonel Blake, reported that:

> A reliable report has been received that the Belgian Government have ordered as much as possible of the oil reserves at Antwerp to be moved. This applies particularly to the stocks held at Kiel, down river from

> Antwerp, from where tanks at Ghent and Brussels are to be filled to capacity. Available aviation spirit in reserve at Antwerp is being moved to Bruges, and as a result rail and road oil-tank vehicles have been marshalled in the sidings of the former town.[42]

Back in England, with the German threat to the Low Countries diminishing, the 'Special Squads' of 55 Field Company had been standing-by on two hours' notice to move to Chatham, but come 17 January and with no sign of an imminent German move against the Low Countries, this was updated to eight hours.[43] Also on eight hours' standby for the XD missions were three officers of the 12th Division Royal Engineers at Milton Barracks, Gravesend. Their instructions now were, on receipt of orders to proceed direct to Chatham Dockyard without waiting for the 55 Field Company squads. They were to travel with three lorries loaded with all the equipment needed for the operations. On arrival at the dockyard's main gate, they would come under the orders of the Royal Navy, whose officers would direct them to their respective ships where their equipment would immediately be loaded on board.[44] By 19 January, with the winter weather in western Europe deteriorating even further, it was obvious that Germany would be unable to launch any immediate offensive, so all the XD RE units reverted to twenty-four hours' stand-by.[45] Their status remained unchanged until 11 February, when 55 Field Company were once more ordered to prepare for operations in Scandinavia, and all responsibility for XD operations was transferred to 12th Division RE at Gravesend.[46]

12th Division themselves had always been earmarked for service overseas, with the BEF in France, but only once they had completed their training in Kent, which was estimated would take twelve months. However, the recent scare on the Western Front had highlighted significant manpower shortages among the BEF's rear-line units, and so 12th Division was ordered to prepare to move to France, along with its full complement of Royal Engineers, to complete its training there, while also assisting with labour and other general duties in the BEF's rear areas. Obviously, this would mean the Director of Military Operations, Lieutenant Colonel Hayman-Joyce, now needed to find yet another unit to take over responsibility for the XD operations. His eventual choice was a certain Territorial RE unit that had been spending the winter manning searchlights along the bleak shorelines of the Thames and Medway rivers, and who we left, moving into their new headquarters in Sheerness, at the end of Chapter 2.

Chapter 9

'BLIMEY, SOMETHING IS HAPPENING!'

In early 1940, the HQ Staff of the Kent Fortress Royal Engineers, freshly installed in their new location at Sheerness, were being joined by more of their unit's personnel as the KFRE's searchlight crews were gradually being replaced by gunners from the Royal Artillery. The KFRE then formed a Field Works Training Section and began extensive drill and fieldworks training. Whilst the former included musketry, anti-gas warfare, and bayonet fighting, the latter comprised pontoon building, bridging, trench digging and, most notably, demolitions.[1]

The accommodation available for the KFRE at Sheerness was very limited, so on 14 February an advance party of two officers and twenty other ranks from the Field Works Training Section moved to Milton Barracks at Gravesend,[2] where they continued their training with the 12th Division RE, who were at that time on stand-by for the XD operations. These were joined, five days later, by the main body of the Training Section comprising a further two officers and eighty other ranks.[3]

The KFRE War Diary contains very little information on the Gravesend Detachment and its XD preparations during the following weeks. Fortunately, Claude Brazier and Bernard Buxton later documented their recollections to provide an authoritative (and in Bernard Buxton's case, sometimes amusing) record of these times. The War Diary continued to be kept on behalf of the Adjutant, by Second Lieutenant W.R. Phillips, who remained at the Sheerness HQ, where he was mainly concerned with the unit's remaining Fortress Duties, and the training of the RA gunners in DEL operations.

In early March the KFRE's CO, Lieutenant Colonel Brazier, its Adjutant Captain Buxton, and captains West and Willmott, attended a five-week Field Works training course at the School of Military Engineering (SME) at Brompton Barracks, Chatham.[4] Whilst there, the decision was taken that the KFRE would take over responsibility for the XD operations. On 11 March the Director of Military Operations at the War Office, Lt Col Hayman-Joyce, wrote to the CO of 12th Division RE at Gravesend, Lt Col Dewdney, confirming the transfer of responsibility from his unit to the KFRE.[5] Two days later at the SME, Brazier was sent for by the Chief Engineer to be informed of his unit's new responsibilities. Capt Buxton (who did not appear to have very much respect for his CO) described Brazier's reaction to the news: 'Just before lunch he re-appeared, coming across the field in full Service Dress, field boots and spurs, everything except his sword. A wag in the squad said, 'Blimey, something is happening'.

The four KFRE officers were immediately pulled out of the training course, with Brazier, Buxton, and West returning to Gravesend, while Willmott was sent to Sheerness to oversee the DEL training of the Royal Artillery personnel.[6]

The next day at Milton Barracks, Buxton and West took possession from the CRE 12th Division of all the plans and details for the XD operations which were then kept secure in what became known as the 'Black Box', with instructions from Brazier that one of them must always have the box in their possession. Brazier, Buxton and West proceeded to study the plans in detail and by 16 March, Brazier's 'Operation Order No.3', replacing that inherited from 12th Division RE, was safely locked away in the Black Box ready to be issued when the time came.[7] This Operation Order differed little from that issued by the 12th Division RE. The main change was that the port of embarkation for the missions was now Dover. In his memoir, Bernard Buxton later recalled some basic details of the operation order:

> A number of sections, each comprising one officer and ten other ranks, and virtually self contained, would be formed to carry out the operations. The number of sections sent to one place would depend on the size of the oil farm. The R.E. party would – on joining the destroyer – come under the command of the Naval Officer i/c Demolitions. The R.E. first priority would be the oil. Only when the oil was destroyed would they help in general demolition.
>
> The withdrawal would in the first place be by Destroyer, but the Navy were under very strict admiralty orders not to risk losing a Destroyer without very good reason. Should the Destroyer have to put out to sea, then the general plan would be to go to the seashore, take the largest boat available and put to sea. If a larger boat was met, transfer to that

> and continue. The Destroyer would be patrolling and on the lookout. If not picked up, then carry on home.
>
> Each section would take 40 old blankets and 20 tins of kerosene. Two large Felling Axes, two Sledge Hammers, two Picks, three large Shifting Spanners, one Shovel, one Crowbar, one Very Pistol (with nine Cartridges), and twelve Steel Wedges would be added to the load. All this would be packed and carried on a stretcher. A box of Guncotton (14 slabs) with Primers and Detonators, carried in our packs would be taken, together with a large roll of Elastoplast for sticking the Guncotton to the side of the Oil Tanks. Chalk and torches were not forgotten.
>
> All this, with two Boy's [*sic*] A/T Rifles with ammunition and our own personal weapons, made a hefty weight to be moved. We hoped to annexe transport for this.
>
> These were our ideas and all we could think of to do the job. We lived with them and they guided our training over the two months run-up period.[8]

Buxton also took over the responsibility for all the stores that had been acquired ready for use on the operations. These were kept locked away in a Nissen hut on the barracks ready for loading onto lorries for transport to Dover. To help cope with his new responsibilities, Buxton was replaced as KFRE Adjutant by Captain Peter Keeble, an enthusiastic young officer who had recently completed a course at Staff College and was also the nephew of the KFRE's honorary colonel.

In the following days another four officers and twenty-five other ranks were transferred from Sheerness to Milton Barracks to join the XD teams, together with Captain Goodwin and Captain Hawes, both of whom were transferred from the Cinque Ports Fortress Royal Engineers. Hawes eventually took over Keeble's duties as Adjutant, freeing the latter to command one of the XD sections.[9,10]

Weeks of intensive training followed for the XD detachment at Gravesend, which included route marches with full packs and weapons, practising demolitions and target shooting on Milton Ranges where they were introduced to the 0.5 Boys anti-tank rifle for the first time. This weapon was of particular importance as it had previously been highlighted for use against the oil tanks in the Dutch and Belgian ports.*

The training also included unarmed combat movement by night, and practising the silent 'liquidation' of sentries. The troops also needed to be familiarised with the environment they would be expected to operate in. However, this presented some security problems as Brazier later

* See Chapter 6

recalled: 'We visited certain industrial plants, docks and quays that may have put Heligoland* into the men's minds. Because of the secrecy of the proposed operations, it was impossible to carry out any specific training that would suggest the destruction of bulk oil installations.'[11]

The junior officers were told they were in training to destroy oil supply installations, but without any specific location being mentioned. To give them some idea of the layout of the type of installation they would encounter, a visit for them was arranged to the oil storage site at Shell Haven, on the north bank of the River Thames at Thurrock in Essex, where Capt Buxton caused some consternation: 'The Manager was very helpful and showed us round, but was visibly shaken and almost physically sick when, just before leaving, I asked him what would be the best way to set it all on fire. He had spent all his [working] life trying to avoid this.'[12]

The visit did however, impress upon the officers, the importance of firing each individual oil storage tank in order to ensure complete success.[13] The method of firing to be employed was:

> ... to find out the type or types of oil to be dealt with and exactly where they were, mark them with chalk and then check the wind direction.
>
> The breaching of the tanks would be done by the following methods, used one at a time in the order given, or by a combination if circumstances called for hasty action.

(i) Open water drain cock
(ii) Take off or partly take off manhole covers
(iii) Smash hole in tank outlet pipe by exploding a slab of guncotton
(iv) Puncture the tank from as many shots from the A/T rifle as could economically be put in, followed by tracer bullets. This method to be used when the operation could only be carried out from a distance
(v) Any other way suggested by local conditions

Having got a nice lot of oil into the open air the firing would be: -

Petrol
(a) From a distance, fire a very Cartridge into it, or
(b) Make a torch of blanket strips fixed to a shortened pick handle, soak it in kerosene, light it and throw from as far away as possible, or

---

* Heligoland is a small archipelago in the North Sea that had been part of the German state of Schleswig-Holstein since 1890. It was extensively fortified and used as a U-boat base in the Second World War.

(c) Make a 'wick' of blankets, soaked in kerosene, leading up over the bund from the inside so as to be as far away as possible and light the far end.
It was realised that this would be a rather dangerous job and one should turn one's back to the tank immediately the process was initiated.

Diesel and Heavier Oils
Light a blanket, soaked in kerosene, gently lay it on the surface of the oil. Repeat the process if extinguished. If a slight blue wisp of smoke started to rise, get out smartly.[14]

By the end of March, Capt Hawes had taken over responsibility for the Black Box, allowing Buxton and West to concentrate on training their respective sections for the operations. At the same time, all the other units' captains were let into the secrets contained in the famous box.[15]

Buxton became responsible for the proposed Rotterdam XD operation, with six sections of troops allocated to his command. He knew all his men well, and they him. They all lived locally and could often spend their evenings at home which no doubt boosted their morale and made Buxton's job far easier. However, on 8 April Brazier decided to change all the sections and removed many of the senior NCOs from them and placed them in 'Reserve'.[16] Although this gave the junior NCOs opportunity to take on more responsibility, it would have also increased pressure on their superior officers.

The following day, news came through that Hitler had launched Operation *Weserübung*, the German invasion of Norway and Denmark. The KFRE Gravesend Detachment were confined to barracks for the next few days, awaiting further instructions, until it was clear that Belgium and the Netherlands were not coming under immediate threat as well.

On 17 April two officers from the RE's 5th Training Battalion at Chester joined the Gravesend Detachment,[17] and in early May they had been joined by five newly commissioned officers from the RE's Officer Cadet Training Unit (OCTU):[18] second lieutenants Ashwell, Baker, Martin, Wells, and Whitehead, who proved to be valuable additions to the detachment.[19] As a result, Buxton and West were removed from their sections and placed in the Corps Troops Pool, which had been formed by Brazier as a precursor to the larger unit the KFRE were destined to be merged into later in the year.

The men in the Milton Barracks were now well-trained and prepared for their mission for which the clock was starting to tick-down. On the morning of 8 May, Brazier received a message ordering his sections to be confined to barracks and held at twenty-four-hours' notice to await further instructions. This notice period was reduced to twelve hours later that day and to six hours the following day.

Despite being on such short notice for deployment, the sappers arranged for a dance to be held in the barrack gymnasium on the evening of 9 May. The dance would be a welcomed diversion from all the drill and training, and a relief to the boredom of being confined to barracks for twenty-four hours a day, as well as offering the chance to get to know some of the local girls. However, their opportunity to do some socialising was doomed to be short-lived, when at 22:00 the message came through headed with the code-name 'BINNEY PRECAUTIONARY', informing them that they were now on just two-hours' notice for Operation *XD*. Mustered by Buxton and West, the KFRE men were quietly ushered out of the gymnasium, first to be paraded and then to check all their equipment. It was not until 02:00 the following morning, Friday, 10 May, that they eventually managed to get to bed, wondering just what situation they would be facing when they awoke.[20]

Chapter 10

ANOTHER 'FALSE ALARM'

While the KFRE sappers in Kent had been preparing for their military mission, in London ministers and their officials were continuing to work on the political and diplomatic preparations. However, relations had been strained with both the Dutch Government, over the 'Venlo Incident' in November,* and with the Belgian Government, since the serious misunderstanding with King Leopold of the Belgians in the aftermath of the 'Mechelen Affair' in January (see Chapter 8).

As a result of the latter, Foreign Secretary Lord Halifax asked Sir Roger Keyes to call on him on 21 February to talk over the misunderstanding that had occurred with King Leopold over his presumed 'invitation' for Allied troops to enter Belgium prior to any German invasion. Halifax showed Keyes the text of the communication received from him by Churchill in the exact form it had been communicated to the War Cabinet by the First Lord on 14 January, with Leopold's requests for certain guarantees from the Allies, along with Churchill's comment that 'If these were promised Sir Roger thought that the King would be able to persuade his Ministers to invite French and British troops into Belgium at once.'

Keyes told Halifax that this had not been Leopold's intention. What had been in his mind was that to receive such undertakings would just make it easier for him to persuade his government to make an immediate appeal for Allied assistance, in the event of a German invasion or Belgian neutrality being threatened. Keyes went on to suggest three minor amendments that could now be made to the original British response to Leopold's requests which, he was

* The Venlo Incident was a covert operation carried out by the German Nazi Party's *Sicherheitsdienst* (SD) on 9 November 1939, which resulted in the capture of two British Secret Intelligence Service agents 5 metres (16 ft) from the German border, on the outskirts of the Dutch city of Venlo.

convinced, would make it more acceptable to him. Keyes also told Halifax that he proposed to send a personal letter to Leopold urging the desirability of Belgium appealing for Allied assistance should the Dutch frontier be violated by Germany. However, at the same time, Keyes begged that no such approach be made through official channels as the object of his letter would be to try to secure such a request for assistance from the Belgian Government themselves. Keyes then went on to offer his services by making another personal visit to Leopold on behalf of the British Government but, in view of the embarrassment caused by his previous visit, he thought it should best to wait until he received an invitation from the king. Halifax agreed with all Keyes' suggestions and prepared a report of their meeting with details of the revised response to Leopold, ready to present to the War Cabinet on a future date.[1]

Hankey and Jacob had been hopeful of setting up another unofficial channel of communication with the Belgian Government, through the person of the mysterious Monsieur de Samblanx, to persuade them to make arrangements to deny important industrial, fuel and transport assets to the Germans in the event of an invasion. Unfortunately, these efforts had to be abandoned when Samblanx was disowned by the Belgian Government, who refused to confirm his credentials. However, on 16 March, Hankey received a note from Jacob, who had been talking with the Foreign Office with a view to using the Military Attaché in Brussels, Colonel Blake, who was still in communication with Leopold's military adviser, van Overstraeten:

> ... I have recently spoken to the Foreign Office on this subject and I suggested we might now make use of the channel of communication which has been opened for military matters through our Military Attaché to General Overstraeten, to attempt to make progress on our precautionary measures. I thought that we might pass to General Overstraeten the Note which was to have been handed to M. de Samblanx, in the hopes that, by so doing we might lead up to direct contact between the appropriate authorities in the two countries. The Foreign Office have now informed me that they see no objection, provided you give your approval. They would, of course, have to obtain the concurrence of our Ambassador that it would be wise at the present time to make this approach.
>
> ... I do not think that the reasons which led the War Cabinet to veto an approach in January would hold good now, especially as the approach is through an informal military channel and is worded in such a way as to bring out the hypothetical nature of the situation which we wish to

discuss. I suggest, therefore, you could safely give your approval to the proposed action.

... There does not appear to be any hope of making progress with the Dutch.[2]

Hankey approved Jacob's suggestion, but then, two days later, at the War Cabinet on 18 March, Halifax reported on a recent development which seemed to indicate a change in attitude with the Belgian Government. Two days previously, British Ambassador Sir Lancelot Oliphant had reported that the Belgian Foreign Minister, Paul Spaak, had asked him about his views on a possible German attack on Belgium:

M. Spaak had said that the report that vast quantities of German troops were opposite the Belgian frontier was disquieting and that the number of German infantry units had recently been increased. The fate of Finland* made him wonder what the position of the Netherlands might shortly be. One of the troubles in the case of Finland had been the difficulty of getting foreign troops to the country across neutral territories. If, for the sake of argument, the Germans attacked the Netherlands without attacking Belgium, what would be the attitude of Great Britain and France? He had already, on 19th December 1939, said that the position of the Netherlands would not be a matter of indifference to Belgium, but he had then purposedly used vague phraseology, since Belgian aid would not be entirely automatic. In his opinion, however, it would be parlous if the Netherlands were to apply to Great Britain and France for assistance and nothing had been decided in advance.[3]

Although Spaak had made no reference to discussing cooperation on denying oil stocks and other assets to the Germans, he, at least, had 'opened a door' to discussing the possibility of allowing the passage of Allied troops through Belgium to aid the Netherlands in the event of a German attack on that country.

Halifax suggested sending Oliphant a telegram instructing him to communicate with the Belgian Government along the following lines:

If, in the event of a German attack on the Netherlands, Belgium went to the assistance of the Netherlands, His Majesty's Government have no

* The 'Winter War' between Finland and the Soviet Union had recently ended with the signing of the Moscow Peace Treaty in which Finland ceded 9 per cent of its territory to the Soviet Union. The Finnish Government, realising that the hoped-for Franco-British military expedition would not arrive in time, as Norway and Sweden had not given the Allies rite of passage, had little choice but to accept the Soviet terms.

> doubt that the Allies would at once come to the help of Belgium. If, in the event of a German attack on the Netherlands, the Belgian Government gave no active assistance to the Netherlands, His Majesty's Government think that the Allies would, if appealed to by the Netherland Government, have no alternative but to go to their assistance, by operating air forces across, and by sending troops into, Belgium. In either event, the extent and method of our assistance would depend largely on the dispositions taken by the Netherland Government, and without knowledge of these dispositions immediate and effective assistance was not possible. Any reply made along these lines would have to be provisional, pending discussion with the French.[4]

Halifax said that he would consult with the Chiefs of Staff to obtain their comments before submitting the final draft of the telegram to the War Cabinet for their approval. Prime Minister Chamberlain also suggested that it would be advantageous to inform the Dutch Government of the Belgians' approach and the British response, and to ask what their attitude would be to the Allies coming to their assistance through Belgium in the event of a German attack. The War Cabinet agreed to both Halifax and Chamberlain's proposals.[5]

When the Chiefs of Staff met on 18 March, they reviewed and agreed the draft of the telegrams Halifax proposed to send to Oliphant in Brussels and Bland at The Hague.[6] They also discussed Halifax's report of his meeting with Sir Roger Keyes on 21 February and the proposed revised response to the Belgian king. The Chiefs thought that it might help to 'promote the exchange of military information and increase the hope of an invitation to the Allied troops before Belgium was invaded or perhaps if Holland were attacked.'[7]

At the War Cabinet meeting the following day, Halifax presented the draft telegram to Oliphant in Brussels as he had outlined at the previous meeting, together with a draft of the telegram he intended sending to Bland at The Hague. The latter, referring to the exchanges between London and Brussels, stated:

> [...] His Majesty's Government think that it is desirable that the Netherlands Government should be made aware of what has passed between themselves and the Belgian Government on the question of possible action by the Allies in the event of a German attack on the Netherlands.
>
> 2. Unless you see serious objection (in which case I should be glad to receive your observations and recommendations at the earliest possible moment) please convey in whatever manner you think best the general sense of the two telegrams under reference. In so doing you should add

> that while His Majesty's Government are not asking the Netherlands Government in the present circumstances to engage themselves definitely in advance, we should be glad to know what is likely to be their attitude to a proposal that the Allies should come to the assistance of the Netherlands through Belgium, in the event of a German attack. […][8]

The War Cabinet agreed the drafts of the telegrams with just minor amendments. They also discussed and agreed to Halifax's proposed amended response to King Leopold's request for certain guarantees and invited the Foreign Secretary to authorise Oliphant to hand the revised response to the king.[9]

Although there now seemed to be a greater air of optimism regarding the possibilities of cooperation between the Allies and the Dutch and Belgians on strategic military matters, there was still no sign of talks about denying their economic assets to the Germans. This situation became more urgent following rumours received from the Dutch Government in early April of impending German action against the Low Countries and Denmark. The War Cabinet was informed on 6 April that the new British Naval Attaché at The Hague, Vice Admiral Gerald Dickens,* had reported that 'according to information received by the Dutch, a serious move by the Germans was to be expected the following week'.[10]

Just three days later, on 9 April, German forces moved into Denmark and Norway. Denmark surrendered within the day, but Norwegian troops continued to resist with Britain and France immediately pledging their assistance. The question now was would Belgium and Holland be next? In an attempt to forestall a German move into the Low Countries, the Allied Supreme War Council, meeting that day, decided to send a joint note to the Belgium Government urging them to invite the Allies to enter Belgian territory 'before it was too late'.[11] The Belgians rejected the Allied note, with Foreign Minister Spaaks saying that he was 'emphatically opposed' to the proposals it contained. The Belgians, however, were prepared to consider the Allied proposals more favourably if they could be assured that French and British forces

---

* Gerald Charles Dickens (1879-1962) was a grandson of the author, Charles Dickens. He joined the Royal Navy as a cadet in 1894 and was promoted to midshipman in 1896; sub lieutenant in 1899, lieutenant in 1901, commander in 1914, captain in1919, rear admiral in 1932, and vice admiral in 1936. He was appointed Naval Attaché to The Hague in succession to Captain Schofield on 8 February 1940. (*https://www.unithistories.com/officers/RN_officersD3.html*).

would take up more advanced positions, thus preventing fighting in the heart of their country.[12]

Nothing could be decided without the agreement of the French, so Halifax instructed the British Ambassador in Paris, Sir Ronald Campbell,* to ask the new French Prime Minister, Paul Reynaud† to obtain the views of Gamelin on the Belgian Government's suggestion. Gamelin had responded saying, 'We can promise to do everything in our power to give satisfaction to the Belgian desideratum'.[13] However, Gamelin was also in full accord with the British Chiefs of Staff view, expressed in their meeting on 10 April, that if the Germans were to invade the Netherlands and the Belgians still did not invite the assistance of the Allies, then they should march into Belgium regardless.[14]

The Chiefs of Staff Committee's report on actions to be taken in the event of a German invasion of the Netherlands or Belgium, including its suggestions of a pre-emptive Allied move into Belgium if Germany attacked the Netherlands alone, was the subject of lengthy discussion at the War Cabinet held on 12 April. An agreement was eventually reached that 'in the event of a German invasion of Holland, the right policy to pursue would be to march into Belgium at once.' Further discussion followed on whether to inform the Belgian Government of this decision. Given that the Belgians would undoubtedly reject such a proposal if put bluntly to them, it was argued that it might be best to just provide them with a broad hint of the Allied intentions. However, a somewhat more forceful hint was eventually adopted:

> [...] That the Allied Governments are unwilling to believe that, if Holland is attacked, the Belgian Government would not go to her assistance; but

---

* Ronald Hugh Campbell (1883-1953) was a British diplomat who was appointed Ambassador to Paris in July 1939 after serving as British envoy to Yugoslavia, a considerable jump in promotion that was extremely rare in the diplomatic service. However, it was long recognised that Campbell possessed outstanding abilities. Following the fall of France in June 1940, he was evacuated through Saint-Jean-de-Luz on HMS *Galatea* on 24 June and returned to London.

† Paul Reynaud (1878-1966) was a French politician and lawyer. He held several cabinet posts in the early 1930s but clashed with members of his party after 1932 over French foreign and defence policy. He strongly opposed appeasement in the run-up to the Second World War. He also clashed with his party on economic policy, backing the devaluation of the franc as a solution to France's economic woes. Reynaud returned to the cabinet in 1938 as Minister of Justice under Édouard Daladier. The Sudeten Crisis, which began not long after Reynaud was named Minister of Justice, again revealed the divide between Reynaud and his party. Daladier appointed him Finance Minister in November 1938. Following the fall of Daladier's government over its refusal to aid the Finns in their war with the Soviet Union, Reynaud was appointed Prime Minister.

> that, if the Belgian Government did not do so, the Allied Governments would be obliged to order their forces to enter Belgium, with the object of assisting Holland, and of safeguarding the security and vital interests of Belgium and of the Allies.[15]

Although the Dutch Government considered recent German moves serious enough for them to declare martial law, the Belgians took a different view and were greatly disturbed to discover that British and French forces had closed to their border without having informed them first. The result of this was a very embarrassing meeting for Sir Alec Cadogan when the Belgian Ambassador, Cartier de Marchienne,* called on him on the evening of Saturday, 13 April.[16] Cartier told Cadogan that the Belgian Government had no certain information that the situation had deteriorated or that the German forces on their border had been reinforced during the last four days, and so questioned why it was that British and French forces had moved closer to their frontier over the previous forty-eight hours without any consultation with the Belgian Government. Cartier also expressed concern over recent increases in British troop levels in France, which had gained much attention in Belgium. Cartier requested an assurance from Cadogan that there was no intention on the part of the Allied governments to move their forces into Belgium without first receiving an invitation from the Belgian Government. Cadogan denied any knowledge of these Allied troop movements, but said that if any such movements had taken place, they were certainly not intended as a threat to Belgium. Cadogan added that he would, however, report the ambassador's concerns to Lord Halifax with a view to furnishing a response for transmission to the Belgian Government.[17]

At the following day's War Cabinet meeting, Halifax reported that he had written to the Belgian Ambassador assuring him that if any movement of Allied troops had taken place, then it was due solely to counter the German menace and not as preparation for them to enter Belgium. He had gone on to tell Cartier that 'We assumed that if the Belgian Government were attacked by Germany, they would certainly desire that our troops should be as well placed as possible for coming to their aid. Similarly, the Belgian Government should welcome any increase of the strength of our forces in France.'[18]

---

* Baron Emile-Ernest de Cartier de Marchienne (1871-1946) was a Belgian diplomat and Envoy Extraordinary and Minister Plenipotentiary in: China and Siam 1910-17, the United States 1917-27, Cuba, Haiti and the Dominican Republic 1926-27, and the United Kingdom 1927-46.

The increase in tensions on the Western Front, together with the continued reluctance of the Belgian and Dutch governments to engage in any meaningful discussions with the Allies regarding preparations for possible German invasion, particularly in respect of denying their oil and gold to the enemy, prompted Lord Hankey to write to Oliphant in Brussels and Bland at The Hague:

> I am dropping a line privately to you as an old friend to ask that, if and when the flag falls on the Belgian [Dutch] frontier, you will not overlook the plans we have made for trying to secure that the Germans do not, in the event of success, get more loot than need be in Belgium [Holland]. Oil is especially important. The Germans have secured 200,000 tons in Denmark and perhaps, another 100,000 tons at Oslo, as well as a certain amount at Trondhjem [*sic*] and Stavanger which they cannot hope to get away. We do not want then to get a lot more in Belgium [Holland].
>
> The Bosch have also most likely acquired between twenty and thirty million pounds in gold between Denmark and Norway, though there are rumours that the Norwegians got some of it away. I suspect, however, that the Belgians [Dutch] are pretty well on their toes in this matter.
>
> I do not think our plans involve very much work on your part. It is just a matter of giving the Belgian [Dutch] Government the right kick at the right moment and in the right place. I expect most of it will fall on your staff, but if the Chief is interested it makes all the difference.
>
> I hope you will not mind me writing you a private line: I did not want to worry you officially at the present time when you are so deluged with official telegrams.
>
> I am glad you are where you are, though possibly you may not think the most salubrious or attractive post in the world. But it must be very interesting.
>
> Anyhow, I wish you the best of luck.[19]

Bland was the first to respond, writing in his own hand to Hankey on 19 April:

> My dear Maurice,
>
> Very many thanks for your letter of April 15, read at a late hour last night. I take it, perhaps presumptuously, as a great compliment that you should have written to me personally on this matter.
>
> You will have seen from my recent telegrams the difficulty, or rather impossibility, of making any advance arrangements with the Dutch about even preliminary precautions, and how far they will collaborate when, to use your words, 'the flag falls', it is hard to say, though they constantly assure me that they are alive to the dangers and are taking adequate precautions. At least as regards gold I am reliably informed

that more than half is already in America or South Africa and that the rest is behind the water-line.*

Anyway, we have, all written out, the statement of our own precautionary measures and it is only a question of signing & dating the documents before they are handed in to the Dutch Govt. What their reactions will be thereto when the blow comes remains to be seen: one can only pray that they will be less unaccommodating than (I again refer to recent telegrams) they have been to similar precautions hitherto. Though as regards petrol & such, it must be born in mind that it would be folly, if so long as they continue to fight, if we asked them to destroy material essential to them for carrying on the war.

Please forgive an illegible scrawl: our two typists have more than they can do as it is without my adding to their burden by dictation. Thank you again for writing so kindly & sympathetically. How I wish we could meet and have a talk before we are driven out of this country, which I love![20]

Oliphant replied to Hankey's concerns, from Brussels on 24 April:

My dear Maurice –

Many thanks for your letter of April 15 Secret and Personal regarding the plans that have been made with a view to ensure the Germans are deprived of as much loot as possible in the event of an attack on this country.

2. Let me say at once that no opportunity has been lost by members of staff of the Embassy in conversations with industrialists, bankers and officials to urge the importance of precautionary measures being taken. Though considerable quantities of contraband raw materials remain in the exposed areas, it is common knowledge that a large amount of wool, cotton and various metals has been removed to what may be considered as relatively safe areas.

3. As regards gold reserves, I do not think we need to entertain any very serious misgivings, since so long ago as October last precautionary measures had been taken and the bulk of gold supplies had been removed to England, New York and possibly Canada. What remains in this country is, I am told, kept in a safe zone, probably in the neighbourhood of Bruges or Ostend. I shall of course lose no opportunity which private conversations may afford to press upon leading bankers, industrialists

* The Dutch Water Defence Lines were a system of military fortifications based on the control of water. The fortifications consisted of a network of forts combined with temporary flooding of polders via a system of canals and locks that were originally built for civil use. The two major defence lines were the New Dutch Waterline and the Defence Line of Amsterdam, built in the nineteenth early twentieth century to protect the economic centre of the country and the capital. (*https://www.worldheritagesite.org/list/Dutch+Water+Defence+Lines*).

> and politicians the vital importance of having all gold stocks and negotiable securities etc. kept in a safe zone or transferred abroad.
> 4. In so far as oil is concerned, the present stocks are believed to be in the neighbourhood of 300,000 tons which we are about to reduce to some 180,000 tons or say three months requirements. I am causing enquiries to be made regarding the main storage zones of this oil, the bulk of which I understand is at Antwerp. There seems to be little doubt that the Belgians, who have had ample time to make their plans, are fully alive to the danger of oil stocks falling into German hands and that they have plans of their own for destroying such stocks should the danger of them falling into enemy possession become imminent.
> 5. If, as well may be the case in the absence of effective Allied support on the Albert Canal and Meuse Lines, a large area of Eastern Belgium including those zones in which sections of the wool, engineering and leather trades are concentrated fall into enemy hands, there is no doubt I fear that considerable stocks, small though they may be in relation to German requirements, of important raw materials will fall to the enemy. But you may rest assured that we will do what we can here to impress upon the authorities the importance of removing as much as possible of them into the safe zones before it is too late.[21]

On 2 May, Oliphant followed his letter up by forwarding to Hankey a copy of a report he had received of a recent meeting of the Anglo-Franco-Belgian Mixed Commission, held to discuss the three nations' War Trade Agreement. In the report, written by Foreign Office official Gerald Villiers,* in surprisingly 'undiplomatic language', the Belgian special representative was described as: '… a Major in the Engineers† – a fat-faced man in the peculiarly monstrous shade of khaki which the Belgians affect.'[22]

However unattractive the Belgian major may have appeared to Villiers, he had still made a strong and favourable impression on him and the rest of the Commission members. When the question of Belgian oil stocks was raised, the French and British representatives expressed concern that the stocks should not fall into German hands. The major was reported to have said:

> … did the Allies understand that the Belgians would dislike it even more? The Allies were no doubt excellent judges of the stocks of oil in Belgium

---

* Gerald Hyde Villiers (1882-1953) was a British diplomat. He was Head of the League of Nations and Western Department, Foreign Office from 1921-28, Head of the Northern Department, Foreign Office 1928-29. (*https://peoplepill.com/i/gerald-hyde-villiers*).

† Unfortunately, I have been unable to identify this 'colourful' major by name.

> and what could or should be done to protect them: was it not arguable that the Belgians were even better judges, since they were in full possession of the facts while the Allies could only guess and estimate.
>
> The Belgians were absolutely determined that if and when Belgium was invaded, their oil should not fall into German hands. They had therefore placed more than half their stocks west of the Ghent-Terneuzen Canal, i.e. in the part of Belgium furthest from Germany and nearest to France, and had concealed them underground. They had reduced stocks in the east of Belgium, even in a centre such as Liége, to the bare amounts necessary for daily consumption. As regards Antwerp they had arranged either to pump oil into the river, or drain it into trenches, or to flood the heavy oils with light oils and set fire to the mixture.[23]

The Belgian major also corrected the Allied estimates of 300,000 tons for his country's various fuel oil stocks. The correct figure, he said, was about 230,000 tons, which would, in the event of war, cover Belgium's requirements for three months. The Belgians had also reduced their stocks of lubricating oils by almost 13,000 tons and any further reduction would leave them with almost no capacity for export.[24]

Villiers reported that the normally 'suspicious and far from Belgiphil [*sic*]' French delegates had said that they were 'quite convinced the Major was telling the whole truth and concealing nothing'. In conclusion, Villiers called attention 'to the fact that the Belgians had abandoned all pretence of being really neutral'.[25]

Hankey replied to Oliphant, thanking him for his letter 'with the interesting and even amusing account' of the Mixed Commission meeting.[26]

Feeling reassured, Hankey forwarded Oliphant's letters and the Mixed Commission report to Ian Jacob with a view to updating the War Cabinet now that 'It looks as if the Belgians and perhaps even the Dutch are beginning to take the matter seriously.'[27] Jacob, however, was a little more pessimistic. Replying, in his role as Assistant Secretary of the War Cabinet, he said:

> … I am inclined to doubt whether there is really much new material which could form the subject of a Note to the War Cabinet. As regards Holland, although we have some reason to think that they have made plans to deal with their stocks of oil, etc., we have nothing sufficiently definite to affect the operations which we have planned, and which remain the same as they have always been. Belgium is a different problem, for two reasons. First, because we sincerely hope to hold that part of the country in which are situated such assets as we could in any case rescue or destroy. Secondly, the Belgian Government and people are

> much more resolute than the Dutch, and more likely to have made and to carry out effective plans; but nevertheless we have so far completely failed to make official contact on these matters, and nothing has come of our unofficial attempts. Our plans, and those of the French, remain as originally prepared. There is therefore very little definite information which we can tell the War Cabinet.[28]

Meanwhile, as Jacob had stated the plans for the XD operations were all still in place and being modified as new information came in. On 6 May, the new embarkation port for the expeditions was confirmed as now being Dover, where on arrival the KFRE demolition parties would report to the CO of HMS *Lynx*, the shore-based headquarters of the RN Patrol Service at Waterloo Crescent in Dover. Once they had reported at Dover, the XD parties would come under the command of their designated, respective RN commanders, and prepare to board the destroyers the Admiralty had allocated to them. Orders for their final embarkation would come from Vice Adm Ramsay, at Dover Castle.[29]

On 7 May Ramsay issued his instructions to the captains of the destroyers allocated to the operation. The four vessels earmarked for the operations were:

HMS *Whitshed*:	Party A (Commander M.G. Goodenough R.N.) to Ymuiden, (7 officers, 121 men, 8 tons explosives and stores).
HMS *Verity*:	Party B (Commander J.A.C.Hill R.N.) to Hook of Holland, (9 officers, 86 men, 6½ tons explosives and stores).
HMS *Wild Swan*:	Party C (This Party was all RN personnel with no R.E. participation) to Flushing, (3 officers, 26 men, 1¾ tons explosives and stores).
HMS *Brilliant*:	Party D (Commander A.C. Stanford R.N.) to Antwerp, (4 officers, 49 men, 4¼ tons explosives and stores).

In addition to its XD party, HMS *Verity* was tasked with transporting a Military Liaison Mission to the Hook, consisting of a major general, nine officers and sixteen men.

The embarkation of personnel and stores at Dover would come under the control of the maintenance captain and the commodore superintendent, respectively. The destroyers would be laying at buoys in Admiralty Harbour, and the stores and personnel would be brought alongside in harbour tugs for embarkation.

Detailed Sailing Orders for each destroyer would be issued before departure and arrivals at the various destinations would be timed for daylight. Every endeavour was to be made to avoid contact or action with any enemy vessels whilst on passage to the ports.

One change to the Binney plan was that no naval captains would be flown out to the ports to take charge of the missions. Instead, command of each operation ashore would be in the hands of the senior RN commander in overall charge of, and arriving on board with, each one of the XD parties.

On arrival and disembarkation at the ports, the destroyers were to keep up steam ready to sail again at short notice. It was hoped that the XD parties would complete their missions and be ready to re-embark within twenty-four hours. The executive signal for the XD operation would be made to the ships and authorities by the Flag Officer Commanding Dover and would read: CARRY OUT OPERATION 'XD'.[30]

With the naval preparations at Dover all in hand and the KFRE Special Parties now well trained and confined to barracks on just six hours' notice in Gravesend, Operation *XD* was primed and ready to go.

For all the concerns about the Low Countries, it was Norway that was under the most immediate threat and the campaign there was not going well for the Allies; a situation reflected by growing unrest in Parliament against the British Government's handling of the campaign. The situation became the matter of a full-scale debate in the House of Commons, which commenced on 7 May, with anger being directed against Prime Minister Chamberlain. Sir Roger Keyes, MP for Portsmouth North, was the first Conservative rebel to speak in the debate. Resplendent in his uniform of Admiral of the Fleet, Keyes, in defending the actions of the Royal Navy in their abortive attempts to retake the now German-held port of Trondheim, strongly criticised Chamberlain for not ordering British forces to seize the port earlier.

When the War Cabinet met on the morning of 8 May, the focus of discussions was, naturally, on operations in Norway and the proposal to land British troops at Narvik, where the Germans had already established themselves in force. The situation on the Western Front, although still tense, seemed to warrant much less attention. The Foreign Secretary Lord Halifax referred to a telegram he had received from Bland at The Hague the previous evening, which reported that a German attack on the Low Countries had been expected at dawn that day or shortly afterwards. However, having made further enquiries, Halifax discounted this now as a probable German feint, with the French regarding as more serious rumours of a German offensive through

Hungary. The Foreign Secretary then went on to refer to a telegram received from Oliphant in Brussels, who had passed on the reports of an imminent German attack on the Low Countries to the Belgian Foreign Minister. Spaak told Oliphant that the Belgian Ambassador in Berlin had been informed that the German Government was drafting a note to the Dutch and Belgian governments, which would be presented to them at an 'appropriate moment'. The details of the note were not known so it was unclear if it would contain any form of ultimatum.[31]

Some further discussions ensued about what should be done to prevent the Dutch airfields falling into German hands and if the RAF bomber force should attack German railway marshalling yards and oil installations to pre-empt any move against the Low Countries, but it was agreed that nothing would be done until German forces crossed the Belgian or Dutch frontiers.[32]

Later that afternoon, the Norway Debate resumed in the House of Commons, which was followed that night by a division that saw the Chamberlain Government's majority reduced from 213 to just 81. Such was the level of discontent in the House, it seemed that some change in government was inevitable if confidence was to be restored in it. Chamberlain came under immediate pressure to form a Coalition Government, and began talks with the leaders of the Labour Party with a view to inviting them into it. If the talks failed, then Chamberlain knew he would be forced to resign. Chamberlain's preferred successor was Halifax, but he lost the opportunity to shape events during a further crucial meeting that evening.

Winston Churchill, Lord Halifax, Neville Chamberlain and Captain David Margesson (Chief Whip) met to discuss who should become Prime Minister in the event of Labour refusing to join the government under Chamberlain. Accounts of this meeting vary. Churchill always maintained that he kept silent at a crucial juncture, and that Halifax discounted himself from the premiership because of his peerage. The meeting ended with an agreement that Chamberlain would advise the king to send for Churchill if Labour relayed the message the next day that they refused to enter the government under Chamberlain's leadership.[33]

At the following day's War Cabinet, with Chamberlain still in the chair, there were reports on the continued fighting in Norway but there was still no confirmation to report of any German ultimatum to either Belgium or the Netherlands, and it seemed that the latest dramas on the Western Front might be yet another 'false alarm'. However, the next twenty-four hours would see a dramatic turn of events in Europe, and Britain with a new Prime Minister.

Chapter 11

FALL GELB

In the early hours of 10 May, Dutch observers spotted German aircraft in the skies above them, heading, they presumed, in the direction of England. However, once over the North Sea the aircraft turned back into Holland and released their bombs over airfields at De Kooy, Amsterdam and The Hague, destroying many aircraft on the ground. Then at 04:00 local time a battalion of German paratroopers began to land near the three Dutch airfields, while another paratrooper battalion seized the vital Moerdijk bridges in southern Holland, and twelve seaplanes deposited about seventy troops on the Nieuwe Maas river in central Rotterdam to capture important bridges there.

While the first paratroopers were landing in Holland, a daring glider-borne assault was taking place on the vitally important Fort Ében-Émael and other fortifications along the Albert Canal, the primary line of defence in Belgium. Operation *Fall Gelb* (Case Yellow), the German offensive on the Western Front, had begun.[1]

At 06:00, the Dutch Foreign Minister, Eelco van Kleffens, received the German Envoy to the Netherlands Count Julius von Zech-Burkersroda, in his office at The Hague. The envoy handed him a message from the German Foreign Minister, Joachim von Ribbentrop, stating:

> We announce to you the deployment of an enormous German military force. Any resistance is perfectly futile. Germany guarantees the territorial integrity in Europe and Overseas, as well as the dynasty, if any resistance remains absent. If not, then a danger exists of complete annihilation of the country and its form of government. Therefore, we admonish you urgently to make an appeal to the people and the military forces and furthermore to establish a line of communication with the German military commanders. Motivation: We have irrefutable proof of an imminent threat of invasion by France and England in Belgium, the Netherlands and Luxembourg, which had long been prepared with the

> joint knowledge of the Netherlands and Belgium, with the purpose of attacking the Ruhr area.[2]

The German envoy also handed over a note from Heinrich Himmler, head of the SS (*Schutzstaffel*), accusing the Dutch of a breach of neutrality by harbouring and supporting agents of the British Secret Service. In an obvious reference to events surrounding the 'Venlo Incident', Himmler revealed his knowledge of the covert intelligence activities of the British Passport Control Office at The Hague, and of its involvement in recruiting German anti-Nazi dissidents living in Holland to act as British agents.[3]

Van Kleffens rejected all the German allegations with indignation and declared that a state of war now existed between the Netherlands and Germany. Van Kleffens then flew to London to request urgent British military help.

Later that morning, a similar message from Ribbentrop was delivered to the Belgian Foreign Minister, Spaak, by the German Ambassador, von Bulow-Schwante. Spaak read the note and wrote down a few words of his own, which he read out to the ambassador, rejecting it and stating that he had nothing further to say to him.[4]

Spaak had already called personally on the British and French Ambassadors earlier that morning with notes requesting, under their countries' 1937 Guarantees, the entry of Allied troops into Belgium.[5] The British Ambassador, Sir Lancelot Oliphant, immediately telegraphed London with the substance of the Belgian note.[6]

Meanwhile, in Britain, Sir Alec Cadogan had been woken up at 05:40* with a phone call from the Foreign Office with the news of the German invasion of the Netherlands and Belgium. By 07:50 he was at his desk at the Foreign Office and, ten minutes later, he was present at an emergency meeting of the War Cabinet at 10 Downing Street.[7]

Prime Minister Chamberlain, his future now very much in doubt, chaired the War Cabinet. The only subject on the agenda was the situation in the Low Countries. The meeting was presented with the scanty details of what was known so far of the events of the previous few hours. It had been confirmed that Germany had invaded the Netherlands and Belgium and that their troops had also crossed into Luxembourg. It had also been reported that Germany had bombed Nancy and two RAF aerodromes in northern France. First Lord of the

---

* Since 4 May, Britain had been on Double Summer Time, also known as Double Daylight Saving Time (GMT + 2 hours), a wartime measure to exploit the many benefits of lighter working days.

Admiralty, Winston Churchill, speaking in his role as Chairman of the Military Co-ordination Committee, told the War Cabinet that 'The whole plan for the advance of the Allied forces into the Low Countries had been set in motion'. He also confirmed that the Dutch Government had 'appealed for assistance'.[8]

Lord Hankey then informed the meeting that 'the plan for the prevention of Dutch and Belgian resources falling into the hands of the Germans, had automatically been set in motion. His Majesty's Ministers at Brussels and The Hague would already have approached the Belgian and Dutch Governments offering them our cooperation.'[9]

The First Sea Lord, Admiral of the Fleet Sir Dudley Pound, added to Hankey's statement saying that 'the 4 destroyers taking our demolition parties across would sail at 10 a.m.'[10] The War Cabinet then officially 'Authorised Plan XD, for the denial of Dutch and Belgian resources, to the Germans, and Plan Lyster (preparatory measures for the blocking of the Belgian ports) to be put into full effect forthwith.'[11]

Meanwhile at Milton Barracks, the 128 officers and other ranks of Gravesend Detachment of the Kent (Fortress) Royal Engineers, had been woken at 06:00, after having less than four hours' sleep.[12] They were ordered on parade and issued with haversack rations for twenty-four hours and ammunition for their personal weapons. They were then divided up into their relevant Sections corresponding to the XD plan's designated demolition parties:

Section 'A' – 3 officers and 32 other ranks under the command of Captain R. Keeble RE.
Section 'B' – 6 officers and 62 other ranks under the command of Captain T.F. Goodwin RE
Section 'D' – 1 officer and 24 other ranks under the command of 2nd Lieutenant A. Wells RE.[13]

Keeble's section had originally numbered only himself, a lieutenant, and ten other ranks, but the previous day Lt Col Brazier had been ordered to provide an additional officer and twenty other ranks for the Amsterdam operation.[14]

Brazier then called a brief conference of all the officers and handed them a copy of his 'Operation Order No.2', which was just a basic programme for their journey that morning to Dover. However, they were also issued with a sealed envelope that contained 'Operation Order No.3', the detailed instructions for their missions. Brazier ordered that the envelopes should not be opened until instructed by either Keeble or Goodwin.[15]

At 07:00, several specially requisitioned 30-cwt lorries with Royal Army Service Corps drivers arrived at Milton Barracks; men and stores were loaded, and at 07:30 they left the barracks on their way to Dover. After their departure, Capt Buxton, who had been left behind as part of the Corps Troops Pool, pondered the fact that no senior NCOs had been included with the parties, but satisfied himself that they were very good men being well led by some equally good officers, who all knew each other very well.[16]

On the journey to Dover one of the lorries broke down. Capt Keeble, who was in another lorry, ordered his vehicle to stop while he got out to see what the problem was. Realising nothing could be done with the broken-down vehicle, Keeble flagged down another, larger lorry that was just passing them. He requisitioned the lorry and ordered the driver to load the stranded sappers and their stores and take them to Dover. The larger vehicle was already well-loaded with gas cylinders, destined for the barrage balloon units at Dover, but somehow all the sappers and stores managed to squeeze on board, and they resumed their journey.

When the convoy arrived at Dover, the section commanders reported to the Officer Commanding HMS *Lynx*, the HQ of the RN Patrol Service, who directed them to their designated destroyers awaiting them in the harbour. As they were already running late, due to the vehicle breakdown, all the stores and equipment were hurriedly cross loaded onto the ships by their crews. Unfortunately, in their rush, they also loaded the barrage balloon gas bottles. When the mistake was realised, they equally hurriedly off-loaded them back onto the quay, leaving them there for the unlucky lorry driver to re-load onto his vehicle himself.[17]

There had been a slight change in Vice Adm Ramsay's original orders, with HMS *Wild Swan* now taking Party B, including Capt Goodwin's KFRE section, to the Hook of Holland, with Rotterdam as its final objective, and HMS *Verity* taking the all-RN Party C to Flushing. Lieutenant Mills and his twenty-four-man section joined Party D on board HMS *Brilliant*, bound for Antwerp as planned.

Keeble's expanded section was planned to be part of Party A on board HMS *Whitshed*, sailing to Ymuiden. However, when Keeble and his thirty-two men arrived on the quay, Party A's naval commander, Commander Michael Goodenough RN, was surprised to see so many of them. The amended plan had not filtered down to him, and he was still only expecting a military party of one officer and ten men. After talking to Keeble, it now seemed uncertain whether it had really been the intention to send all the larger party to Dover. However, after considering the many 'attractive targets' he felt certain they would find at their destination, and the number of possible casualties they could suffer, Goodenough decided to embark all the extra personnel.[18]

The destroyers were now ready to sail but were still awaiting their final orders. At the War Office, Ironside wrote a note to the Secretary of State for War, Oliver Stanley, anxious to get the missions away:

> R.E. Demolition parties are prepared to sail in destroyers from DOVER to AMSTERDAM (Party A), ROTTERDAM (Party B), and ANTWERP (Party D) to destroy oil stocks.
>
> H.M. Ambassadors in BRUSSELS and THE HAGUE have asked the Government to which they are acredited [*sic*] whether they are prepared to receive these parties.
>
> A reply has been received from THE HAGUE agreeing to receive the parties, no reply has yet been received from BRUSSELS.
>
> You and the First Lord [Churchill] will wish to raise the question in the Cabinet as to which of these parties should proceed. I consider that notwithstanding that no reply has been received from BRUSSELS we should authorise all the parties to sail. The stocks will not actually be destroyed except, on the initiative of the Belgian and Dutch authorities respectively, or in an emergency on the authority of the man on the spot.[19]

The next War Cabinet meeting, held at 11.30 that morning at 10 Downing Street and chaired again by Chamberlain, was a particularly busy one. Many messages were received and read out during the meeting as events on the Western Front unfolded and German bombing attacks on the Netherlands, Belgium and France intensified. It was reported that German parachute troops had landed at numerous places throughout Holland and that the aerodrome at Rotterdam was now under German control. Ironside reported that German ground forces were advancing through Luxembourg and the Ardennes to the line of the Meuse, and through Belgium to the line of the Albert Canal. Allied troops were due to begin their advance into Belgium at 13:00. Halifax reported that the Dutch Foreign and Colonial Ministers were arriving in London by air later that day.[20]

Hankey informed the meeting that:

> His Majesty's Representatives had already impressed on the Dutch and Belgian governments the need for dealing effectively with the following: -
> Gold and securities.
> Dock and harbour facilities.
> Raw materials, including oil.
> Rolling stock.
> Mechanical transport.
> Shipping, barges, &c.

> Aircraft and aerodrome facilities.
> Machine tools.
> Power stations.
>
> We had not yet heard from His Majesty's Representatives whether the Dutch and Belgian governments would welcome our cooperation in this work, but the Admiralty had heard from the Naval Attaché at The Hague that our forces would be received in Dutch ports.
>
> [...] destroyers with military parties were ready to sail to Ymuiden, Hook of Holland, Flushing and Antwerp to deal with dock and harbour facilities, oil and coast defences (Operation XD). Detailed arrangements had been made for the destruction of oil stocks by this party, but, in addition, there was a scheme held in reserve for oil destruction to be carried out by the R.A.F. The destroyers would sail during the course of the day. If the French Army arrived successfully in Flushing and Antwerp, they would take over the responsibility for demolitions at those places.[21]

Churchill informed the meeting that the Admiralty were taking steps to remove the remaining gold from Holland and that block ships would be in readiness from the following day for blocking Zeebrugge and Ostend if necessary (Operation *Lyster*). Further discussions included preparations for dealing with the expected 300,000 Dutch and Belgian refugees and Churchill suggested offering asylum to the former German Kaiser, who had been living in exile in the Netherlands since his abdication in 1918;* a suggestion to which the Cabinet agreed.[22]

The War Cabinet meeting ended with Chamberlain, now feeling more confident about remaining in office, proposing that he stayed on to see through the present crisis, and maintaining that now was not the time for a change of leadership. However, Kingsley Wood, the Lord Privy Seal, insisted that it was time for the Prime Minister to go. Apart from Samuel Hoare, the Secretary of State for Air, no member of the War Cabinet spoke up for Chamberlain and even his close friend, Halifax, made it clear he agreed with the Lord Privy Seal.

That afternoon the Labour leadership broke the news to Chamberlain that their party would not join any coalition Government with him as leader. The Prime Minister's fate was now sealed.

The third War Cabinet meeting of that tumultuous day was held at 16:30 at 10 Downing Street, with Chamberlain continuing in the Chair. The meeting was updated on the situation in the Netherlands and Belgium. Reports had been received of German bombs falling

* The former Kaiser Wilhelm II chose to remain in the Netherlands with his family, where he lived until his death on 4 June 1941, aged 82.

on many locations in both countries as well as in France and even in neutral Switzerland. The advance of Allied troops into Belgium was going according to plan, and although large numbers of parachutists had been dropped in that country, there was no sign yet of any rush of German armoured units across the frontier. Halifax informed the meeting that he had met with the Dutch Foreign and Colonial ministers who had arrived by air earlier. Their aim was to provide the nucleus of a Dutch Government here in the event of their country being overrun by the Germans, but no decision had yet been made whether the Queen of the Netherlands should come to Britain. The Dutch Foreign Minister said that the Dutch now regarded themselves as one of the Allies.[23]

Finally, the Prime Minister informed the War Cabinet of the results of his negotiations with the leaders of the Labour Party regarding their cooperation in the Government: 'The Labour Party are prepared to take their share of responsibility as a full partner in a new Government, under a new Prime Minister, which would command the confidence of the nation.'[24]

Chamberlain added that he had reached the conclusion he should tender his resignation to the king, which he proposed to do that evening.[25] Chamberlain arrived at Buckingham Palace at 18:00 for his audience with King George VI. He tendered his resignation, advising the monarch to send for Winston Churchill, and request that he form a new government. Shortly after Chamberlain left the palace, Churchill arrived and there he received his Commission from the king to form a government. Britain now had a new Prime Minister.

Earlier that day, the destroyers at Dover had finally received their orders to sail to their destinations. HMS *Whitshed*, under the command of Commander E.R. Conder, was the first away, sailing at 12:00 with Party A to Ymuiden, followed shortly after by HMS *Verity*, under the command of Lieutenant Commander A.R.M. Black, with Party C to Flushing, and HMS *Brilliant*, commanded by Lieutenant Commander F.C. Brodrick, with Party D to Antwerp; and finally HMS *Wild Swan*, commanded by Lieutenant Commander J. L. Younghusband, with Party B, setting sail for the Hook of Holland.

While the ships were at sea a report was compiled by the War Office, based on figures obtained from the petroleum industry, detailing the latest estimates of stocks of petrol held in Holland and Belgium. The Dutch estimates amounted to 567,500 tons, of which 75 per cent were located in Rotterdam; while Belgian stocks amounted to 206,000 tons, with 75 per cent located in Antwerp.[26] With the fate of these stocks in mind, it was imperative for Operation *XD* to succeed.

Chapter 12

YMUIDEN AND AMSTERDAM (10-14 MAY)

On board HMS *Whitshed* at sea on 10 May, the naval commander of Party A, Commander Goodenough, pondered on his forthcoming mission. Approaching his thirty-sixth birthday, Michael Goodenough had joined the Royal Navy at 14, attending the naval colleges at Osborne and Dartmouth. He joined his first ship, the battleship HMS *Benbow*, as a midshipman in 1922 and was rapidly promoted through the junior ranks. By 1936 he was a lieutenant commander attending the RN Staff College at Greenwich. He was promoted to commander in June 1939 and in the August of that year, just before the outbreak of the war, he joined the Plans Division at the Admiralty.[1] He had been closely involved in Binney's planning for the XD operations and was delighted to be informed in January that he had been designated the commander of the Ymuiden XD party, a mission he had been preparing himself for ever since.[2]

Goodenough had received his final orders at 06:00 that morning whilst still at his barracks in Chatham. The first paragraph read: 'The object of the expedition is to assist and stimulate the Dutch to carry out demolitions of their property which, without the presence of the British parties, they might be disposed to keep intact.'[3]

Obviously, much would depend on the level of cooperation Goodenough would receive from the Dutch authorities and even then, there could be elements sympathetic to the Nazis that could oppose or hamper his operation. He had been sufficiently concerned about this to lobby the Admiralty for additional forces to ensure the security of his party once they were ashore.[4] He eventually succeeded in obtaining two extra platoons of seamen, comprising two officers and sixty-four men, added to his original complement, all of whom would remain under his orders until the completion of his mission.[5]

Goodenough's orders went on to state:

> On arrival you are immediately to get in touch with the Dutch authorities, explain why you have come and the numbers of men and amount of explosives which you have available. You should then act in close cooperation with the Dutch authorities. No demolitions are to be carried out without Dutch permission except on the near approach of the enemy. An important part of your duty is to persuade all shipping which may not be preparing to go, to leave harbour as soon as possible.[6]

His orders warned Goodenough that the safety of the destroyer was paramount. It would not be able to remain at Ymuiden for longer than 'one period of daylight', to minimise the danger from enemy bombing, and that her commanding officer had been given complete discretion to return to England at any time if they considered that damage from enemy action was possible. Unless there was good reason otherwise, the demolition parties, including the RE Sections, should return to the destroyer by two hours after sunset that day. Failing that they must make the best arrangements they could to return to the UK as soon as possible.[7]

Goodenough fully understood that if they faced any delays or opposition ashore, there was every possibility he and his party could be left stranded in Holland.

As Michael Goodenough considered his possible fate, Captain Keeble RE and his second-in-command Lieutenant Don Terry opened their sealed orders. Robert Keeble, known to all as 'Peter', was born in 1911 in Kenilworth, Warwickshire and attended the King Henry VIII's School in Coventry. After his schooling he was indentured to Alfred Herbert Machine Tool manufacturers in Coventry. He later moved to Kent, where his family had strong connections with the cement industry and joined Bevan's Cement Works. Bevan's managing director, Charles Davis, was Keeble's uncle by marriage. When the KFRE were reformed from men employed at Bevan's in the 1930s, Keeble was one of those who signed up, receiving his commission in 1936.[8]

Keeble began briefing the KFRE demolition team, crowded on the deck of the destroyer, which was also packed with stores, weapons, explosives, and equipment ready for use on the demolition missions. Keeble told his men that once they had reached Ymuiden, they would make their way to Amsterdam by launch, where their objective would be to destroy the vast oil stocks in the various 'tank farms' located there. He then went on to explain their general plan of attack which was to use their Boys anti-tank rifles to breach the oil tanks and then ignite the effluent, using the methods they had practised in training. If the A/T rifles did not prove effective, then they would fall-back on the option of using explosives. He outlined the procedure that was to be followed for the attack and informed his men that, when their tasks were completed, they would return to HMS *Whitshed* by launch. Keeble warned them that if the destroyer had already left then they may have to make their own way back to England, either direct by launch or alternatively by withdrawing to France using motor transport or any other available method, paid for by using Dutch currency that would be issued to them. Keeble then handed out the guilders to the equivalent of £50 per officer and £5 each for other ranks. He also said that, although they hoped to complete their mission in twenty-four hours, they would be issued with three-days' emergency rations. If they had to stay longer, they would then have to seek accommodation. This accommodation and any extra food would have to be paid for out of the currency issued to them.[9]

In the early afternoon, HMS *Whitshed* neared the French coast, with the KFRE contingent now settled down on her deck. Despite the heavy seas, they appeared to be enjoying the voyage so far: 'Everyone was gay and it seemed like a pleasure trip' recorded one of the junior NCOs, Lance Corporal Twocock. However, the mood began to change when a lone German bomber was spotted high overhead. The aircraft released its bombs but fortunately they all missed the destroyer, and the aircraft was beaten off by the ship's anti-aircraft gunners. At 17:00 the sappers received a very welcome tot of rum followed by corned beef sandwiches and tea from the ship's galley. Enjoyment of their refreshment was tempered by the acute awareness that they could be attacked again at any time. Their fears were soon realised when more enemy aircraft appeared overhead and began dive bombing them. L/Cpl Twocock described the scene: 'More planes overhead and things began to fly – all guns were manned and we took cover. Had those sailors got guts! We could hear from the whistle of the bombs as they hit the water – two Portside and one Aft. We had a marvellous skipper [Conder] – the ship was doing [?] knots and twisting and turning like an eel. All we could do was hang on and pray.'[10]

More attacks followed and again Conder proved his skill in limiting their effect with the expert handling of his ship, even impressing his naval colleague Michael Goodenough to record: 'The majority of these attacks were ineffective due to the very skilful handling of the WHITSHED by her Commanding Officer E.R. Conder, R.N. Not only was the enemy aim thrown out by manoeuvre, but, by well judged use of the helm, additional elevation was given to the main armament thus allowing barrage fire to be employed.'

Whitshed's gunners managed to down at least one German bomber, believed to be a Junkers Ju 88, but the bombing continued relentlessly. The destroyer managed to avoid any direct hits, but one particular salvo of high explosive bombs had a devastating effect when they detonated close by the ship on its portside, lifting it clear out of the water, blowing four sailors overboard and showering those on deck with deadly splinters and shards, killing one seaman and causing numerous casualties. The flash from the bomb explosions ignited some of the considerable stocks of ready-use cordite stowed on the destroyer's gun deck.[11] The flames from the burning cordite threatened the demolition parties' explosives stores that were stacked nearby, and had already charred some of its wooden boxes, when two of *Whitshed*'s crew displayed extraordinary bravery, one of them grabbing a bundle of the burning cordite and throwing it overboard, while the other got hold of the other ignited bundle and jumped off the ship, clasping it in his arms, into the churning sea below.[12] Due to the coolness and prompt action by two more of the crew, the flames from the fire were extinguished within a minute and repairs to the ship's holed side and superstructure quickly effected.[13]

Conder, after consulting with Michael Goodenough, made the incredibly difficult decision not to stop to pick up those that had gone overboard. Goodenough advised him that any delay could further endanger the ship and jeopardize the object of the operation. Instead, 'Carley' floats and life buoys were thrown overboard to the beleaguered seamen, and the destroyer pressed on towards Ymuiden at full speed.[14]

As the *Whitshed* approached Ymuiden at speed and still under attack from about twenty German aircraft, a tug was spotted towing some barges across the harbour entrance, forcing Conder to pull his ship fast astern, bringing it to an abrupt halt to avoid a serious collision. This proved a fortunate manoeuvre as at that same moment, the German aircraft released their bombs, aiming them forward of the destroyer to allow for its continuing headway, causing them to fall into the sea in front of the halted ship without producing any further damage.[15]

Remarkably the KFRE contingent survived the air attacks without suffering any casualties, but Goodenough's RN demolition sections were not so fortunate. Four officers, including Goodenough himself, and two seamen suffered injuries. The most seriously injured was Goodenough's demolition officer, Lieutenant Hogg, who had sustained severe burns to his face and hands that required urgent hospital treatment, ruling him out of any further participation in the mission.[16]

HMS *Whitshed* eventually managed to enter the harbour without experiencing any further trouble. It was still unclear how serious the situation was at Ymuiden; just what the mood of the Dutch authorities would be and how they would welcome them. As a precaution, Goodenough disposed his naval party on deck so as to be ready to carry out their demolitions immediately should the situation demand it.

The destroyer was eventually met by a pilot boat carrying a Dutch naval officer, who requested to come on board. He explained that friendly Dutch forces were still in full control of the harbour and that no immediate action was necessary. Before the Dutch officer left, Conder told him about the six men circumstances had forced him to leave behind in the sea. The Dutchman agreed to send the pilot boat to look for them. It was later reported that one man out of the six had been picked up by the pilot boat, but there was no sign of the other five.[17]

When the *Whitshed* eventually pulled alongside and tied-up, Goodenough sent a small naval party ashore under the command of Lieutenant Madden RN, to seize some suitable merchant ships from among those lying at the nearby iron ore quay to use as blockships in case early blocking operations of the harbour entrance were required. Madden had been a late addition to Goodenough's party having joined just four days previously, originally as a replacement for Lieutenant Michael Hemans RN who was due to attend a gunnery course. In the event Goodenough decided to take both officers along on the operation in view of the heavy casualties he was expecting.[18]

Colin Madden had been born in 1915, in Bilbao, Spain where his father was the British Consul. He began his education at Aldbrough Lodge prep school before entering the Royal Naval College at Dartmouth. He was serving on the cruiser HMS *Liverpool* in the Far East when war broke out in September 1939. He had already volunteered to become a navigating officer, and his course was due to start in England in June 1940. He left Hong Kong on 1 April and had arrived back in England on 1 May. During his voyage home, Madden had a change of heart about doing the long navigation course and when he arrived in London, he reported at the Admiralty to see if he could be granted a small command instead. Unfortunately for Madden there were no vessels available for him, but he was told that if anything else came up they would be sure to let him know. He was staying with his mother in London at the time, so he left her telephone number with the Admiralty clerk. On 6 May, after lunching with a friend at his club, Madden returned to his mother's house to find a message waiting for him instructing him to report to the Admiralty the following morning. There he was given instructions to report to Commander Goodenough at Chatham. When Madden arrived at the naval barracks at Chatham on 9 May, he met Michael Goodenough, who briefed him on the Ymuiden operation that he was to join and told him to familiarise himself with the details of the proposed demolitions. At 07:30 the following morning, Madden found himself travelling down to Dover with the rest of Goodenough's RN party to join HMS *Whitshed*.[19]

While Madden and his detachment were at the iron ore quay, the rest of the RN party assisted with the unloading of all the stores and equipment for the demolition teams from the *Whitshed*. Their main concern was to get the explosives under cover before they were subjected to any further air attacks. One of the seriously injured from the *Whitshed*'s crew was taken by ambulance to the local hospital for treatment, but the seriously burnt Lieutenant Hogg could not be moved and was left on board ship. Hogg's place on Goodenough's party was taken by Lieutenant Charles Wilkinson, the torpedo officer of HMS *Keith*, who had been assigned to the *Whitshed* for this voyage.[20]

Once the destroyer had been unloaded, Goodenough ordered Keeble to set off for Amsterdam. Keeble's KFRE party consisted of himself, Lt Don Terry and sixteen of the sappers. They were accompanied by Lieutenant Bowden-Smith RN and eighteen ratings from Goodenough's naval platoons, who would provide armed protection for the party. There were no suitable launches available to take them on the canal, so they all had to travel by train, with their stores following in three commandeered lorries which were provided with another naval escort. By the time they arrived at Amsterdam station it was already 21:00. They were met by Dutch naval officers who insisted that they must proceed to the Amsterdam naval barracks. Keeble protested that he was anxious to get to his objectives that evening, but the Dutch officers would not permit it. Keeble then demanded to be allowed to visit the British Consulate in Amsterdam. The Dutch agreed to Keeble's demand, and he and Bowden-Smith were taken under escort to the Consulate, leaving the rest of the British party kicking their heels under guard at the railway station. When they arrived, they met with the Consul General Sir Gerald Shepherd and Captain Ree, the British Naval Control Service Officer. Unfortunately, they could offer little assistance as they had received no official confirmation from either the British Legation or Dutch GHQ at The Hague that Operation *XD* had been activated. Talks went on until 23:30, by which time Keeble decided he had no alternative but to return to his men and for them all to spend the night at the naval barracks, leaving Shepherd to continue negotiating with the Dutch authorities through the night.[21]

Back at Ymuiden, on board *Whitshed*, Conder and Goodenough had agreed that in view of the wounded left on board, and the structural damage she had sustained, plus her lack of ammunition combined with the probability of further air attacks, the destroyer should sail for home without any further delay. HMS *Whitshed* left Ymuiden at 22:15, leaving Goodenough and Keeble with their parties in Holland, and with no other vessel as yet assigned to bring them home when the time came.

Goodenough spent the rest of the night around the port establishing the location of his objectives, posting sentries and sending out patrols. He also took over responsibility from the Dutch authorities for the arrest of any Germans known to be working on some of the tugs and barges. The Dutch police and military had proved unwilling to continue performing this duty, fearing reprisals if the Germans took over the port.

The British force had been given permission to spend the night at the local militia headquarters, and once Goodenough had settled his men in there, he made his way to see Ymuiden's fortress commander, who was another Dutch naval officer, Commander Cornelis Hellingham. Goodenough described their meeting as 'a distasteful interview'. Hellingham presumed that Goodenough's party was just the forward party for a much larger British force that would soon be arriving to help defend the port. Goodenough had the difficult task of explaining to him that this was not the case and that they were only there 'to prepare for the expected defeat of the Dutch'. Hellingham accepted this, albeit unwelcome, news and pledged his loyalty to the Allied cause. Goodenough then returned to the Militia HQ to try to get some sleep.[22]

Early the following morning, on Saturday, 11 May, Keeble was collected from the naval barracks in Amsterdam by Captain Ree and the British Vice Consul, who took him to meet with Captain Nico Rost van Tonningen, Commandant of Maritime Resources, Amsterdam and the officer responsible for the overall defence of the area. The commandant had just received a telegram from the Dutch GHQ at The Hague stating: 'British Demolition Party which has reported to you will place themselves in your command for the purpose of preparing and executing demolitions eventually to be ordered by higher authorities.'[23]

With the commandant's blessing, Keeble, along with Bowden-Smith, Ree, and some Consular staff, visited their three main objectives: 'A1' – Petroleum Haven, on the southern bank of the North Sea Canal; 'A2' – the Shell oil storage installation; and 'A3' – Benzine Haven. The British officers managed to collect most of

The war memorial commemorating the Bevan's workers who lost their lives in the First World War. (*Gravesham – Bevan's War Memorial in Northfleet Cement Works*. Photo by David Anstiss, licensed under Creative Commons Attribution-ShareAlike 4.0 International. Available via Wikimedia Commons)

Clifford Claude Brazier as a graduate in Electrical and Mechanical Engineering at Manchester University. (Gravesend Historical Society)

Grove House, Northfleet – Headquarters of the Kent (Fortress) Royal Engineers, 1934-39. (Gravesend Historical Society)

Bevan's chairman, A.C. Davies, seeing the KFRE off to their first annual summer camp from Northfleet Station in 1933. (Gravesend Historical Society)

Major Brazier with General Edmund Ironside, GOC Eastern Command [later Field Marshal and Chief of the Imperial General Staff] at the KFRE summer camp at Weymouth, 1936. (Gravesend Historical Society)

Major Brazier with his officers at summer camp, Wyke Regis, 1937 [Brazier – front row, 3rd right; Tommy Goodwin – back row 2nd left; Bernard Buxton – back row, 4th left; 'Peter' Keeble – back row 2nd right]. (Gravesend Historical Society)

The KFRE band marching through Northfleet, 1938. (Gravesend Historical Society)

The KFRE shooting team at summer camp, Sandown, Isle of Wight, 1939. Keeble and Brazier are seated in the front row. (Gravesend Historical Society)

Sir Maurice (later Lord) Hankey. (*Sir Maurice Hankey*. Photo from the Library of Congress, Prints and Photographs Division. Digital ID: npcc 05489. Public domain.)

Admiral Hugh Binney as Governor of Tasmania, 1945. (Government of Tasmania, Public domain, via Wikimedia Commons)

Milton Barracks, home to the Gravesend detachment of the KFRE in 1940.

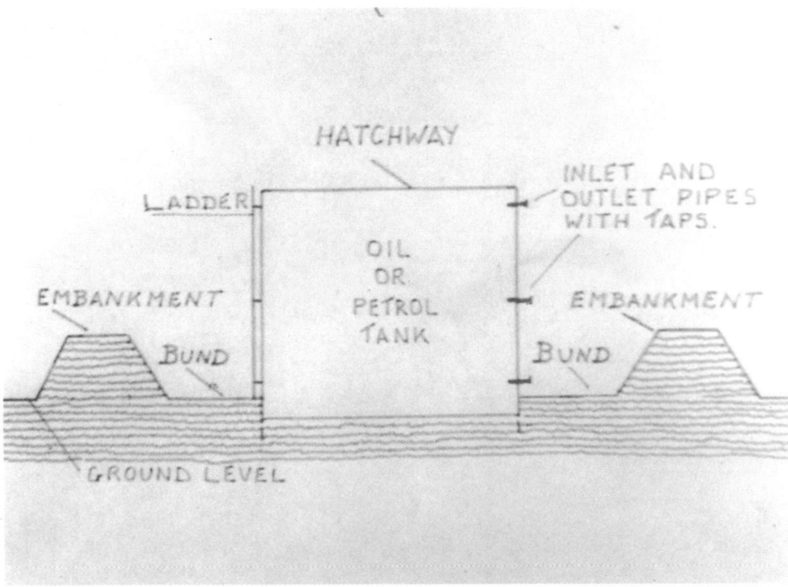

Diagram of an oil tank installation produced by the KFRE for training purposes. (Gravesend Historical Society)

Aerial image of Ymuiden / IJmuiden. (Courtesy of the Netherlands Institute of Military History - Collectie: NIMH. Used with permission)

The Harwich ferry quay at the Hook of Holland. (Courtesy of the Netherlands Institute of Military History - Collectie: NIMH. Used with permission)

Aerial image of Petroleum Haven, Rotterdam. (Courtesy of the Netherlands Institute of Military History - Collectie: NIMH. Used with permission)

Aerial image of Flushing / Vlissingen. (Courtesy of the Netherlands Institute of Military History - Collectie: NIMH. Used with permission)

Antwerp port with oil barrels stacked along the quayside. (Author's collection)

Oil tanks ablaze following the demolitions at Ymuiden / IJmuiden. Photographed by KFRE Sapper Vic Hugget, 11 May 1940. (Gravesend Historical Society)

KFRE sappers Vic Huggget and Frank Huelin at Ymuiden / Ijmuiden, 11 May 1940, with blazing oil tanks in the background. (Gravesend Historical Society)

the information they required for their operations from the Dutch management at the installations, without alerting them to the true intent of their mission. Obviously, the managers would not have been pleased that the British were there to destroy their oil and would not have been so cooperative had they known the truth.

When he returned to the naval barracks, Keeble arranged with the Dutch Naval Staff for the requisition of three motor launches to use to get to their objectives, together with more food to tide them over the extra time they now expected to need to complete the mission. The commandant then sent for Keeble and Bowden-Smith and told them not to leave the barracks unless ordered to do so by him. Keeble insisted that all the parties should be permanently stationed at the objectives from now on to avoid surprise action by the enemy to seize them. After a long discussion, the commandant eventually backed down on the strict understanding that no operations were to commence without his instructions, for which a code word was agreed.

At dusk the three sections departed in the launches to their respective objectives, ready to carry out their allotted tasks. Keeble proceeded, with his A1 Section, to Petroleum Haven, arriving there at 23:00, having already seen the other two sections installed at their objectives and given them their final verbal orders. Keeble then left his men under shelter while he made a reconnaissance of the exact layout of their objective, before returning to get some sleep.

While Peter Keeble had been out visiting the KFRE objectives, Michael Goodenough had been busy at Ymuiden making a detailed survey of his RN demolition team's targets around the port, including the canal entrance lock gates and machinery, and the huge Hoogovens iron ore complex. They would also be responsible for the sinking of blockships to prevent the Germans using the North Sea Canal. Goodenough then had another long interview with Hellingham, who told him he had insufficient troops to man the defensive lines around the town, or to maintain street patrols against German paratroopers or any 'Fifth Column'* attack. There had been a lot of firing in the streets and suburbs at night, and rumours of parachute landings abounded. To meet these threats, Hellingham had been forced to strip the crews from three of his minesweepers, leaving them unable to operate. Goodenough agreed to relieve the minesweeper crews of this duty,

---

* A fifth column is any group of people who undermine a larger group or nation from within, usually in favour of an enemy group or another nation. There was an active National Socialist movement in the Netherlands, strongly sympathetic to Nazi Germany, which was the prime 'fifth column' threat.

using his men to take their place, feeling confident his demolition teams could perform their tasks without needing armed cover. To perform this duty, he moved his men to quarters on the south side of the fishing harbour, where they could also take their place in the defensive line, facing an area of dunes that offered an ideal drop zone for enemy parachute troops.[24]

During the evening, the *Luftwaffe* dropped magnetic mines at Ymuiden in an attempt to close both the inner and outer harbours. However, they failed to close all the channels, allowing two Dutch merchant ships carrying 76 tons of the National Bank's stocks of gold bullion from its vaults in Amsterdam, to escape into the North Sea where they were met by Royal Navy destroyers and safely escorted to England.[25]

At 08:00 the next morning, Sunday, 12 May, Keeble telephoned Goodenough, reporting on the arrangements he had made with Commandant Rost van Tonningen to await his code word before carrying out the demolitions. However, he reassured Goodenough that he would still act on his (Goodenough's) instructions, or on his own initiative should the situation warrant it.

Later that morning, Goodenough called Keeble back with the news that Rost van Tonningen had been shot. The commandant had been visiting a unit of marines that had just arrived to take their place in the defence line. The marines had already come under attack from Dutch fascists the previous evening while moving through Amsterdam, and one of their number had been shot and killed adding to the already high tensions running through the unit. The leader of the *National Socialist Bund* (NSB, the Dutch equivalent of the German Nazi Party) at the time happened to be the commandant's brother, Meinoud Rost van Tonningen. Despite Nico Rost van Tonningen being completely loyal to his country, when he arrived to inspect the Marines, their commanding officer, Captain van de Hend, shot him in the neck. Whether this was a case of mistaken identity by van de Hend, or revenge for his killed comrades, is unclear. Either way he was by then in a very disturbed state and before he could be overpowered, he ran out into the street, shooting and killing three completely innocent civilians. Fortunately, Commandant Rost van Tonningen's wounds had not proved fatal, but he had been seriously wounded and would not be resuming his duties.[26]

Keeble immediately contacted the naval barracks, who confirmed the story and informed him that Ros van Tonningen's second-in-command had taken over as the commandant. Keeble then proceeded to make a further reconnaissance of the petroleum site with his section, which he now split into three, three-man teams, each being given respective areas of the site for demolition. Keeble then instructed each team in the methods they should employ and distributed his stores accordingly.[27]

Ymuiden was subjected to an almost continual series of bombing attacks throughout the day and night of the Sunday, as result of which Michael Goodenough hastened the dispersal of his explosives around the port, placing them under guard and then employing his few spare men in making elementary air raid precautions.

Later that evening Goodenough was telephoned by Sir Gerald Shepherd with a request to help prepare the British merchantman SS *Dotterel*, which had just berthed at Ymuiden, for the evacuation of British refugees who were already on their way to the port by road and rail. An alternative plan for the evacuation of the refugees was put forward by the British Naval Attaché at The Hague. This plan entailed the refugees to be embarked on any of the four RN destroyers that were then on their way to Ymuiden. However, Goodenough successfully argued against that idea saying that having the refugees on board a destroyer would hinder the vessel's operational capabilities.

With the assistance of the *Dotterel*'s Master Captain Green, Goodenough and every man he could muster hurried to make the vessel as comfortable as possible for the refugees. It was very late on the Sunday evening before the refugees began to arrive, and then their embarkation in the *Dotterel* was very slow due to the considerable amount of luggage and the continuous air attacks. However, by 01:00 the next morning, with over 150 refugees safely embarked, the *Dotterel* was on her way to England, with two of the incoming destroyers, HMS *Hyperion* and HMS *Windsor*, now detailed to act as her escorts.

Meanwhile, another of the incoming destroyers, HMS *Kimberley*, was bringing a British military mission to Holland. The mission had originally been due to sail on HMS *Wild Swan* with the 'XD' Party B to Rotterdam but had missed that vessel's departure from Dover on the Friday.[28]

The fourth destroyer was HMS *Codrington*, which was arriving at Ymuiden to embark some 'VIPs', and it arrived in the harbour at 21:00 on the Sunday evening. Michael Goodenough had been kept completely ignorant of the identity of the VIPs the destroyer was there to collect. It was left to Hellingham to inform him that the *Codrington* was embarking members of the Dutch Royal Family in the persons of the Crown Princess Juliana, her husband Prince Bernhard, and their two daughters the princesses Beatrix and Irene, together with members of their household: about ten people in total.* Goodenough was horrified that the port was being used for this important mission despite the extreme danger posed by the mines and the constant air attacks.[29] His worst fears were almost realised, as Lieutenant Colin Madden, who was standing on a jetty in the harbour to witness the event, later recalled:

> [...] and I saw the destroyer coming in, and it really was an absolutely super sight, she came in very fast, brand new white ensign, all the sailors fallen in, and came straight along the side, stern first, beautifully. Within seconds the gangway was out, a car drew up, and there was Princess Juliana with her family. They were ushered onboard, everybody bowed and saluted and the destroyer let go, slipped [anchor] and proceeded fast out of harbour. But, just as she was leaving, a determined [air] attack was made on the CODRINGTON. [...] But by extreme skill on the captain's part, he missed all the bombs and shot out of the harbour, and a few hours later, we were all happy to hear that they had all arrived safely in England.[30]

It was a busy Sunday night for Goodenough, with various vessels arriving and departing for him to contend with. Three RN motor-torpedo boats (MTBs) arrived in the port at 21:30. They had been sent there, at the request of the Dutch authorities, to engage on 'reconnaissance duties' in the North Sea Canal. Goodenough was concerned for their safety operating in the shallow waters of the canal and their vulnerability to air attack by day. However, after some deliberation he decided that they might be of value for night patrol and reconnaissance and agreed to send them through, and they duly departed through the lock gates into the canal at 22:30.[31]

The Dutch merchantman, SS *Perseus,* then arrived to load up with the last of the National Bank's gold bullion from its Amsterdam vaults.

---

* Crown Princess Juliana's mother and Dutch Head of State, Queen Wilhelmina of the Netherlands, was determined to remain with her people. She was eventually persuaded to leave from the Hook of Holland, onboard the British destroyer, HMS *Hereward,* on Monday, 13 May 1940, but only on condition that she could then be taken to Flushing, where she intended to disembark and remain there. However, the minefields surrounding Flushing prevented the *Hereward* entering the port and her captain received orders from the Admiralty to proceed instead to Harwich. When they arrived at Harwich, the queen refused 'to budge' and telephoned King George VI to insist she be returned to the Netherlands. The king refused and she was eventually prevailed upon to be taken by train to London, where she was met by the king at Liverpool Street station and taken by car to Buckingham Palace. (Keyes, Roger – *Outrageous Fortune,* p.209-210).

Perseus departed at 04:00 the next morning, with 1.37 tons of gold on board, escorted by the British destroyer HMS *Vimy*.[32]

It was 02:00 on Monday, 13 May before Goodenough eventually returned to his quarters hoping to get some much-needed sleep. When he got there, he received reports that his patrols and posts had been fully engaged throughout the night in backing-up the Dutch forces with arresting suspects in the streets. He then retired only to be woken at 03:30 by a Dutch officer informing him that German parachute troops had landed just 10 km away. Most of them had been shot, but some were still at large. Goodenough reinforced his guard posts and put the rest of his men on stand-by for the night.[33]

Somehow during that eventful Sunday night, Goodenough found the time to contact Peter Keeble at Petroleum Haven to check that all was well and that his parties were ready to act, warning him that 'time was short'. The following morning, Monday, 13 May, was spent by Keeble and his section on checking their equipment, while the consulate provided them with more food and stores during the day. Goodenough phoned again that evening to warn Keeble to be 'very ready' to carry out his operations.[34]

Back at Ymuiden, Goodenough had experienced yet another hectic day organising operations, with his naval demolition parties completing placing charges on their various objectives around the port. Colin Madden and his team were detailed to lay charges at the Hoogovens iron ore complex, while Charles Wilkinson and his men did the same with the canal lock gates and machinery. Further suitable blockships were requisitioned and prepared. One of these was the Dutch passenger steamer SS *Jan Pieterszoon Coen,* which Goodenough ordered Madden to prepare ready for scuttling at the entrance to the harbour. Madden and his team loaded their cordite into empty fish boxes and divided it up into four lots. Once on board the ship, one lot was placed in the bow, one lot in the stern and the remaining two lots were placed either side of the engine room main water circulators. They then prepared the fuses and disembarked from the ship, ready to return when instructed.[35]

The destroyer HMS *Kimberley* then arrived at the port with the British Military Mission to Holland, headed by General Thomas Heywood. Goodenough welcomed the general and his staff and managed to find some cars to take them to The Hague. Meanwhile, the flow of refugees into the port was unrelenting and Goodenough found himself besieged by British and other nationals seeking passage out of Holland. He did his best, with the assistance of Hellingham and his staff, to provide help, particularly to the British, eventually directing them to a large hotel in the suburbs in an area that had been mostly free from bombing. He told them to wait there until he could find ships for them. Then at 23:00, Captain Ree, the Naval Control Officer, arrived from Amsterdam with his staff ready for evacuation. Goodenough put them up at his HQ at the barracks for the night and they were evacuated the following morning.

From 21:00 Goodenough also found himself having to deal with reports of shooting in the streets and parachute troops landing at various points. It became necessary to reinforce all his defence posts and take over others from the Dutch, eventually employing his entire force on these duties for most of the night.[36]

As dawn broke over Holland on Tuesday, 14 May, Dutch resistance was on the verge of collapse. The destroyer HMS *Vesper* arrived at Ymuiden at 07:00 with three very important signals requiring action from Goodenough. Two were from the C-in-C The Nore warning him not to allow the three MTBs to be cut off up the canal, and requesting him to provide transport for a Captain Davies, arriving that morning on HMS *Havock*, for a 'special mission', the details of which were completely unknown to Goodenough. The third signal was from the Admiralty stating that 'H.M. Government had decided on the immediate destruction of the oil stocks at Amsterdam'. Goodenough was now doubtful, given the current situation, if the latter could be accomplished in full without the concurrence of the Dutch authorities. He was also concerned about Sir Gerald Shepherd, who was still at his desk in Amsterdam. Any precipitate action by Peter Keeble and his team without Dutch consent could jeopardise Shepherd's escape from the city. Goodenough considered his options and decided to give Keeble two hours to try to obtain Dutch concurrence, destroy the remaining petroleum stocks and then get back to Ymuiden. Goodenough telephoned Keeble at 08:00 and gave him his instructions, ordering him to try to obtain the permission of the Dutch authorities to 'blow', failing that he was to act on his own initiative and begin destruction of the remaining fuel stocks. When that was done Keeble and his sappers, together with Bowden-Smith and his naval escort section, were to evacuate by road to Ymuiden. Goodenough then telephoned Shepherd at the consulate, advising him to get to Ymuiden immediately.[37]

The situation at Ymuiden was becoming increasingly difficult with more German bombing and mining, making shipping movements almost impossible. Goodenough, realising that the evacuation of the port would now be a very risky operation, sent a signal to the Admiralty stressing his opinion that the danger of mines and air attack made it unjustifiable to send destroyers into the harbour to aid the evacuation. He then called a final conference of his officers and ordered the whole of his force to their pre-determined action stations.[38]

Meanwhile, at Petroleum Haven, Keeble, pre-empting possible problems with getting the Dutch authorisation, contacted his other two sections at the Shell and benzene installations and ordered them to commence their respective operations. He then went to see the new Dutch commandant, seeking his authority to 'blow', describing the position as 'very urgent', but the commandant responded with an emphatic 'No'. Keeble then took it upon himself to telephone the Dutch GHQ at The Hague. Speaking to the Duty Officer there, Keeble explained that he was in command of the XD operations in Amsterdam and considered that a start should be made on them now. The Duty Officer replied with some agitation 'Do it. Yes, do it at once!' Keeble relayed the Duty Officer's response to the Dutch commandant, who refused to believe it and had to phone the Duty Officer himself before he was convinced. The whole official authorisation process had now taken over ninety minutes, but unbeknown to the Dutch commandant, the XD operations at the Shell oil storage farm and at Benzene Haven had both been proceeding during that time. Keeble and his section then proceeded to commence work on their target, the vast Petroleum Haven storage site. By 11:30, half the petrol stocks were 'on the ground' and four of the tanks had been fired.[39]

Keeble delayed the firing of the rest of the petroleum stocks to avoid cutting off the withdrawal of his other two sections, A2 and A3, from their objectives further up the canal. It was then that Michael Goodenough phoned to tell him that the lower reaches of the canal had recently been mined from the air by the Germans to restrict any movement out of Amsterdam. His withdrawal to Ymuiden would now have to be made by road. Unfortunately, he lacked any motor transport to do that. Realising the seriousness of the situation, Keeble rushed to a nearby Dutch anti-aircraft gun battery and gave their officers a story that some German parachutists had been taken prisoner nearby and he needed three lorries to take his men to collect them. Keeble's ruse obviously worked, for within twenty minutes he had three Dutch army lorries at his disposal. Meanwhile, Keeble took a launch upstream to assist his other two sections with their withdrawal from their objectives. He was within 500 yards of the first section objective when he came across both groups, having completed their respective tasks, travelling in launches in the opposite direction. Keeble then contacted Goodenough to tell him all his men were safe and that they would be returning to Petroleum Haven to finish operations there and would be leaving for Ymuiden by 13:30. When they reached Petroleum Haven, Keeble loaded most of his sappers, together with most of Bowden-Smith's naval escort party, onto two of the waiting lorries and ordered them to make their way to a rendezvous point half a mile along the road to Ymuiden and to wait there for the remainder of the party. Keeble, along with four sappers and six naval ratings, then proceeded to empty and fire the remaining fuel tanks. By 13:12 Keeble and his small party were on their way to the rendezvous point in the remaining lorry. From there the entire party began their journey back to Ymuiden, with Petroleum Haven and the other objectives ablaze in the distance behind them.[40]

Although not on the mission himself, the KFRE's CO, Lt Col Claude Brazier, later received Keeble's written report, and heard many verbal accounts of the operation at Petroleum Haven from those that partook in it. After the war he wrote up an account of all the XD operations, which was subsequently added to by his son 'Jock' with information gained from later research and interviews and eventually published as a book. The book describes the firing and subsequent conflagration at Petroleum Haven:

> They exclusively adopted the system of blowing off the cocks to the tanks with gun cotton to flood the areas between the tanks and the bunds. When they fired Very light cartridges into the air over the bunds the fuel would ignite and burn furiously about fifty foot above the pool of petrol. This phenomenon was caused by lack of sufficient oxygen until it reached this height. Eventually, with an enormous whoomph a whole tank would take off into the air, roll over and fall down. This tickled the sappers' imagination no end! The flames grew higher and higher and the back smoke denser and denser. The flames eventually reached several hundred feet and the smoke drifted slowly over the city [Amsterdam].[41]

At Ymuiden, HMS *Havock* arrived in the harbour at 13:30, after making her way safely through the mined channel. She disembarked Captain Davies, for his 'special mission', and embarked some of the British refugees, before hastily departing, with Goodenough's orders to return at 22:00 to assist with the final evacuation.[42]

Davies and the purpose of his mission were still very much a mystery to Goodenough. All Davies told him was that he needed to use a telephone to contact someone in Amsterdam and a car to get him there. Goodenough explained that the demolitions had taken place, and all the British, including the demolition teams and the Consul General, had been evacuated from Amsterdam in view of the serious situation developing in the area, and so there was no British official left in the city he could contact. Nevertheless, Davies insisted on using a telephone, while Goodenough found him a car.

It was not a British official that Davies wanted to phone, it was Dr Adriaan De Jong, a director of *De Nederlandsche Bank* (DNB), the Dutch Central Bank. Davies's mission was to ensure that Dutch bearer bonds, securities and other financial assets did not fall into the hands of the Germans. This had been one of Lord Hankey's major concerns and had prompted Davies's secret mission. Davies eventually got through to Dr De Jong and advised him that he was coming to Amsterdam. In the meantime, Goodenough had, with the cooperation of Commander Hellingham, managed to obtain a car, military permit and armed escort for Davies, who was soon on his way to Amsterdam, with a stern warning to return before nightfall.

When he arrived at the DNB offices, Davies was met by Dr De Jong and the bank's president, Leonardus Trip, to whom he presented his credentials and explained the purpose of his mission. From his discussions, it was apparent to Davies that little, if any, thought had been given by the Dutch to the question of the fate of their bearer bonds and other securities in the current circumstances. Davies found both men depressed with the failure of the Allies to come to Holland's aid, and the entire atmosphere of the meeting was 'charged with defeatism'. In view of the impending fall of Amsterdam, Davies urged on the two Dutchmen the urgency of taking some rapid drastic action to safeguard their assets. Trip agreed to call an immediate meeting of his co-directors to which he also summoned the chairman of the Amsterdam stock exchange executive. The meeting agreed to block all trade in stocks until the end of hostilities and to urge all stock exchange members to advise their clients to transfer bearer bonds into safe custody outside Holland. Davies then took Trip to one side and strongly suggested that he take more drastic action, such as the actual physical destruction of the bank's own bearer certificates and paper currency. Trip agreed and arranged for slabs of TNT explosives to be moved into the bank's vaults for this purpose. He also agreed to contact the other banks in the city to advise them to do the same.

Davies had hoped to remain in Amsterdam until he had seen some action on his suggestions initiated, but it was now 18:30 and he realised he would have to leave to get back to Ymuiden in time to be evacuated. As he prepared to leave, news came through that the Dutch garrison in Amsterdam had surrendered and that German paratroopers were landing along the Amsterdam – Ymuiden road. Despite this unwelcome news, Davies decided to take his chances and headed off to the port.

He ended up having to shoot his way through two German roadblocks before arriving safely back at Ymuiden at 19:30 that evening.[43]

Keeble and the Amsterdam party also had problems with roadblocks on the same road when they were travelling along it earlier in the day, their three lorries crashing through several on the route. However, they came through unscathed and arrived in Ymuiden at 14:30 with their mission successfully completed. Keeble reported to Goodenough, who asked him if he and his sappers would be prepared to help with the demolitions at the port. Keeble readily agreed saying that they 'were only too anxious to help'. A2 Section was allocated to Charles Wilkinson to assist in blowing all the lock gates; A3 Section to Colin Madden to blow the blockship *Jan Pieterszoon Coen* in the north entrance; and A1 Section, with Keeble himself, to Michael Hemans to demolish cranes, floating docks, and to blow the blockship in the southern entrance.[44]

Goodenough then joined Hellingham at his HQ so he could keep updated on his latest intelligence and, if necessary, influence any decisions he would be making. While Goodenough was there, the three RN MTBs arrived back safely at the port. He immediately ordered them to take cover by the lock walls ready to assist with the final evacuation. At 16:30, with news coming in of an imminent Dutch surrender and continued German bombing and mining of the harbour, Goodenough, with Hellingham's agreement, ordered the demolition teams to commence operations.[45]

Before he could see to the *Coen*, Madden first had to deal with the huge Hoogovens iron works over the other side of the port. Madden, with three of his party, had only the use of a rowing boat to reach their objective, and it took them over an hour to row across the harbour to the works. Realising then that time was getting short, and the relative impossibility of the task they were confronted with, Madden and his team decided the best they could do was to throw a depth charge into the giant blast furnace, close the door and run! They were then confronted with another hour-long row to get to the *Coen*.[46]

Meanwhile, Keeble, Hemans and their party successfully destroyed one large floating crane, two floating docks, four tugs and several large lighters, while Bowden-Smith, with the assistance of some Dutch marines placed the blockship across the southern entrance to the harbour and sunk her. When those jobs were completed, Goodenough ordered Keeble and the sappers of A1 Section to relieve the Dutch troops manning various positions commanding the lock approaches from the south. Goodenough intended this outwardly as a generous gesture towards the Dutch, enabling those troops to prepare for evacuation. However, he also regarded it as a precaution against any sudden surrender by the Dutch authorities which would leave the British force exposed.

At 17:30, the information came in that everyone was dreading – the Netherlands had surrendered.* Commander Hellingham broke the news to Michael Goodenough, telling him that the orders from his headquarters were for all Dutch troops to lay down their arms, all demolitions to cease, and the British evacuation to be halted. There was a lot of confusion and doubt in the minds of the Dutch officers as to the validity of the orders. Some began to waver, but Hellingham himself stood firm in his duty to the Allied cause, cancelling the orders, and then going around the port with Goodenough in a Dutch MTB to rally his troops.

Meanwhile, the demolitions continued apace. Charles Wilkinson's party sank a dredger and several hoppers, while three of his men were despatched to the iron works to do what more damage they could there. As well as achieving some extra structural damage they also managed to destroy the work's main control board before returning. Wilkinson then commenced blowing up all the lock gates machinery. The main power station for the gates was blown-up; the machinery for the both north lock entrances, and all the machinery for the north entrance of the Middle Lock was destroyed, while the hand-worked gates of the smaller South Lock were jammed by dumping hundreds of tons of stone ballast and iron ore into them. Two tugs were then sunk in the approaches to complete the job. The lock gates themselves were not destroyed but just left shut. Goodenough was concerned that destroying them would do nothing to hinder shipping but would cause flooding to the poorer quarters of Amsterdam.

Wilkinson achieved the bulk of his tasks by 19:30. He then sent most of his party, including Don Terry and the sappers of A2 Section, off in a tug, while he and a few men remained to finish work at the last lock, which was done by 20:30. They then left in a rowing boat for the harbour's south entrance to join up with Colin Madden's party, while sinking two abandoned pilot vessels along the way.[47]

That evening, Peter Keeble and his section covering the approaches to the South Lock received instructions from Michael Hemans to withdraw to a small vessel he had commandeered, where they

---

* Although the Commander of the Dutch armed forces, General Henri Winkeklman, surrendered all his armies north and east of the River Schelde (an area that encompassed virtually all of the Netherlands), on 14 May, the official Dutch surrender document was not actually signed until the following day, 15 May. It was several more days before the remaining Dutch forces in Zeeland finally capitulated.

proceeded to load their stores into the boat and by 19:35, were all on board and heading out to sea.[48]

The final job was left to Colin Madden and his party. By 20:00 they had cast-off the *Coen* and were now being towed towards the southern pier by a trawler. The small trawler struggled with the 11,000-ton *Coen*, but with some gentle assistance from Hellingham, who was using an even smaller vessel, the harbour tug *Atjeh*, to occasionally nudge the giant ship's stern to keep her straight, she made her way slowly across the harbour to her final position. All the time this was going on, German mine-laying aircraft were flying overhead and when they realised what was happening, in Madden's words, 'all hell broke loose'. The German planes dropped mines all around to try to prevent the progress of the *Coen* and even tried to bomb her directly with them, while other aircraft strafed the vessel with machine-gun fire.[49]

However, Madden managed to run the gauntlet without suffering any serious casualties, and by 22:00 he was on his final approach to the southern pier. There he was joined on board by Goodenough, who had been touring the harbour and locks on a motorboat, checking that no stragglers from his various parties had been left behind. As he went around on his tour, he observed that there was now shooting in the streets, and the last of the Dutch minesweepers were leaving the port while all other vessels had either left or been sunk.[50]

On board the *Coen*, Goodenough ordered Madden to 'Stand by to blow, and blow when you think you should'. Madden, in his recollection's years later, described the ensuing action:

> So, I went down with my chief torpedo gunner's mate, sent all the sailors to the stern of the ship, and when we felt her touch [the pier], we lit the Bickston's [*sic*]* fuse in the bow. And then we raced up all the ladders and rushed about and went to the stern of the ship. The moment we got to the stern, there was a muffled explosion, and the ship shook. Down she went aground for'ard. Then it was a question of blowing up the stern, and the whole thing was to get across the entrance, and of course, we had nothing to get her across the entrance with. It had to be all done by working in the tide, and the tide was beginning to flood, if I remember rightly, and we were beginning not to be square across. How we got across in the first place was sheer skill on behalf of the trawler. But

* I think Madden here means a 'Bickfords fuse', essentially a safety fuse made from strands of rope, wound around a central core of gunpowder. The rope used in the fuse was known to burn at a constant rate, thus by adjusting the length of the rope you could accurately adjust the delay before detonation of the explosives. (*https://www.bbc.co.uk/ahistoryoftheworld/objects/uX4fb8QkQpSZgs5lYvgxQg*)

> I realised as soon as we got the stern down on the bottom, the better. So without any further ado, I sent my sailors for'ard and I and the torpedo gunner's mate, once more, lit the Bickston's [*sic*] fuse and rushed for'ard. [...] When we got there, there was a muffled explosion, down she went. She was, as far as one could do, across the entrance, about 20 [degrees] wrong, but it was all a bit difficult at the time. One certainly couldn't have done really much better.[51]

However, Madden's business on board the *Coen* was still not complete. To ensure that the vessel could never be re-floated, it was essential that her 'bottom side' was blown out. With German bombs and parachute mines raining down around them, Madden and his team prepared to fire the final explosion. The explosives this time needed to be detonated electronically using a switch box that Madden already had his doubts about. When his team had first unpacked their equipment on board the *Cohen*, the battery for supplying the current to the electronic switch was found to be missing. After searching around the ship, they found a similar battery in the back of the captain's personal wireless, but had no time to test it. To his horror, when Madden came to fire and he threw the switch, nothing happened. Either the battery was flat, or the switch was faulty. After some hurried discussions it was decided to dispense with the switch and try to induce a current by way of a direct connection to the battery. Lacking any connectors, Madden wrapped one bare wire around the negative terminal of battery, then rubbed the other bare wire against the positive terminal and:

> ... after two or three shots there was the most enormous explosion [...] and the bottom of the ship blew out. [...] this huge ship, 20,000 tons, catapulted over from a vertical position to about thirty to forty degrees, which is quite a lot. And all the machinery [was] all over the place, winches and wires, anything that was in any way loose broke apart [...] The ship slowly settled back in a vertical position, well and truly on the bottom.[52]

Although the *Coen* was now securely sunk between the pier heads on the seabed, there was still a gap of about 20 yards under her stern. After some discussions between Goodenough and Madden, it was thought that the gap could be filled by scuttling another vessel in it. The only vessel left afloat large enough to fill the gap was the trawler that had been towing them. The problem was that the trawler was the same vessel they were planning to use for their retreat. However, it was decided they had no choice but to use it to fill the gap and then take their chances by all crowding onto the small tug. The trawler got underway and manoeuvred into the gap, its sea cocks were then opened, and she gradually went down. The trawler crew were subsequently taken off and joined everyone else on the *Atjeh*, which finally proceeded westwards into the open sea, with Amsterdam now left inaccessible to large sea-going vessels for the rest of the war.[53]

By 23:00 all the XD parties had left Ymuiden, but in vessels which were both totally unsuited to the voyage back to England and vulnerable to attack by any roaming German aircraft or E-boats.

Peter Keeble and his party were already well out to sea in their open motorboat when they spotted Don Terry with A2 Section and several sailors in their tug heading further out to sea. Terry's tug soon became lost but was later fortunate to be seen by a Belgian destroyer, whose captain put them on course for Dover, where they eventually arrived the following day.[54]

Meanwhile, on the motorboat, Keeble and his party were coming under constant machine-gun attack from German fighters. They responded as best they could with rifle fire but to no effect and only made things worse by drawing the attention of the aircraft to them with the flashes from their rifles. Keeble took a chance and ordered his men to cease firing. His hunch paid off as the fighters now lost them in the pitch darkness.

At 21:30 a Dutch trawler was sighted, which they came alongside and boarded, leaving the tug to be scuttled with all their stores still on board. They continued in the trawler, coming under air attack again until 23:45 when they made contact with HMS *Havock*. Keeble and his party all boarded the destroyer, which then proceeded to Harwich, arriving there safely at 07:00 the next morning.[55]

At Harwich the returning sappers were directed to the local RN shore establishment, where the Royal Navy proved to be most generous hosts, congratulating them all on a job well done, and providing food, tea, hot water for washing and shaving and most welcome of all, a comfortable bed for the night before their return to Gravesend the next day.

Meanwhile, the *Atjeh* was still at sea with over seventy men on board a vessel designed for a maximum of just twenty-five passengers and crew. The small harbour tug could only make about 8 knots and had to keep stopping to avoid being spotted by German aircraft. By dawn on 15 May they were still only about 40 miles off the Dutch coast when the engine stopped: they had run out of fuel. The crew found some spare fuel and managed to carry on, but by mid-afternoon the tug only had enough left for less than 20 miles' sailing.[56] It was then they found themselves being joined by a Dutch lifeboat, the *Zeemanshoop*, carrying forty-six Jewish refugees escaping from the Nazis. They were all from Scheveningen, a beach resort and fishing harbour near The Hague, and included several children and elderly among their number. Both small vessels, equally helpless with no navigation charts between them and almost out of fuel, were reduced to risking further air attack by firing off distress flares. Fortunately, the flares were spotted by the lookouts on the destroyer HMS *Venomous*, which was sailing near the Goodwin Sands escorting two auxiliary minesweepers, the requisitioned Southern Railways paddle steamers HMS *Sandown* and HMS *Ryde*. The *Zeemanshoop* was spotted first, and *Venomous* lowered her whaler, which set off to meet the lifeboat to instruct it to come alongside her where the destroyer's crew helped the refugees to climb aboard. Then, at 16:00, the *Atjeh* was sighted, and she too was called alongside. All the British contingent, together with some Dutch officers, including Commander Hellingham, climbed on board the destroyer leaving just the three-man Dutch crew on the tug. The *Atjeh*, now supplied with more fuel and accurate directions, took the *Zeemanshoop* under tow and headed off to Harwich, while HMS *Venomous* sailed at high speed to Dover, arriving there late that afternoon.[57]

Chapter 13

THE HOOK OF HOLLAND AND ROTTERDAM (10-15 MAY)

HMS *Wild Swan*, under the command of Lieutenant Commander John Younghusband, sailed from Dover just after mid-day on 10 May, bound for the Hook of Holland.

Born in India in 1899, Younghusband joined the Royal Navy at the age of 13 and within five years was an acting sub lieutenant. When he was serving on board the battleship HMS *Commonwealth*, the captain noted that he 'Should make a capable officer with more experience. Active, intelligent and efficient, [with a] quiet manner.' He was promoted to lieutenant commander in 1927, and in 1932 was the commanding officer of the destroyer HMS *Vimiera* in the Mediterranean – his first command. He had been the commanding officer of HMS *Wild Swan* since July 1939.[1]

On board *Wild Swan* was a twenty-eight-man RN demolition party, and the KFRE Section B with Captain Thomas Goodwin in command of five junior officers and sixty-two other ranks. Tommy Goodwin was 36 years old. He had been born, raised, and educated in Durban, Natal in South Africa, where he later became an engineer. He then emigrated to England where he was employed by Bevan's Cement Works in Northfleet and recruited into the KFRE. He married Louise Pike in 1933 with whom he had three daughters. He was a keen and competitive recreational rifle shot and was Kent County Small Bore Champion in 1935.[2]

The *Wild Swan* had also been due to take the twenty-six-man Military Mission No.10 to the Hook, but the mission had been delayed on its way to Dover and had subsequently missed embarkation. It was now due to follow later, sailing on board HMS *Wivern*.

In charge of the combined RN/RE demolition force was 39-year-old Commander James Hill RN, who had joined the Royal Navy at the age of 13. At the outbreak of the war, he was serving on the China Station as commanding officer of the destroyer HMS *Westcott*, but for the last few months, he had been attached to the Plans Division at the Admiralty, working with Michael Goodenough on the planning of the XD operations.[3] Hill now found himself in overall command of XD Party B with orders to ensure the destruction of the estimated 400,000 tons of oil and petrol stocks at Rotterdam and to carry out demolitions of various port installations at the Hook, including the coastal defence gun batteries, various mine and torpedo stores, and any navigational aids that could be identified.[4]

Just before the *Wild Swan* sailed, and completely unbeknown to Hill, the War Cabinet meeting held at 11:30 that morning had been discussing the XD missions and the question of the security of the Dutch gold reserves. The meeting decided that the gold held at the Rotterdam branch of the *Nederlandsche Bank* should be secured by Hill's XD party and brought to England.[5]

The *Wild Swan*'s passage to Holland was uneventful, with no enemy air activity recorded. A hot meal was served to all on board before she arrived off the Hook at 16:30. Despite signals from the Admiralty indicating the presence of magnetic mines, Younghusband decided to attempt to enter the Hook. Fortunately, a pilot boat was sighted nearby and Younghusband summoned it to approach his ship. The pilot came on board, accompanied by a Dutch naval officer who demanded to know the purpose of the destroyer's visit. Younghusband told him that he was 'bringing a party to assist local authorities'. The naval officer appeared satisfied and left, after warning Younghusband that a Dutch armed trawler was patrolling in the area. The pilot confirmed the presence of the magnetic mines but said that he knew where they all were. He then returned to his boat to guide the destroyer as it entered the mine-infested channel at what Younghusband later described as a 'hair-raising 20 knots the wrong side of the channel buoys'. They negotiated the channel safely and moored up at the LNER Harwich ferry quay, where they were met by crowds of people cheering from the shore.[6]

Now they had arrived, and with enemy aircraft appearing overhead, the priority for the demolition teams was to disembark their stores as quickly as possible. While they were doing that, a Dutch officer, Commander Logger came on board the *Wild Swan*. Logger announced himself as the second-in-command of 'Fort aan den Hoek van Holland', the fort defending the Hook and its port. He proceeded to interview

Younghusband and Hill, briefing the two RN officers on the current local situation and told them that he was confident of holding the port, but was worried about Germans landing by parachute or from landing craft. He then became considerably concerned about the demolition stores that were being off-loaded from the destroyer. Hill reassured him by saying that they were only there to prepare demolitions and he would not fire them unless requested to do so by the Dutch authorities. Seemingly satisfied with that, Logger took Hill off to meet the fort commandant.[7]

With all the demolition party and their stores safely ashore, Tommy Goodwin briefed his sappers on the orders for their operation. These were to ensure the destruction of the oil and petrol stocks at Rotterdam. As with the Ymuiden / Amsterdam mission, the safety of the destroyer was to be considered of paramount importance. Unless there was any good reason to the contrary, all the parties should return to the *Wild Swan* two hours before sunset the following day. If anyone failed to rejoin the ship in time before she sailed, then they would have to make their own way back to the UK as soon as possible using the Dutch currency they had been issued with.[8]

James Hill returned from his meeting with the fort commandant and told Goodwin that his RE party should proceed at once to Rotterdam to try to contact someone in authority there who could authorise the destruction of the oil tanks. The only problem was that no arrangements appeared to have been made to provide them with the launches they were expecting to make the journey in.[9]

Hill went off to speak to Commander Logger and Commissioner Van Dienst from the Hook of Holland pilotage to arrange for the use of a pilot boat to transport the sappers to their objectives. After receiving permission from his superiors, the commissioner gave his approval and shortly afterwards, the appointed vessel pulled up alongside the quay ready to embark Goodwin's sappers and their stores.

As a precautionary measure, all the civilian pilot boats at the Hook had been taken over by the Royal Dutch Navy, just before the outbreak of the war, in August 1939. Pilot Steamer No.19 was one of those boats. Built in 1923, she was 152 feet from bow to stern, with a beam of 25 feet, and powered by a steam engine that could make a maximum speed of 10 knots. Although unsuitable for the open sea she was ideal for the coastal waters, sea inlets and ports. After being commandeered by the navy, she was assigned as a surveillance craft, re-named 'HM SC 19A', and equipped with two 3.7 cm guns, mounted on her port side. She was commanded by an officer of the Royal Dutch Reserve Special Forces, Lieutenant I.J. Smit, and had an armed crew. As a surveillance craft, its duties were to inspect and search suspicious vessels attempting to enter the Nieuwe Waterweg, the ship canal that connected the Hook of Holland to the port of Rotterdam via the Scheur and the Nieuw Maas. In between these military operations she was still used as a pilot vessel and placed back under the command of a civilian pilot. All these routine operations were now put on hold as HM SC 19A prepared for her new special assignment.[10]

At 19:30, while the steamer was being loaded, a message came through to Younghusband from the Admiralty ordering himself and Hill to secure the gold bullion held in the Rotterdam bank vaults and send it back to England. The two commanders then discussed the best course of action to take. They eventually decided, due to the time, tides, and known dispositions of German troops, aircraft, and mines, that the pilot vessel would have a better chance of getting through to collect the gold than the destroyer would. Then, when the pilot boat returned, Younghusband would take the gold on board the *Wild Swan* and sail for England.

Although this was obviously an extra burden he could have done without, Hill resolved to take personal responsibility for securing the gold. Taking three of his RN party with him, he joined Goodwin and his sappers on the HM SC 19A, which set off for Rotterdam at 20:15.[11]

The situation in Rotterdam was already very serious. German seaplanes had been landing on the river and disgorging troops into rubber boats and onto the quaysides since the early hours of the morning. These were followed by landings by parachute troops attempting to seize control of the airfield at Waalhaven. To add to the problems of the Dutch military, armed members of the NSB had also taken to the streets in support of the invaders, and the city and port had already been heavily bombed.

Much of the activity at Rotterdam was being witnessed by an officer of the Royal Naval Reserve, Commander F.C. 'Fred' Hartley. A 52-year-old Lancastrian, Hartley had been in Rotterdam for the last five and a half months as an officer in the Naval Control Service (NCS), monitoring and controlling the movements of British merchant shipping at the port. In that time, he had travelled extensively all over the Netherlands by canal, road, and rail on both duty and pleasure. He had visited all the major towns and cities paying particular attention to the defence measures the Dutch were putting in place to counter any invasion. From his travels and observations, he later recalled, 'All over the country they were preparing but no place seemed to be quite ready'.[12]

Hartley had been on duty in the Shipping Control Office since the early evening of Thursday, 9 May and had heard the first German aircraft fly over Rotterdam at 03:50 on the Friday morning. The invasion had come as no surprise to Hartley as his superior, Captain Charles Cartwright RN had been summoned to the British Legation at The Hague the previous day to receive a warning from the Naval Attaché of a German ultimatum to the Dutch Government and to be prepared to move all British merchant ships out of Rotterdam at a moment's notice.

At the time of the invasion, there were five British ships at Rotterdam, two of which, the SS *Malines* and SS *St Denis*, had been chartered by the British Government from the London & North Eastern Railway and sent to Rotterdam ready to evacuate its consular staff and other British citizens from the city. The evacuation would be controlled by the NCS and by 08:00 on Friday, 10 May, all the British ships were reported by their captains to the NCS office to be ready for sea at five minutes' notice. Fred Hartley and the other NCS officers began to muster the evacuees at the local Mission to Seamen's building, under the supervision of the resident padre Mr Day, and some of the consular staff.[13]

At 11:00 Captain Cartwright telephoned Hartley from the consulate to inform him that he was returning to The Hague to receive further instructions, leaving Hartley in charge of the evacuation. Unfortunately, on the drive to The Hague, Cartwright's car was ambushed by German parachute troops, and he suffered multiple gunshot wounds. He was rushed to the Red Cross hospital at The Hague but died from his wounds later that day.

By the early evening, Hartley had collected over 260 evacuees at the Mission, who he then transferred to the *Malines*. The LNER vessel set sail from the port for England at 20:00 and would have passed HM SC 19A with James Hill, Tommy Goodwin and the demolition party on board sailing in the opposite direction.[14]

The situation awaiting the British party at Rotterdam was a very tense and dangerous one, as Hartley later recalled:

> There was a 'curfew' each night from dusk to dawn except for those who had special passes.
>
> Other orders that were issued were: - No intoxicants were to be sold and only one day['s] supply of food could be purchased at one time.
>
> People in the streets were told not to conceal their hands; they were not allowed to have them in their pockets or behind their backs. All windows were to be kept open and no one was allowed on the house tops. These latter regulations were made of course against the NSBs.

> About 1600 the Germans made a bomb attack on the guns at Wester Kade and the Boomje, on the latter place they obtained several hits and set the district on fire. On the Wester Kade however they missed and the bombs fell in the river. Every piece of glass for a mile around was blown to powder.[15]

At the Hook, the RN party began laying demolition charges underneath the rolling stock standing at the port's railway station, while Younghusband made contingency plans to torpedo the Hook's northern breakwater if unfavourable circumstances forced them to leave before the port demolitions could be completed.

As the evening wore on there was increasing enemy air activity overhead and Younghusband's main concern was that they could be laying mines in the river. However, as he watched them through the gloom, none appeared to be doing so, but he then realised that they could be landing more troops at nearby captured airfields. To add to his concerns Younghusband now found himself responsible for the safety of a small Dutch Military and Naval Mission that had just arrived requesting passage to England. They had experienced considerable difficulty making their way to the Hook since leaving The Hague at 05:00 that morning and were now all very tired, hungry, and thirsty. Younghusband showed them to his cabin and ensured that they all received a good meal, something to drink, and a place to rest up for the night.[16]

It was 23:00 before HM SC 19A eventually arrived at Lekhaven Wharf in Rotterdam. Hill and Goodwin went ashore with the aim of contacting the relevant authorities for their respective missions. Such was the febrile atmosphere at the port, it was not long before Goodwin, in company with 2nd Lieutenant Paul Baker, was arrested by the Dutch military and taken to the nearest guardhouse, where they were interrogated by a captain. Unfortunately, the captain spoke very little English and the KFRE officers could not speak Dutch. However, Goodwin did his best to try to resolve the situation by speaking in Afrikaans, a language he had picked up from his time in South Africa. Far from improving things, it just made the situation even worse as the Dutch captain could not understand a word of Afrikaans, but instead thought Goodwin was talking German.[17]

Shortly afterwards Hill was brought in to join them, having been arrested as well. Between them the British officers eventually managed to convince the Dutch captain that they were English, and of the urgency and importance of their missions. He allowed them use of his telephone and provided Hill with a contact number for the Governor of the Rotterdam branch of the National Bank, and Goodwin with that of the manager of the 'Old Matex' petroleum storage site on the River Maas, which was owned by the Batavian Oil Company, a subsidiary of Royal Dutch Shell. Although it was a difficult conversation to have, Goodwin still managed to get the manager to agree to meet him. James Hill was also successful in his attempt to speak to the bank's governor, who gave him permission to collect the gold. Hill had no transport available to him so the governor would arrange for the gold to be transported to the wharf.[18]

In the vaults of the bank lay 937 gold bars, weighing 10.8 tons, and valued at almost 22 million guilders, all packed in wooden crates ready to go. This was less than 10 per cent of the actual stock, but it was all the bank staff had managed to pack as the building was now coming under heavy shellfire and bombing. The commander of the local Dutch garrison provided four trucks and several marines to help load and then escort the gold on its journey to Lekhaven. Coordinating the loading of the gold was the Auditor-General for the *Nederlandsche Bank*, W.C. Roest van Limburg. He later described the final stages of the hazardous operation:

> The trucks are moving out one by one. Every time one crosses a bridge, the Germans get suspicious and open fire. When the last truck has moved out, and the last soldier has left, it is nearing dusk. We learn that the Germans have been pushed back to the Boompjes,* but that they endured that night on the bridges and the left bank of the Maas. There will be attempts to expel them there as well! We are now warned for the fire that approaches our office from the east. The buildings directly across the Maasbrug (bridge) have been set on fire and this fire is nearing us on the eastern wind. We must get out of here. We leave on the Navy Commander's signal, after having securely closed the building. Most officials rush across the bridge on foot. Finally, I left by car with Mr Lagerwey and the present women. The Germans see us off with a volley.[19]

The gold arrived at Lekhaven Wharf at 03:00 on the Saturday morning, 11 May, where the KFRE sappers helped load it onto HM SC 19A stacking it either side of the wheelhouse. The vessel left Lekhaven two hours later to make its way back to the Hook. Apart from its twenty-strong Dutch crew, left on board were Hill and two RN ordinary seamen, T.G. Goshawk and F.G. Higgs. Tommy Goodwin and his sappers were left ashore to proceed on to their objectives.

---

* The Boompjes is an area on the north bank of the Nieuwe Maas, near Rotterdam city centre.

The journey back towards the Hook was largely peaceful, and as dawn broke, the vessel was making good time, expecting to be back at the Hook around 07:00. She had just passed Vlaardingen at 05:30 and was entering the Nieuwe Waterweg, when she activated a German magnetic mine, possibly dropped from one of the aircraft Younghusband had spotted the previous night. The mine's explosive charge shot up and hit the keel of the HM SC 19A under the engine room, exploding with tremendous power, and forcing her out of the water with her decks ripped apart and wreckage flying into the air. The boat's bow and stern fell back separately into the water and immediately began to sink. Soon, all that could be seen of her was the top of the funnel and a few metres of her foremast surrounded by bubbling black water and burning fuel. Then came the yells and screams of crewmen and passengers fighting for their lives in the water.

The crew members in the wheelhouse had been killed instantaneously in the blast, as had those in the engine room. Those who had survived were now in the water, many with terrible injuries. A rowing boat and a port service vessel left the shore to go to their aid, but only six were saved. Among those that perished were Commander James Hill, and Ordinary Seamen Goshawk and Higgs. As for the gold, it all now rested on the bottom of the Nieuwe Waterweg.[*,20]

Earlier, at 02:15 that morning, Younghusband had received a signal from the Admiralty instructing him to contact the British Consul General and Naval Control Service Office at Rotterdam and tell them to sail all British and Norwegian ships at the port 'forthwith'. He managed to contact the consulate by telephone and asked them to pass the message on immediately to the Consul General and the NCSO, as well as the British Naval Attaché at The Hague, Vice Adm Dickens.

---

* 'At the recovery and demolition of the wreckage, 776 gold bars were recovered, 161 were still missing. It was soon decided to turn to dredging to recover the missing bars. From 24 September this was taken up by dredging company Adriaan Volkers Mij. in Sliedrecht. Another forty bars were found in a week's time. The salvage operation was supervised by the *Rijksveldwacht* from Vlaardingen, and every find was recorded. The lost gold was claimed by Germany, however, and sent to Berlin in April 1941. That confiscation gave cause to stop the dredging.' That left 121 bars unaccounted for. Ten bars were found during sand dredging operation in 1946, prompting the bank to commission a dedicated dredging operation in 1947, which soon recovered a further 100 bars. By the time the operation ceased in June 1947, only ten bars were left unaccounted for. Unsurprisingly, it turned out that some bars had been stolen, either during the chaos of 10 May 1940 or the post-war dredging operations. Four of these were eventually traced, but that still leaves to this day six bars missing with a value now of around 2.5 million euros. (*https://www.tracesofwar.com/articles/5315/Lost-gold-on-the-Nieuwe-Waterweg.htm*).

He also asked them to try to find out how Hill was getting on with collecting the gold. The consulate phoned back to confirm that the message had been passed on to everyone stipulated, but they had no news of Hill who, unbeknown to the consulate, was still under arrest at the time.

At 03:00, Younghusband received another signal instructing *Wild Swan* to assist the Dutch defence forces by bombarding nearby Waalhaven, where the Germans had seized the airfield and were airlifting in reinforcements. When he contacted the Dutch naval authorities to coordinate the operation with them, he was told that the bombardment was no longer required as Dutch ground forces were already attacking the airfield. Younghusband's next telephone call was to the Harbour Master at Rotterdam, who was able to tell him that the HM SC 19A was currently embarking the gold at Lekhaven and was almost ready to leave. Relieved at the news that Hill was on his way back, as he put the phone down Younghusband was then confronted by reports of German parachutists advancing down the right bank of the river and around the back of the Hook, with some approaching within 500 yards of his ship. The sound of Dutch artillery and machine gun fire seemed to confirm these reports, but no German troops could be seen, and neither was the destroyer fired on.

At 04:15, just as dawn was breaking, HMS *Wivern* appeared off the entrance to the waterway, carrying the delayed British Military Mission. Younghusband warned them that it was too dangerous for them to land due to the fighting and told them to proceed to Ymuiden and land there. The head of mission, General Heywood, protested and requested to be landed at Flushing instead. Younghusband agreed and saw the *Wivern* on its way. Shortly afterwards two more destroyers, HMS *Hyperion* and HMS *Havock*, arrived off the Hook. Younghusband told them to stay where they were until he could find pilots to guide them in. He eventually found two pilots and the destroyers arrived safely alongside at 07:00. Younghusband went on board *Hyperion* and reported the current situation at the port to her commanding officer, Commander Hugh Nicolson. He told Nicolson that German parachutists were being dealt with by the Dutch and the firing ashore had now abated. He also reported that Dutch torpedo boats had been upriver bombarding various buildings, but enemy aircraft activity appeared to have subsided.

When he came back ashore at 07:45, Younghusband was met by some Dutch officials who gave him the terrible news that the HM SC 19A had struck a mine and sunk. However, there were no reports as yet of either the current status of the gold or of any survivors. At 08:00

Younghusband managed to contact the Admiralty by telephone, on a very erratic line, which he suspected was being tapped, and reported the loss to them. The rest of John Younghusband's morning was taken up with putting Nicolson in touch with the local authorities and overseeing the RN demolition parties who were preparing their charges to be fitted at 'instant notice' in the various forts and gun batteries on both sides of the river. At 09:00 Younghusband was telephoned from Rotterdam by 2nd Lieutenant Ashwell, second-in-command of the sapper party, reporting that Captain Goodwin had left them the previous evening and had not yet returned. Unaware that Goodwin had been arrested earlier, Ashwell requested instructions from Younghusband, who told him to contact the Dutch military commander in Rotterdam and to begin to prepare his demolition charges.[21]

In the early hours of that fateful Saturday morning, after convincing their Dutch captors they were British and on important missions for the Allied cause, Tommy Goodwin and Paul Baker parted company with James Hill to begin a tour of reconnaissance. They were never to see him again. Their first objective was the 'Old Matex' petroleum storage site at Vlaardingen. They arrived there at 04:00 to find the site heavily guarded by troops armed with machine guns. They met the site manager, Mr Baasch, who was prepared to agree to allow the sappers onto his installation to prepare and lay their demolition charges, but that he would need the authorisation of the Dutch Government in order to do so. Goodwin and Baker then found a boat to take them across the Maas to the huge Shell and Standard Oil storage sites at Petroleum Haven. Both sites were deserted, apart from some armed guards, but, to their horror, they saw that German troops were now occupying areas just to the south of them. They completed their recce, crossed back over to the north side of the river, and made their way to the Dutch military headquarters in Rotterdam.

When he arrived at the Dutch HQ and introduced himself, Goodwin found that no one there knew anything about the XD operations. The garrison commander, Colonel Scharroo, telephoned the Dutch army Commander-in-Chief at The Hague, General Henri Winkelman, who flatly refused permission for any demolitions either to be carried out or even be prepared. To emphasise his decision, he ordered that Goodwin and Baker should be returned to the Hook under escort and for them to wait there for further instructions.

The British officers were escorted back to Leckhaven Quay, arriving there at 10:30 to be reunited with the rest of their party who had spent the Friday night under shelter in a local town hall. The sappers reported that German troops had been seen in Hudson Street, just to the south of the quay. The Dutch officer commanding the escort asked Goodwin if he would assist in clearing the Germans from the area. Goodwin rightly decided that he could not take on that responsibility without further instruction, so he telephoned the British Military Attaché at The Hague who told him 'under no circumstances' must he take part in any such operation. Instead, the sappers commandeered some lorries and set off back to the Hook.[22]

During the day at the Hook, Younghusband had continued overseeing the RN demolition parties, and the RN destroyers had engaged enemy aircraft bombing the forts and gun batteries along the river. At the request of the Dutch and with Admiralty permission, HMS *Wild Swan* had also bombarded reported German positions in a wood about 2 miles up-river. The destroyer fired sixty-six rounds of high explosive at the woods, but no German troops could be seen. However, as *Wild Swan* made her way back to the Hook, aircraft were spotted dropping about fifty parachutists, possibly onto the beaches to the north. Younghusband radioed HMS *Havock*, which then set out to sea to deal with any landings, where she came under heavy attack from German aircraft before returning to the Hook, having seen no enemy troops on the beaches.[23]

Tommy Goodwin and the RE party eventually returned to the Hook at 17:00. He immediately reported to John Younghusband that the Dutch authorities had refused to allow his party to place their demolitions and that they had been unable to do so by force as all the objectives had been heavily guarded. He also told Younghusband that he (Goodwin) and Hill had been held under arrest by the Dutch on suspicion of being disguised Germans, and that the south bank of the river and the eastern third of the city were now occupied by German forces. He then gave Younghusband the terrible news that James Hill and the other naval ratings were feared lost in the sinking of the HM SC 19A.[24]

Goodwin and his party were then split up amongst the three RN destroyers now at the port to receive a very welcome hot meal. Goodwin took further advantage of the Navy's hospitality while on board by taking the opportunity to have a hot bath. What he failed to realise, was that his bathroom was directly under one of the destroyer's 4.7-inch guns and that the ship's crew were at action stations ready to deal with approaching German aircraft. Halfway through his bath, Goodwin heard an almighty crash as the gun above him engaged the hostile aircraft. Fearing the destroyer had been hit and might be sinking, he jumped out of the bath and ran up on deck, still completely naked, much to the amusement of the ship's crew.[25]

When he had recovered his composure, as well as his clothes, Goodwin and his party, together with all their stores, found accommodation in a shed on the Fruit Wharf, where they ended up spending the night.[26] During his earlier recce of the deserted Petroleum Haven site, Goodwin had requisitioned a small portable typewriter from one of the offices, which he used that night to write a brief note to his CO Lt Col Brazier, giving it to the commander of HMS *Havock*, to take to England:

> Dear Colonel,
>
> I can't tell you much except we are still standing by, the troops are in excellent health and even better spirits, they are all enjoying it.
>
> Seen quite a lot of Jerry, both on land and in the air, the troops are so used to air raids they don't even bother to look except when one crashes. Am in touch with everyone concerned this side, the Government are not too keen yet, unfortunately had to do all contracting [? contacting] myself, no arrangements had been made for us, and for 24 hours hid the troops on a deserted quay in a large town whilst I spent the best of that time in various jails. We nearly got caught, just vacated [our] position on the quayside before Jerry cut it off.
>
> Vessel is just off to refuel hence this note. Kind regards to all at K.(F) R.E.[27]

With the danger of more German mines being laid overnight, a decision had to be made as to whether it would be desirable for the three RN destroyers to leave the Hook rather than risk being trapped there. After some lengthy discussions, Younghusband and Nicolson decided that *Wild Swan* and *Hyperion* would remain, but HMS *Havock* would return to sea to patrol the waters outside.

German bombers flew overhead all through the night but thankfully without attacking the destroyers, despite being engaged by the ships' anti-aircraft guns. Rifle fire was also heard coming from just beyond the quay where the destroyers were moored, so Younghusband ordered sentries to be posted abreast the ships to prevent them from being rushed.[28]

Meanwhile, in Rotterdam, Fred Hartley had received orders from Adm Dickens at The Hague to sail as many British, Norwegian, and Danish ships as possible. There were no Norwegian or Danish vessels left at the port now, but there were still some British ships including the SS *Dotterel*, which Hartley despatched that afternoon to Ymuiden to evacuate British refugees from there. Hartley also still had Allied refugees at Rotterdam to deal with. He was now using the LNER steamer *St Denis* as a direct refugee base as it was proving impossible to move them from the Mission to the ship at short notice. By 16:00 he had collected about thirty British, French, and Norwegian men, women and children on the ship. At 17:00 the Consul General ordered Hartley to move the refugees to another British ship, the SS *Roek*, and to sail her as soon as possible to England, leaving the *St Denis* in port ready to evacuate the consular staff when the time came for them to leave. However, the *Roek* was lying at berth about 2 miles away from the *St Denis* over dangerous ground which was occupied by the military and coming under frequent bombing attacks. The area was also known to be a 'hunting ground' for the NSB rebel gangs. Hartley decided the safest means to transfer the refuges would be by water, so he contacted the harbour master and arranged for a tug to take them. The transfer was eventually completed successfully, but then Hartley received the news that the river had been mined and the HM SC 19A sunk. Hartley therefore had no choice but to instruct the *Roek* to stay where she was until daylight.

The Dutch Navy managed to have the river swept of mines in the early hours of Sunday morning, allowing the *Roek* to set off at 04:30. Unfortunately, twenty minutes later she struck a mine in the river off Vlaardingen that had been missed in the earlier sweep. Although his ship was sinking, her master, Captain Parkinson managed to run her ashore on the south bank of the river and get all her passengers and crew away in the ship's boats. A police boat appeared and towed them over to the north bank as the south bank was now being overrun with German troops. Parkinson and some of the crew then returned to their stricken vessel and reclaimed all the passengers' luggage. Once everyone was safely ashore again, police buses took them back to the *St Denis*.[29]

Back in England, at 19:00 on the Saturday evening, the buglers sounded 'General Assembly' at the Royal Marines Barracks in Chatham. The famous old Georgian barracks was a fairly deserted place at the time, with most of the active personnel of the Royal Marines Chatham Division on duty at their various War Stations, either on board ship or in shore bases around the Nore Command. Of the few men that fell in on the parade ground that evening, 200 were ordered to be formed as a 'Unit for a defensive role in some unknown place'. The officer detailed to command this new unit was Major B.G.B. Mitchell, who later described its formation:

> Of the two hundred men detailed, every walk in life was represented: there were Small Arms Instructors, Signal Instructors, old age pensioners (the oldest man being fifty-four), barbers, cooks, grooms, clerks, boats crews and last, but not least, men from the King's Squad* which had only just passed for duty that morning. This motley crew were told to go away to their rooms, pack up enough gear in their kit bag for a three-day stay, and fall in on the Parade Ground in fighting order, ready to move at 8 p.m.
>
> At 8.15 after a big rush, a convoy of buses left the Royal Marine Barracks, Chatham containing this Unit, for Dover where further orders were awaiting it.[30]

This hastily cobbled-together unit, dubbed 'Mitchell Force', was to be the advance party for Operation *Harpoon*, an operation conceived at a meeting of the Inter-Service Planning Staff earlier that day, and approved at that morning's War Cabinet meeting, to send a military force consisting of two battalions of infantry, to the aid of Holland. The objective of the operation would be 'to give heart to the Dutch, to resist attacks by German parachute troops at The Hague.'

The Staff had agreed that the only suitable landing place for the operation would be the Hook and that 'time was the essence of the problem'. For this reason, sufficient troops to form a bridgehead to secure the port and its facilities for the main force needed to be established at the Hook within twenty-four hours.[31] The task of forming this bridgehead would fall to Major Bryan Mitchell's 'motley crew' of Royal Marines.

Mitchell Force arrived at the eastern arm of Dover Harbour at 22:00, where Mitchell then reported to Vice Adm Ramsay who, as he later recalled, gave him his orders:

---

* The King's Squad: 'On the occasion of his visit to the 4th Battalion in March 1918, preparing at Deal for their raid on Zeebrugge on St George's Day 1918, HM King George V also visited the Depot and witnessed recruit training. He was much impressed with what he saw and on completion directed that the senior squad of recruits under training should be designated "The King's Squad". As a mark of distinction, it is customary for members of the squad to wear a white lanyard on the left shoulder of their blue uniform and to the chinstrap of their cap "down below the chin".' (https://www.rmhistoricalsociety.org/history/kings-squad-and-kings-badge).

(a) The Force was to embark on two Destroyers, as quickly as possible and proceed to the Hook of Holland.
(b) My Force was to hold the landing place at the Hook, so that further landings could take place unopposed.
(c) I was to get in touch with the S.N.O., Hook,* and local Dutch authorities to get the latest information.
(d) I would probably be withdrawn at the end of three days.

Mitchell and his marines embarked on the destroyers HMS *Verity* and HMS *Venomous* and sailed from Dover at 00:15 on Sunday, 12 May for the Hook.[32]

At the Hook, Younghusband had already been warned to expect the arrival of the destroyers bringing the Royal Marines at about 04:00, so at 03:40 he ordered the *Wild Swan* to leave port to rendezvous with them. Younghusband had also made a request to the Dutch authorities for a pilot boat to be sent to help guide the destroyers into the port, but none had appeared before he left. It was 05:30 before *Verity* and *Venomous* came into view, by which time the pilot boat had caught up with the *Wild Swan* and proceeded to guide the new arrivals into the port, while the destroyer followed them in to cover the landings.[33] These new arrivals were accompanied overhead by three Bristol Blenheim 1F fighters – the first RAF aircraft the British forces at the Hook had seen since they arrived.

As soon as they got alongside at the Hook, Mitchell Force mounted their four Bren guns ready for anti-aircraft defence. Apart from four Vickers machine-guns, and a Lewis gun with a broken bipod, the Brens were the only additional firepower the marines would be able to bring to bear to supplement their personal weapons while they were there. While most of the force was set to work unloading their meagre stores from the destroyers, Mitchell deployed a single platoon to act as a screen around the quay,[34] no doubt hoping that no German tanks would suddenly appear.

Having escorted *Verity* and *Venomous* into port, *Wild Swan* was ordered back out to join HMS *Havock* in patrolling the coast between the Hook and Ymuiden. Within ten minutes of *Wild Swan* departing, three German JU-88 bombers appeared from the clouds overhead, one of which began to dive towards the destroyer. Younghusband later recorded what happened next:

---

* 'SNO Hook: Senior Naval Officer at the Hook of Holland, who at that time was Commander Nicolson on HMS *Hyperion*.

> This E.A. [enemy aircraft] dived at a very steep angle from about Red 120 at the bridge. A salvo of four bombs hit the water about 50 feet abreast the bridge and burst underwater about 30 feet from the ship's side.
>
> Fire had been opened by Pom-Pom, which fired a whole belt[,] and Lewis Guns, the angle was too steep for 4.7". I do not think the E.A. was hit but he did not attack again.
>
> The Channel was too narrow to take avoiding action but on the dive starting I had put the telegraph to "FULL" and the wheel to Hard-a-Port in order that the ship would ground clear of the fairway if hit.
>
> No direct damage was done to the hull, but the most serious result was the rapid development of "condenseritis"* both sides, later, whilst on passage to Dover. The Asdic was put out of action for half-an-hour with broken training drive and the low power circuits came unclipped for about a minute. Mess Deck furniture and crockery was badly smashed up and one or two rivets in No. 2 Boiler Room started to weep.
>
> The attack was beautifully timed and would have sunk the ship in a very tricky position in the channel. This attack took place at 0625.[35]

Whilst he was supervising the unloading of his unit's stores, Major Mitchell witnessed the attack on *Wild Swan* and thought that the ship's anti-aircraft guns had succeeded in bringing down the German bomber. Shortly afterwards he also witnessed the three RAF Blenheims coming under attack from three Messerschmitt Bf-110 fighters, the result of which was the loss of one aircraft from each side. After this engagement, the surviving two Blenheims turned for home and that was the last anyone saw of the RAF until the day of evacuation.

Once all his men and stores were ashore, Mitchell wasted no time in contacting the Dutch Fortress Commander, who informed him that there were at least 200 German parachutists in a wood, no more than 2,000 yards away from the quay, and requested Mitchell clear them out. Mitchell refused this request, but he did agree for fifty of his men to take up defensive positions at three points in front of the quay. Mitchell then returned to the quay and organised his troops accordingly. Those taking over the defensive posts as requested by the commandant were escorted to them by Dutch guides and were all in position by 09:00. Mitchell then set up his headquarters in the railway stationmaster's house on the quay. It was a far from ideal location due to the large number of glass windows. He ordered the windows to be covered by fixing wooden shutters to the outsides and nailing thick blankets over them on the inside to provide some protection from flying glass. By

* Condenseritis [*sic*] is a 'slang' naval term for serious salt-water contamination of a ship's condenser feed-water.

11:00 he had succeeded in establishing wireless communication with Vice Adm Ramsay's HQ in Dover, thanks to a wireless set and two RN telegraphists that had been lent to him by Ramsay to accompany his party over from Dover.[36]

Mitchell's first communication from England, however, had been sent through seven minutes earlier, to Commander Nicolson on HMS *Hyperion*. It was from the Admiralty in London:

> For Major Mitchell R.M. IMMEDIATE.
> War Office can send one composite Guards battalion tonight to support you. This is too small a force to restore a bad or deteriorating situation but by its moral rather than military effect might tip the scales if situation is nearing restoration by the Dutch. Report your opinion.[37]

Whilst Mitchell was reading the signal, at the Hook War Cabinet Chiefs of Staff Committee was meeting in London where they were discussing the deteriorating military situation in Holland, and the question of sending further reinforcements there.

CIGS Ironside had only a composite* battalion of Guards ready to leave at short notice, although others were being prepared. However, Ironside thought that they should not be sent before they had a clearer understanding of the situation on the ground. For this, they would have to rely on the opinion of the Officer Commanding the Royal Marines Detachment already there. Ironside said that instructions had just been sent to the officer, and he was awaiting the reply.

At this point, General Lelong, the French Military Attaché in London, entered the meeting with a message from Gamelin, the Allied C-in-C on the Western Front, emphasising the seriousness of the situation in the Rotterdam – Hague – Hook of Holland area and the need to get help to the Dutch. After further discussion, the Committee agreed that waiting for a response from Holland could lose precious hours and that the Guards should be sent that day regardless. The time taken for the journey to the Hook would allow for Mitchell's reply and any other information received to be considered. If the situation looked too bad when they arrived, they need not disembark.[38]

The Guards battalion consisted of 650 men of the 2nd Battalion Irish Guards, attached to 20th Guards Brigade, which had recently been ordered to the area around Tunbridge Wells to counter rumoured landings by German paratroopers. When the rumours were found

---

* 'Composite' battalion in this sense means that contained men from other units drafted in to bring the battalion up to full strength.

to be untrue, the brigade was then warned to be ready for overseas service. However, 2 Irish were far from a complete battalion, due to having many of its men away on leave for the Whitsun period. There was no time to have them recalled so, to bring the battalion up to full strength in time, a rifle company consisting of ninety men of the Welsh Guards was ordered from London to join them.[39] To ensure secure communications, seven signallers and two wireless trucks from the Royal Signals would join the 20th Guards Brigade at Dover.[40]

The entire force would come under the command of Lieutenant Colonel Joseph Haydon OBE, of the Irish Guards. Included with his headquarters, he would have an officer interpreter, a cipher officer,[41] and an officer from the Royal Army Service Corps, with two NCOs who would be responsible for sourcing local transport for ferrying the Guards to The Hague.[42]

The object of Haydon's mission, as instructed to him by the Vice Chief of the Imperial General Staff, General Sir John Dill, was to:

> ... get in touch with the local Dutch Commander and the Commander of Marines Major Mitchell from whom you will ascertain the latest situation.
>
> Your object will then be to move your battalion towards THE HAGUE and to cooperate with the local commander in his operations to safeguard the Government and restore the situation at THE HAGUE. In assisting in these operations you will carry out any task allotted your battalion by the local commander if you consider the task a reasonable operation of war. You will not, however, come under his orders and will not hesitate to refuse to carry out any requests for assistance which would, in your opinion, entail useless sacrifice of your men.
>
> In the event of the Netherlands Government evacuating THE HAGUE you will endeavour to withdraw to the HOOK for re-embarkation in His Majesty's ships.[43]

At 14:05, just as Haydon's Guards were preparing to leave Tunbridge Wells, a signal came through at the Admiralty from Mitchell at the Hook, responding to their request for his opinion on sending the Guards to reinforce him: 'Am of the opinion that one composite force would not have any material effect without aircraft support being considerably strengthened. General situation still, but appears unchanged in vicinity of the Hook.'[44]

Nevertheless, Haydon's force still departed Tunbridge Wells later that afternoon in two trains taking them to Dover where they embarked, with 100 tons of stores, on two Southern Railway cross-channel ferries: the TSS *Canterbury*, and the TSS *Maid of Orleans*.[45]

Whilst the Harpoon Force was still at Dover, Mitchell's signal was read out and discussed at the meeting of the War Cabinet's Chiefs of Staff Committee, held at 18:30 that evening. Given Mitchell's comments, the committee considered the desirability of proceeding with the despatch of the Guards. Although the committee generally felt that the chances of 'Fortress Holland' holding out for any length of time without increased air support were remote, they were all firmly of the opinion that they could not afford to offer any additional air commitment or anti-aircraft guns, and that any military reinforcements could only be sent on that basis. However, they thought the French may offer some limited air support so they agreed that the Guards battalion should be despatched as arranged.[46]

The ferries carrying the composite Guards battalion left Dover for the Hook at 20:10 that evening, escorted by the destroyers HMS *Keith,* HMS *Wivern,* HMS *Wolsey,* and HMS *Boreas.*[47] The remaining 20th Guards Brigade battalion and a company of 140 Field Ambulance were then put on twelve hours' notice to join them.[48]

Having survived the bombing attack earlier that morning, HMS *Wild Swan* sailed out to join HMS *Havock* in patrolling the waters off the Hook. At 07:50 Younghusband intercepted an 'SOS' from a Dutch ship sailing about 9 miles to the north, saying she was being bombed. He ordered *Havock* to continue the patrol while *Wild Swan* sped off to investigate the distress signal. When the *Wild Swan* arrived at the reported position about an hour later, there was no sign of any ship or wreckage. However, Younghusband now had another concern: when his ship had been speeding above 15 knots, he had noticed a heavy vibration setting in on the bridge. When the vessel reached 20 knots, all the instruments on the bridge were put out of action by the vibration, which was also now causing damage in the W/T office. It had become apparent that the destroyer's starboard propeller was badly damaged. Younghusband decided he had no choice but to return to the Hook.

At 10:30, as the *Wild Swan* returned down the coast, enemy aircraft were spotted dive-bombing a Dutch packet steamer, the SS *Prinses Juliana,* which was ferrying Dutch troops from Flushing to Ymuiden. Although other RN destroyers were already in attendance, Younghusband still ordered his damaged vessel to close at the highest possible speed that would still leave his bridge in working order. As she closed on the stricken Dutch ship, *Wild Swan* opened fire with her main armament and 'pom-pom' gun on the German aircraft. When the destroyer got closer to *Prinses Juliana,* Younghusband could see that although she had not taken a direct hit, she had been damaged by a bomb salvo that had burst under her port quarter. She was now taking on water and had lowered all her boats which were already full to capacity with troops. One of the other RN destroyers in attendance was HMS *Codrington,* the lead ship of the 1st Destroyer Flotilla, commanded by Captain George Creasy. Creasy ordered Younghusband to pull alongside the Dutch ship to rescue about thirty troops that were still stranded on board without any other means of escape. *Wild Swan* came alongside, bow to bow with the Dutch ship, allowing all the troops to successfully jump on board her forecastle. Younghusband then picked up another ten Dutchmen who were either swimming in the sea or hanging onto rafts. Amongst those rescued were five members of the British Military Mission that had landed at Flushing the previous day. *Wild Swan* then headed back to the Hook, arriving there without further incident at 12:30.

Once he had secured his ship, Younghusband reported to Commander Nicolson on board HMS *Hyperion* to be updated on the latest situation at the port. He then received orders again for *Wild Swan* to proceed upriver ready to bombard the airfield at Waalhaven, should the Dutch require it. Nicolson told him to contact the Dutch commandant to see just what, if any, assistance he required. Younghusband telephoned the commandant, who told him he did not need the airfield bombarded at present, but he did need a coastal patrol. Younghusband informed the commandant that any bombardment of Waalhaven would be an impractical operation anyway unless he was given a free hand to shoot up the oil tanks and other demolition objectives along the river. The commandant said he could not agree to such actions at that time. Younghusband reported his conversation to Nicolson and then returned to his ship to await further orders.[49]

Meanwhile, Mitchell Force had established themselves at several positions around the perimeter of the port. However, communications were a problem, as the perimeter units had no radios to keep in touch with Mitchell's HQ at the railway station. Mitchell solved this by commandeering three motorcycles and nominating three of his men as despatch riders.

At midday, Lieutenant Bayley, who was commanding one of the platoons around the perimeter, sent out a patrol of eight Marines accompanied by eight Dutch troops to burn down a row of houses being used by German snipers firing on his platoon. Later that afternoon, Mitchell came along to inspect Bayley's defensive position. The day had now turned colder, and the Royal Marines had forgotten to bring their greatcoats. Mitchell was dismayed to see them wearing coats scrounged from the Dutch troops sharing their position and supping on mugs of hot milk to keep warm. He immediately ordered a rum ration to be brought forward from his HQ so his men could have a 'tot' to add to their milk. Mitchell went on to inspect the other defensive positions, finding himself 'well pleased with the initiative and common sense' shown by all his officers around the perimeter.[50]

Also at the Hook, Tommy Goodwin and his sapper demolition party had been reduced to kicking their heels for most of the day awaiting further instructions. However, with the general situation at Rotterdam now rapidly deteriorating, he had at last received from the Dutch Government the news he had been waiting for – the authority to proceed with his operation. The Dutch officer who had brought his government's instructions to Goodwin also had orders to accompany the sappers on their mission. A tug was rapidly found to transport the party and at 18:15 they set off upriver to their objectives,[51] watched with some concern by John Younghusband from his bridge on the *Wild Swan*.

Younghusband had just received orders from Captain Creasy on HMS *Codrington* to make his arrangements for leaving the Hook that evening, along with HMS *Hyperion*. This would leave no RN ships at the port to bring the sappers out if the situation demanded it.[52] It would also leave Mitchell's Royal Marines without any anti-aircraft cover, apart from two armed naval drifters, one of which only had a jammed 2-pounder gun.

At 18:30 HMS *Wild Swan* followed HMS *Hyperion* out of the Hook steaming northwards to join HMS *Codrington*. Their departure was witnessed by a forlorn Bryan Mitchell, who later recalled feeling 'like a mouse in a closed room with a large and hungry tom-cat'. His mood was not helped when, just thirty minutes later, four German aircraft appeared and bombed the length of the waterfront, causing several casualties in one of the precious drifters.[53]

Out at sea, *Hyperion* and *Wild Swan* rendezvoused with *Codrington*. The three destroyers' orders were to proceed to Ymuiden to evacuate members of the Dutch Royal Family, but when Creasy realised that *Wild Swan* was damaged, he ordered Younghusband to sail her immediately to Dover, leaving the latter officer full of regret for leaving the Hook without having completed the mission he was originally sent there for.[54]

Tommy Goodwin's party was now well on its way to their first objective. However, before they arrived, a message came through on the tug's wireless from the Dutch headquarters at The Hague cancelling Goodwin's previous instructions and ordering the sappers to proceed straight through to Rotterdam instead. Just as the tug was tying up at the Schiehaven jetty, nine German bombers appeared directly overhead and released their loads, destroying all the buildings along the jetty, and forcing Goodwin and his men to run for cover. Fortunately, the attack missed all the sappers and the explosives, which they had been carrying on ambulance stretchers. As darkness fell, they all took shelter in a nearby school that had managed to escape the bombing. They then settled down there to try to get some sleep while awaiting further instructions. However, the bombing raids continued throughout the night, ruining the chances of sleep for any of them.[55]

At the Hook on that Sunday evening, Mitchell watched German aircraft coming over dropping more parachutists into the nearby woods, and mines into the river. He sent a report about the airborne landings to Vice Adm Ramsay at Dover, warning him that the destroyers had sailed, leaving his force without any supporting fire. Mitchell then spent the rest of the night preparing for and looking forward to the arrival of the Guards.[56]

Around 02:00 on Monday, 13 May, the destroyer HMS *Hereward* was approaching the Hook. Fortunately, Mitchell had just arrived at the Dutch Fortress HQ to make sure they were ready to receive the Guards battalion and was just in time to prevent the Dutch coast guns from opening fire on the British destroyer.[57] *Hereward* eventually entered the port without further incident.

By 04:30, and probably much to Mitchell's great relief, the ships carrying the main 'Harpoon' force, together with their destroyer escorts, safely arrived in the port. Within ten minutes the Guards were disembarking and taking up defensive positions along the quay. The disembarkation was completed without incident despite the constant overflying of enemy aircraft. While the Guards were coming ashore, Mitchell held a conference on board HMS *Hereward* with Harpoon's commander, Colonel Haydon. Haydon told him that he proposed to advance to The Hague as soon as he could get transport.[58] However, Haydon also had instructions from the War Office: 'Should you find Germans strongly posted between Hook and Hague you must use your discretion as to the most useful action you can take to assist Dutch in dispersing of enemy within their gates.'[59]

At 05:30 Mitchell witnessed another RN destroyer, HMS *Malcolm*, the lead ship of the 16th Destroyer Flotilla, arrive with its commander, Captain Halsey who was detailed to take over from John Younghusband as the Senior Naval Officer at the Hook.[60] Once *Malcolm* had tied up on the quay, Halsey went on board the *Maid of Canterbury* for a conference with Haydon and Mitchell. Haydon told Halsey that he intended to advance through the Marines' positions to The Hague, leaving Mitchell Force to secure bases at the Hook ready to bring in reinforcements who would then relieve them. Halsey assigned one of his officers, Lieutenant Robertson together with W/T set, to act as his liaison officer with the Guards.[61]

Once the 'Harpoon' force was safely ashore with all its stores and equipment, the two LNER ferries left the Hook with their destroyer escort, sailing for Dover and leaving HMS *Hereward* and HMS *Malcolm* at the port.[62] *Hereward*'s radio room then intercepted a signal from the C-in-C The Nore, which indicated that there were four other destroyers available in the area. Halsey ordered two of these, HMS *Mohawk* and HMS *Versatile*, to join him at the Hook to support the troops ashore and to be ready to assist with any evacuations.[63] Then just before midday, a fleet of long, black cars arrived on the quayside. A rather flustered-looking Dutch army officer stepped out from one of the cars and spoke to the adjutant of the Irish Guards detachment who was standing on the quay. He told him that Queen Wilhelmina of the Netherlands and other members of her family and household were in the cars requesting passage in a Royal Navy ship to Breskens, a harbour town near Flushing. The adjutant took the officer to see Halsey, who immediately put HMS *Hereward* at the queen's disposal. The destroyer left the Hook at 12:10 with the royal party on board.*[64]

In Rotterdam, at 06:00 on that Monday morning, Fred Hartley was woken by a call from Eric Cable, the British Consul General, telling him that German troops could be seen from the consulate unloading stores from barges along the waterfront. Hartley informed the Dutch commandant, who sent two officers to investigate. When they arrived at the consulate the officers decided to use the building as an observation post and ordered its evacuation. The consulate had already become untenable having been coming under fire since the Friday morning. All the windows had been shot out, and the walls were riddled with bullets. The only way in and out of the building now was through a second-floor window reached by going up and down five different ladders, over garden walls and across refuse barges moored along the river, so evacuation would not be easy. Hartley also had those people still stranded on the *St Denis* to worry about. There were 110 refugees and crew on board who were almost out of food. Hartley got into a taxi and went around all the small shops he could find still open and

* See footnote Chapter 12.

bought whatever food was available then, with the help of the police, had it sent to the *St Denis*.

About midday, Hartley received another call from Eric Cable saying that the situation in the city was now desperate and they would all need to get away on the *St Denis* that afternoon. However, when Hartley checked with the Harbour Master, he was told that the river had been mined again overnight and no ships could leave. After discussing the situation with Cable, Hartley arranged for coaches to take everyone from the *St Denis*, together with all the consular staff, to the Hook. Unfortunately, he could not be provided with any military escort, nor could he get any drivers to take the coaches outside the city limits, so if they were going to get away, they would have to drive themselves. Meanwhile, Hartley received orders from Adm Dickens at The Hague to scuttle the *St Denis*. Once Hartley had carried out the admiral's orders, the whole party left Rotterdam in three large touring coaches and the Consul General's car. Cable drove his car himself while the two vice-consuls each drove one of the coaches. The third coach was driven by a Dutch volunteer who had only ever driven a baker's van before. The small convoy was clear of the city by 12:30 and, after frequent stops at military checkpoints, managed to reach the Hook a few hours later without serious mishap. Describing his thoughts about the coach journey for the conclusion of his report a week later, Fred Hartley said: 'I am not yet convinced which was the most hair-raising - the worst of the German air raids or the drive from Rotterdam to the Hook.'[65]

At the Hook, Halsey had been trying to achieve clarification on the current military situation and on the number of refugees he could expect to handle. During the afternoon he had been in touch with the Naval and Military Attachés at The Hague, the Vice Consul in Rotterdam, and the Dutch Fortress Commander, but none had a clear idea of the situation. However, it soon became evident that a considerable number of people, mostly from legations and military missions, would soon be arriving at the Hook for evacuation. It also became apparent to Halsey that without more fighter support in the air, the use of the Dutch ports would soon become impracticable, the landing of troops hazardous, and their positions after landing untenable. Halsey signalled Ramsay at Dover requesting fighter cover, transports and more destroyers to assist with the evacuation. Although no fighter cover was forthcoming, by 18:00 the destroyer HMS *Janus* had arrived on station just outside the Hook to provide anti-aircraft protection, and the destroyer HMS *Windsor* had joined *Malcolm* and *Mohawk* alongside the quay.[66]

Meanwhile, Colonel Haydon was also unsure what his next steps should be. When he spoke by telephone with the British Military

Attaché at The Hague, he was told that in view of the departure of the queen and her household from the capital, the Dutch commander-in-chief considered it best for the Guards to stay put and support the Dutch forces at the Hook. Haydon had little option but to stay at the Hook as the transport he had been promised by the Dutch army had so far failed to materialise. In addition, Haydon's communications were now hampered by irreparable damage to his wireless sets incurred on the voyage across. He was therefore reduced to using HMS *Malcolm* to send a message to the War Office in London asking whether he should continue with his advance to The Hague or stay where he was.[67] The Dutch transport column eventually arrived at 14:00 but even then valuable time was wasted in arguments with the local Dutch commander, who wanted the Guards to move into Rotterdam, and who then came back with another request for Haydon to move his whole force to Amsterdam. Haydon refused both requests, insisting that they would remain and hold their bridgehead until he received instructions from London. The Dutch commander eventually agreed to leave six vehicles with Haydon ready for him to use if needed when his instructions eventually came through. Meanwhile, the Guards were being deployed to join Mitchell's Royal Marines in defensive positions around the perimeter of the quay.[68]

To add to all the uncertainty, Captain Halsey received a signal from the Admiralty that evening stating that the second Guards battalion would 'probably' be arriving that night and that the ships bringing it would 'probably' be used to withdraw Mitchell's Royal Marines force.[69]

Although the focus was now on all the naval and military activity at the Hook, there was still the outstanding question of the fulfilment of one of the primary objectives of the original 'XD-B' mission: the destruction of the fuel stocks at Rotterdam. On Monday morning, with the Dutch resistance almost at an end, Tommy Goodwin had at last received the final authority to proceed and destroy the Shell installations and the American Petroleum storage site at Rotterdam. However, the Dutch Government, with a view to the post-conflict food situation, had also given strict instructions not to destroy any vegetable or mineral oil installations.

Goodwin and his men, together with a Dutch military escort, immediately proceeded to Vlaardingen where they crossed the Maas to the Shell installations on the south side of the river. When they arrived, Goodwin went straight to see Mr Baasch, the site manager, who denied having received any instructions for the destruction of his precious installations. With his patience now at an end, Goodwin wrote out an order, handing it to Baasch, stating that he was going to destroy the installation at 15:30, by which time he expected all the manager's employees to have withdrawn from the area.

It was then that Goodwin mysteriously lost his Dutch military escort, which left him having to find cover for his demolition operations from his own already limited manpower resources. Another problem soon became evident: because of the vast size of the Shell refinery installation, it would be impossible to demolish it all with the limited quantity of explosives the sappers had been able to carry with them. The only alternative was to try to burn all the buildings down while smashing up as much machinery and plant as they could with sledgehammers. Goodwin set his men to work with their sledgehammers and then flooded the main refinery buildings with oil from a nearby large storage tank, which was then ignited to burn off.[70]

The sappers then turned their attention to the 'Old Matex' petroleum storage tank farm. Here they mostly used their preferred method of demolition, which entailed blowing off the main stopcocks on the tanks with gun cotton, allowing the petrol to flow out into the surrounding bunds, and then firing it with Very pistol flares. However, the cocks on some tanks proved stubborn to blow, so the alternative method of puncturing was applied, using a Boys anti-tank rifle to fire a round into the tank. Goodwin had a 'close encounter' with one of these rounds while he was examining a particularly difficult stopcock, unseen by Lance Corporal Baker, who decided to puncture the tank with the anti-tank rifle. Goodwin's subsequent comments on the incident remained unreported![71]

The sappers then moved on to their final objective – the American Petroleum Co. tank farm, where they repeated their performance. This time, however, they encountered German troops, so some of the party had to break off from the demolitions to provide cover for the rest. By the time this final demolition task was completed, the flames from all burning fuel installations had reached several hundred feet high, with clouds of black smoke that could be seen from miles around. One of the KFRE's NCOs, Lance Corporal Alf Blake, later recalled his memories of the demolition operations:

> Set to work demolishing oil and petrol storage tanks, breaking valves and pipes and blowing holes in tanks, started fires, sometimes with a fire of blankets soaked in kerosene, sometimes by firing tracer or Very light shells into the petrol, causing great fires and explosions. There was one incident of some of our chaps trying to cross to an island or

> promontory upon which were storage tanks. Germans were on there and opened fire. Someone had the idea to fire at the tanks with anti-tank rifles, making holes – out poured the petrol, then we fired tracer across – terrific explosions, fires and destruction – up went the lot, enemy too.[72]

Their job finally done, the sappers withdrew back across the river by boat to Vlaardingen, where the lorries they had commandeered earlier were waiting for them. When they reached the vehicles, Goodwin was told by a Dutch officer that German parachutists had landed on the road back to the Hook and were now occupying several houses and farms along the road. Goodwin decided he needed to check out the situation for himself, so he divided some of his party into two teams, one for each side of the road. These teams proceeded to move from house to house, while a rear party followed up with the lorries. Progress back to the Hook, inevitably, proved slow but thankfully uneventful, save for the occasional burst of fire from some unidentified sources.[73]

Meanwhile, streams of refugees, including Fred Hartley's party, had been arriving at the Hook from various legations, military missions and government offices at The Hague and Rotterdam. An evacuation operation was swiftly set in motion and about 400 refugees, including the British Minister at The Hague Sir Nevile Bland and his staff, were quickly and efficiently embarked on HMS *Mohawk* and HMS *Windsor*. The two destroyers departed from the Hook at about 19:20 with their places in the port being taken by HMS *Versatile* and HMS *Vivien*.[74] Just as *Versatile* was coming alongside, three German bombers appeared approaching from the south. All the RN destroyers opened fire with their AA guns but failed to stop the bombers one of which dropped a bomb, hitting *Versatile*'s upper deck above her engine room. All three bombers then returned and raked the destroyer's bridge and upper deck with machine gun fire. The attack left many dead and wounded among *Versatile*'s crew, and the damage caused left her without any steering and unable to make steam.[75]

Other bombs fell onto the quay where Bryan Mitchell had established his HQ at the railway station:

> My Battalion Headquarters was straddled by six bombs and heavily machine gunned. My servant was inside cooking some potatoes for my supper at the time. These went sky-high and a row of tins on the shelf above him, containing tea, coffee and sugar, were riddled with machine gun bullets. A Bren Gun post, which the [Irish] Guards had placed on

> top of my Headquarters, opened fire on the enemy, who promptly flew back again and wiped them out.[76]

The bombing set the depressing scene that greeted Goodwin and his sapper demolition party when they eventually arrived back at the Hook at 20:00 that evening, as he later recalled: 'The place by this time was a complete shambles after long and continuous air bombardment.' The mood was not helped when Goodwin realised that the *Wild Swan* had already left the Hook and, as yet, no other ship had been detailed to take them back to England. Goodwin and his men had no alternative but to resign themselves to spending yet another night in Holland with all the dangers that would entail. The sappers eventually found cover in the railway yard, some sheltering under wagons and others under a locomotive turntable where they settled down for the night and attempted to get some sleep.[77]

Mitchell also sought refuge in the railway yard, locating a large dugout under a coal bunker into which he moved his headquarters. By some miracle, his Royal Marines had so far suffered no casualties. However, Lt Col Haydon's Guards had not been so fortunate, with seven men killed and twenty-one injured.[78] Haydon also had to contend with the continued uncertainty about his mission, and having to rely on the navy's destroyers to send and receive messages compounded his already considerable difficulties. Although Haydon had earlier sent a signal to the War Office informing them that he had not moved to The Hague, he still presumed he was to be reinforced by a second Guards battalion which was expected to arrive that night. With the situation deteriorating, Haydon sent another signal to the War Office: '[I] Am very strongly of the opinion that a second battalion without carrier or supporting arms and the continuous help of fighter aircraft will not be sufficient to make any change in a situation which appears to be deteriorating.'[79]

With more than three hours' delay in communications between London and the Hook, unbeknown to Haydon the War Office had already decided to terminate his operation and a signal was on his way to him to that effect: 'Report situation and your proposed future action. In view of the reported evacuation of Dutch Government it would appear your task will then be finished and we are consequently making preliminary arrangements with the Admiralty for your withdrawal.'[80]

In the meantime, Haydon's wounded guardsmen, together with a party of foreign diplomats, were embarked on HMS *Janus*, which departed the Hook at 21:30 with the stricken HMS *Versatile* secured alongside her.[81]

It was almost midnight before Haydon received the latest War Office signal to which he replied: 'I agree that as Dutch Government left here today and as Diplomatic Corps followed them that I have no task to perform so far as they are concerned. My recommendation is that this place [the Hook] should either be strongly reinforced immediately or that the forces now here should be withdrawn at the earliest possible moment.'[82]

At 00:30 on Tuesday, 14 May, the only official British presence remaining at The Hague was Gen Heywood's Military Mission which had been monitoring the deteriorating military situation from the Dutch headquarters in the capital. Reports had been coming through there that the Germans were preparing for an imminent assault on The Hague. Heywood, realising his Mission and the British position at the Hook would become untenable if the Dutch surrendered, sent a telegram addressed to the War Office, Admiralty and Air Ministry in London stating:

> German attack from Rotterdam on The Hague expected tomorrow. Am evacuating Mission to HOOK daybreak to join Irish Guards. Request every effort be made to send fighter patrols over Hook area from 0300 to 0700 B.S.T. Arrangements should be made for evacuation of 800 Irish Guards and Marines and Mission earliest possible. Evacuation from Hook depends on result of German attack.[83]

As the sun began to rise on that Tuesday morning, four German JU-88s flew in, bombing and strafing the waterfront causing several casualties amongst the Guards. The air attacks continued throughout the morning, and at 09:30, just as he was completing a conference with his company commanders, Haydon's battalion HQ was struck, inflicting several more casualties amongst his officers.[84] The bombers were also now targeting the columns of civilian refugees streaming out of Rotterdam, heading to the Hook, seeking any vessel that would help them escape the hell being visited upon them.

As an all-out assault on Rotterdam appeared to be imminent, the decision had been made overnight to evacuate the Royal Marines and Guards from the Hook, and at 05:06 the Admiralty in London instructed Ramsay in Dover to commence arrangements for the evacuation, codenamed Operation *Ordnance*. Ramsay ordered six destroyers to be despatched from Dover for the operation.[85] Later that morning, the War Office signalled Haydon, informing him of the evacuation plan and the navy's preference for it to be undertaken after dark. However, they also told him that if he thought an earlier evacuation essential, then it could be achieved at three hours' notice. When he received the signal Haydon went into a meeting on board HMS *Malcolm* to discuss the evacuation plans with Captain Halsey, Naval Attaché Adm Dickens, and Gen Heywood; the latter having arrived with his Military Mission from The Hague earlier that morning. All agreed that an early evacuation was essential, but that could only be achieved successfully if adequate fighter cover was provided. However, even then there would not be time to embark all the Guards' stores, which would have to be abandoned ashore. After the meeting, Dickens departed the Hook on board the destroyer HMS *Wessex*, leaving Halsey to send a message to Ramsay: 'Evacuation by day preferred in any event particularly if fighter protection is available. Consider that transports will have difficulty getting alongside by night especially without tugs. Fighters and anti-aircraft is vital, suggest anti-aircraft cruiser.'[86]

Halsey then sent another message to Ramsay for him to pass on to the Director of Military Intelligence at the War Office, this one on behalf of Heywood: 'In view of political and military situation do not consider Irish Guards or Mission can fulfil useful purpose by remaining at the Hook. Propose Mission should return to London unless you wish it to proceed to Walaheren [*sic* – Walcheren?]. Dutch C.S. [Chiefs of Staff?] inform me that Rotterdam is likely to fall this afternoon.'[87]

Back in London, at a hastily convened mid-day meeting of the Inter-Service Planning Staff, the fighter cover for Operation *Ordnance* was approved to be made available for one and a half hours preceding, and for half an hour after the operation.[88] Following the meeting, the Admiralty signalled Ramsay at Dover giving the final order for *Ordnance* to proceed and informing him about the fighter cover that would be made available for it.[89]

Although all the preparations for the prompt execution of Operation *Ordnance* seemed to be well in hand, two situations had not been foreseen. The first was the weather: thick fog in the Downs that morning had prevented the Dover destroyers from venturing any further into the Channel, so Ramsay had to call on six destroyers from Harwich to be ready to take their place, with a consequent long delay in the evacuation timings. Fortunately, the fog soon cleared allowing the Dover destroyers to proceed to the Hook.[90]

The second 'unforeseen' was the attitude of the new Prime Minister, Winston Churchill to the evacuation. At that morning's meeting of the War Cabinet the Foreign Secretary, Lord Halifax, stated that he had earlier been approached by the French Ambassador, who informed him that the French Government had been very disturbed by a message sent to their President by Queen Wilhelmina, which indicated that the Dutch Government might be contemplating negotiations with the Germans. However, now the Dutch Government had all left the country, and reinforced by the impression he had received from conversations with the Dutch Foreign Minister, Halifax was now convinced that the Dutch were determined to fight on. Churchill, inspired by his Foreign Secretary's optimism, pointed out that if Dutch resistance was continuing, then it was very important that the Guards battalion at the Hook should not be withdrawn too hastily. After some discussion, the War Cabinet agreed that the War Office should wait to see how events unfolded.[91]

The War Cabinet discussions prompted a flurry of signals between London, Dover and the Hook, cancelling *Ordnance*.[92] However, the signal did not reach Captain Halsey in HMS *Malcolm* until 13:10, by which time the first of the Dover destroyers, HMS *Whitshed*, which had arrived at the Hook an hour before, was already on her way back to England with 300 of the Guards and Heywood's Military Mission.[93] It was another thirty minutes before the evacuation cancellation signal was seen by Heywood on board *Whitshed*. He immediately sent a response from the ship to Ramsay's HQ, and to Halsey back at the Hook, confirming that he was already on his way home with the 300 Guards and asking if they were now expected to return to the Hook, while at the same time warning to accept heavy casualties if they were required to do so.[94]

Naturally, everyone at the Hook was horrified when the signal cancelling the evacuation came through, particularly Haydon, who had now lost over half of his force. Halsey quickly responded to the cancellation by signalling Ramsay to inform him that over half the Guards had already left and that Haydon now considered it 'impossible to hang on here'.[95]

After further consultation with Haydon, Hasley decided to take matters into his own hands. He called on the destroyer HMS *Vesper* to come alongside the quay and then signalled Ramsay, informing him of his intention to embark all the remaining troops on the newly arrived vessel.[96] Halsey's signals pointing out their now desperate situation at the Hook prompted some hurried consultations between the Admiralty and the War Office in London, as reported by the Director of Military Operations Major General Richard Dewing in a note to his boss, the VCIGS, Lieutenant General Sir John Dill:

> At 2.5 p.m., V.C.N.S.* rang up. He had received a message timed 1319 hrs. from the S.N.O. at the Hook to the effect that the Colonel of the Guards battalion regretted that it was becoming impossible to hold on. A second message timed 1346 hrs. reported that he intended to embark the remainder of the battalion as soon as possible and asked for approval of this action.
>
> After consultation with me, V.C.N.S. signalled approval. He added [to the signal] that the War Office appreciated that the situation had deteriorated more than had been appreciated when your message to "Harpoon" was despatched. V.C.N.S. also instructed the S.N.O. to take off as many Dutch troops as possible.[97]

Within thirty minutes, a signal came through to all the commanders involved: 'Carry out operation Ordnance that is evacuation forthwith'.[98] This was followed ten minutes later by a further signal from the Admiralty sent just to Halsey: 'Your 1346 to V.A. Dover approved. War Office appreciate that situation has deteriorated more than they anticipated when message V.A. Dover 1302/14 was despatched. As many Dutch troops as possible to be given opportunity to leave if they wish.'[99]

In anticipation of receiving approval for the final evacuation, Hasley had already embarked the remaining Guards on HMS *Vesper* and, on receiving the above signals, ordered her to sail at 14:15.[100] Unfortunately, there was no room or time to load any of the Guards' stores, so they all had to be left abandoned on the quayside.

Tommy Goodwin's sapper party, still holed up in the railway yard with their rations depleted and by now very hungry and dehydrated, had spent the early hours of Tuesday morning foraging for food from a nearby farm and various ruined buildings. The results enabled them to enjoy a hearty breakfast of cocoa, bread, and some fried duck and chicken, rounding off their meal with a nice smoke thanks to the discovery of a box of cigars in the ruins of a police post. However, they were all acutely aware that there was still no destroyer to take them back to England, and so they were in great danger of being taken into captivity by the rapidly advancing German forces. Once they had finished their breakfast Goodwin convened a 'council of war' with all his officers at which they decided that rather than face capture by the enemy, they would wait until dusk and then seize a small vessel they had spotted tied-up nearby and sail her back to England themselves. Unfortunately, their plans were upset when they saw the vessel set sail

* Vice Chief of the Naval Staff – Vice Admiral Sir Tom Philips.

with her own crew later that morning, leaving Goodwin pondering on how they could now make good their escape. However, salvation was soon at hand with the arrival of HMS *Malcolm* alongside the quay.

When the destroyer had tied up, Goodwin went to see Captain Halsey to request permission for his party to embark on the destroyer when the time came for the port to be evacuated. He also asked the captain to send a message to London, stating that his team had destroyed 400,000 tons of oil and petrol on the south side of the river, and reporting the Dutch authorities' refusal to permit the destruction of the storage installations on the north side. Goodwin then returned to the railway yard to rejoin his men sheltering from the bombing, and to await Halsey's further instructions.

In between the bombing raids, the sappers took over some of the defensive positions that were gradually being vacated by the Guards as they made their withdrawal. They remained in these positions until 13:00 when a message came through to Goodwin from Halsey with implicit instructions for him to commence his withdrawal immediately. Goodwin got his men together and they made their way to the quayside where they were embarked on HMS *Malcolm*. Unfortunately, like the Guards, they had to abandon most of their remaining stores but were able to take all their weapons and ammunition on board with them [101]

Once the sappers were safely embarked, the Royal Marines of Mitchell Force, who were still defending the perimeter around the quay, were ordered to begin their withdrawal. Mitchell had spent much of the morning making careful preparations for this and had already taken the precaution of loading most of the surplus stores, including their unused rum ration, on board HMS *Malcolm*. All that was left was to bring the Marines' rear guard back from their outlying defensive positions. Those Marines defending the right flank were closest to the quay, so Mitchell sent out one of his men on a bicycle to them with instructions for them to make their way there by foot. The left and centre defensive positions were located further out, so Mitchell commandeered a bus and driver to drive out to them and bring them back. However, a Dutch officer warned Mitchell that the bus driver was a well-known Nazi sympathiser; a warning that was borne out when the driver refused to cooperate with Mitchell's orders. He was eventually persuaded to do so by having a revolver pointed at his head by a sergeant major of the Irish Guards, one of a small Guards party that had been attached to Mitchell Force the previous day. Along with the bus, Mitchell also commandeered a lorry and two private cars. With his transport all assembled, Mitchell gave the order 'Go' and the convoy set off for the Marines' out-lying positions.

The right and centre parties were successfully withdrawn to the quay, where they embarked on HMS *Malcolm*, but the left position party, consisting of three Marine platoons and twenty Guardsmen under the command of RM Lieutenant Bishop, had still not appeared twenty minutes after the time Mitchell had anticipated for them. Without any radios, Mitchell had no way of contacting the missing party and had no idea why they were delayed. He now had to make an agonising decision: whether to wait and risk being overrun by the Germans or embark with the rest of his men now so that *Malcolm* could get on its way. Being unable to contemplate abandoning Bishop's men to their fate, Mitchell decided to wait a further five minutes and if they had not appeared by then, he would disembark his whole force and go to their rescue. Fortunately, the bus with Bishop's party arrived with just a couple of minutes to spare and they were all then safely embarked on the destroyer.[102]

The only British personnel left on the quay now were Captain Halsey and a small naval demolition party who were busy placing charges around the various wharves. However, the Dutch commander-in-chief refused permission for the demolitions to be carried out, so the charges were left unblown, leaving the demolition party to return to the destroyer.

Halsey finally embarked on HMS *Malcolm* at 15:10 and, with German bombers still marauding above, immediately ordered the destroyer to leave port. In his haste to leave the Hook, Halsey forgot an order from Ramsay to torpedo the port's northern breakwater. As the final demolitions at the Hook had failed to be completed, the only way left to sabotage the port was the destruction of the breakwater that protected it from silting up. Halsey only realised his oversight when he re-read Ramsay's orders when the *Malcolm* passed out into the open sea. Fortunately, HMS *Keith*, the lead ship of the 19th Destroyer Flotilla was waiting off the Hook, so Halsey was able to pass Ramsay's instructions onto its commander, Captain David Simson. Simson then ordered *Keith* and three of his other destroyers to carry out the torpedoing operation. Despite suffering intensive air attack by German bombers which inflicted severe damage and killed ten men and left over thirty severely injured, the destroyers still managed to fire off twelve torpedoes at the breakwater.[103]

At 17:08, while she was still 16 miles off Dover, HMS *Malcolm* also came under attack from German bombers. The destroyer had already suffered some damage from bombing while she was at the Hook and could only make a maximum speed of 15 knots. However, she managed to escape any further damage from this latest attack and was able to continue her slow journey home without further incident, arriving safely in Dover's Admiralty Harbour at 23:57 on Tuesday, 14 May.[104]

Once ashore, Tommy Goodwin and his sappers looked utterly spent. Unshaven, filthy, and exhausted, their uniforms were soaked through with petrol and grime. They found some respite that night, settling into the barracks at Dover Castle, where a hot meal and the promise of a full night's sleep awaited them.

Meanwhile, Bryan Mitchell's Royal Marines were just as weary and bedraggled. Hungry and caked in dirt, they first had to unload all their stores before beginning the long road journey back to their own barracks in Chatham, finally arriving home at 04:10 on Wednesday, 15 May, utterly worn out by the ordeal.[105]

This, however, was not the final act of the Hook operations: at 12:30 on Tuesday, 14 May, two Royal Navy torpedo boats, MTB 15 and MTB 16 under the command of Lieutenant Philip Gould RN, left their base in Felixstowe for the Hook of Holland. Gould's instructions were to place his boats under the orders of the Commander of the 16th Destroyer Flotilla, Captain Hasley, on arrival at his destination, where he understood they were to assist with the embarkation of the XD demolition parties.

The MTBs proceeded at 22 knots for the first hour but then, with the situation deteriorating at the Hook, they received a signal ordering them to increase their speed to 30 knots. At 15:30 MTB 15 developed engine trouble and was forced to return to Felixstowe while MTB 16 proceeded to the Hook alone. At 16:30 MTB 16 began to suffer severe vibrations from her port propeller. Gould judged the problem to be either a loose bracket or a damaged propeller blade. Not one to be deflected from his important mission, Gould reduced speed to 15 knots and proceeded on towards his destination with the centre propeller shaft still slightly vibrating. Now approaching the Hook, Gould could see RAF fighters and German bombers overhead, together with bomb explosions and heavy anti-aircraft fire coming from the port.

It was 18:15 before MTB 16 eventually entered the Hook. Gould could see no other RN ships in the port, so he secured his boat alongside a small Dutch naval vessel at Berghaven lifeboat station, near the LNER quay. By now the Dutch forces were evacuating the port, using whatever vessels they could find. A Dutch naval officer, who appeared to be controlling the evacuation, came on board MTB 16 and told Gould that all the British destroyers had left, and he was not expecting any to return. He also did not know if any British troops or naval ratings remained in the town, which was now being heavily bombed. Gould went ashore and telephoned the Hook's military commander, who told him that the Germans were only 10 kilometres from the town. He also thought that there were still some British troops remaining, but he had not seen any sailors. Gould asked the Dutch commander to try to locate the remaining British troops and order them to come to the quay and board MTB 16, unless they had any other firm orders preventing them to do so. The Dutch commander agreed to do this but would first need to locate them.

With no British Consul at Rotterdam to assist with any information, Gould decided to telephone the American Consul General in Amsterdam, who told him that there were still British nationals there waiting to be evacuated and that two RN officers, Captain Ree and Commander Goodenough, were still at Ymuiden. Gould tried to phone them but could not get through.

Gould returned to MTB 16 to await news of the remaining British troops. While he was waiting, a Dutch civilian came on board and asked Gould if he could take him and his family to England. He produced his Dutch passport with a visa from the British Passport Control Office at The Hague, authorising 'a visit of 12 months for employment by Messrs Philips Lamps Ltd., valid ONLY in the event of a National Emergency, for four persons, Mr and Mrs Adrianus Helms van der Ven and two children.' The Dutchman and his family had been escaping from the Germans since the morning of the invasion and were now at the end of their tether. Gould took pity on them and agreed to take them to England.

Another Dutch naval officer, Commander den Hoedt, then appeared on board. He was the second-in-command at the Hook, and he told Gould that the remaining British troops were still being searched for, but the Germans were now only 4 kilometres away, and that the two Dutch ships remaining at the quay were waiting to complete evacuation of the Dutch forces. He asked Gould if he would wait for ten minutes after the two Dutch ships sailed, to take off himself and his commanding officer. Gould agreed to do this, but refused to take any more Dutch troops until he knew just how many British troops were left to evacuate.

Despite the continual air raids, the Dutch evacuation proceeded in an orderly manner and their two ships sailed at 19:50. There were still a few Dutch troops left on the quay, but they told Gould they preferred to stay and take their chances under German rule.

At 19:55 Gould was relieved to see five British troops arrive on the quay. Among them was Corporal McClean, who told Gould that they were the sole survivors of a detachment of Irish Guards who were left behind after the rest of their battalion was evacuated earlier that day. He confirmed they were the only British troops left in the town. They had been under air attack all day and had suffered many casualties. Gould asked McClean if they had left any equipment behind, which he admitted they had but had been too exhausted to bring it with them. With the Germans now in the town, Gould and McClean agreed it was now impracticable to try to retrieve it.

By 20:10 the Dutch commander had still not appeared. Den Hoedt, who was by now in a semi-hysterical state through exhaustion, told Gould he could not get hold of his superior, and that it was useless to remain. Gould agreed and slipped MTB 16 at 20:12. As they were leaving, they came under shell fire from the shore. Fortunately, all the shells fell about 100 yards astern of the MTB, but in time many parts of the Hook were ablaze either from demolitions or bombardment.

MTB 16 made it out into the open sea where, at 20:30, she passed a British destroyer that appeared to be on her way to the Hook. Gould signalled the destroyer, telling her 'Have evacuated all remaining British troops', to which the destroyer replied, 'Am going in for the [Dutch] Army'. Despite Gould signalling back that there were no Dutch troops left that wanted to leave, the destroyer continued on its course, while MTB 16 continued on hers, arriving safely at Parkeston Quay, Harwich at 05:40, on Wednesday, 15 May, with her crew, five Irish Guardsmen, a Dutch officer, and a Dutch family of four, all relieved just to still be alive.[106]

Chapter 14

FLUSHING (10-17 MAY)

At 06:18 on Friday, 10 May, the destroyer HMS *Verity*, under the command of 41-year-old Lieutenant Commander Arthur Black RN, had been on the North Goodwin Patrol off the Kent coast where she had already engaged several German bombers, when she received orders to return to Dover 'with all despatch'. By 10:45 that morning she was in Admiralty Harbour, having fully refuelled, and embarked XD Party C and all its stores ready to sail for the Dutch port of Flushing.[1]

Party C was an all-RN demolition party under the command of Commander Peter Cazalet RN. Cazalet was born in 1899 and had joined the Royal Navy as a midshipman in 1917. In 1919, he was serving on the battleship HMS *Thunderer* when he was described as an 'average officer' by his commanding officer. However, just a year later he was promoted to sub lieutenant and being 'Strongly recd. for promotion to lieutenant'. He was promoted to commander in 1934 and had been serving with Binney's team at the Admiralty when he was appointed to lead the Flushing XD party.[2]

Cazalet commanded a naval party of three officers and twenty-six ratings, whose objectives at Flushing were the destruction of the coast defence guns, the oil storage tanks, navigational aids, the seaplane base at Veere, the lock entrance into the Verbreed Canal, any other locks and lock gates, bridges, the railway station and rolling stock.[3] As the French had been given the responsibility for Allied operations in Zeeland, Cazalet was ordered to place himself at the disposal of the French C-in-C at Flushing when he arrived. It was considered unlikely that *Verity* would be able to remain at Flushing for more than one period of daylight, on account of the risk of enemy bombing. Black had been given complete discretion to return to England at any time if he considered his vessel to be at risk of serious damage. This meant that if Peter Cazalet's team had not completed their mission and returned to the destroyer within two hours after sunset on Friday, they would have to make the best arrangements they could to return home.[4]

At 11:51 the *Verity* slipped her moorings and left Dover Harbour, along with *Wild Swan, Whitshed,* and *Brilliant*. She passed through 'The Downs' at 28 knots until she reached the North Goodwin Light Vessel, where she increased her speed to 30 knots until she arrived off the Dutch coast at 13:57. From here *Wild Swan* and *Whitshed* proceeded north-eastwards to their respective destinations, while *Verity* and *Brilliant* headed towards the Wandelaar light vessel anchored off Ostend. As the two destroyers approached the lightship, Lt Cdr Black could see German dive bombers attacking Zeebrugge and Flushing. He was expecting a pilot vessel to meet them at the Wielingen Buoy, but none appeared. However, he did manage to establish communications with a Dutch warship, HNLMS *Johan Maurits,* whose commander was able to summon a pilot to come out to the *Verity*. The Flushing pilot was embarked on *Verity* and she continued her approach into the port with *Brilliant* following close behind. The pilot had warned Black that there were both German and Dutch mines laid across the Wielingen Channel, but by staying close to the southern shore they were able to avoid them. As they entered Flushing, which had just been bombed again, they were met with a loud cheer from the crew of the Dutch cruiser *Sumatra* that was anchored off the port. The Dutch sailors were under the impression that the two RN destroyers were arriving to help them fight off the German invaders. If they had known the true reason for the mission, they may not have been so welcoming.

As *Verity* entered Buiten Haven at 16:20, she parted company with *Brilliant,* which proceeded on her way to Antwerp. The quay at Buiten Haven was a floating pontoon and being almost level with her deck, an ideal height for *Verity* to secure alongside. By 17:00 *Verity* was secured and the demolition stores and two electrically charged depth-charges were safely landed on the quayside. Cazalet and his XD party then disembarked and were shown to the accommodation the Dutch had prepared for them, in the naval gymnasium near the guardship inside the Basin. They were also allowed to store their explosives in the naval magazine and their food on a nearby training ship.[5] Thanks to the cooperation of the Harbour Master, telephone communication facilities and other harbour services were quickly organised and set up, and calls were exchanged with the Dutch naval and military authorities.[6]

Once he had seen his party safely established ashore, Cazalet made a reconnaissance of two of his team's targets: the oil tanks at Flushing and the seaplane base at Veere.[7] He then visited the Dutch Naval HQ in Middelburg where he met with the commander-in-chief of all the

Dutch forces in the Zeeland Province, Rear Admiral Hendrick Van der Stad. Cazalet explained his mission to Van der Stad, who received it well but also warned Cazalet not to carry out any demolitions without his permission. The Dutchman left a very poor impression on Cazalet, who described him as 'a man completely lacking in intelligence and personality and was quite ineffective'. To Cazalet's surprise, he was informed that the Dutch had practically no stocks of explosives on Walcheren to use for the demolition of the island's coastal defences. Cazalet immediately agreed to supply the Dutch Colonel of Engineers, Colonel Beckman, with enough charges to destroy all twelve coastal guns. Cazalet also expressed serious concerns about the number of merchant ships at Flushing. He had seen at least sixteen large vessels waiting in the 'Flushing Roads' when he arrived, which, Van der Stad explained, were refusing to move because of the danger from the magnetic mines the Germans had dropped in the harbour the previous night. Cazalet urged the Dutch admiral to order the ships to leave, which he eventually agreed to do. When Cazalet returned to Flushing at 18:00 he was relieved to see that the merchant ships had already begun to depart.[8]

While Cazalet had been away from the port, a steady stream of French mechanised army units had begun arriving, with ferries landing troops and vehicles every half hour. At 20:45, with the dark of night closing in, Lt Cdr Black took *Verity* out into the Flushing Roads to be in a better position to provide anti-aircraft fire cover to the incoming ferries. It turned out to be a timely move as from 21:45, German bombers began appearing in the skies above the port and for the next hour *Verity* engaged them with fire from her 'pom-pom' and Lewis guns.

When dawn broke on Saturday, 11 May, it brought with it the danger of further, and probably more intensive, air attacks. During an 04:30 consultation, Black and Cazalet agreed that *Verity* could not risk being caught in daylight by German bombers, so at 05:45 she left Flushing and resumed her North Goodwin patrol, leaving Cazalet and his party at the port still awaiting permission to commence their mission.[9]

Despite the threat from air attacks, French troops continued to arrive at Flushing throughout the morning. Just before midday, the commander designate of the French forces in Walcheren, Brigadier General André Durand, arrived at the port. Cazalet met with Durand as he arrived to explain his presence and, as per his mission orders, placed himself and his XD party at the disposal of the French commander. Durand accepted and told Cazalet to meet him at his headquarters that evening. Cazalet came away with a low impression of Durand, whom he thought did not take the possibility of requiring any demolition operations at Flushing seriously, having told him that he already had the situation at the port well in hand.[10] Cazalet's thoughts then turned to his XD party 'kicking their heels' at the naval gymnasium. He spoke to the local naval authorities and managed to arrange some recreation for his men in the form of a supply of footballs and the use of a pitch to play on while they were waiting for orders to commence their operations. However, although a welcome relief from boredom for Cazalet's men, it must have been a somewhat incongruous sight for any Dutch civilians watching the British sailors playing football while their troops and the French were hectically unloading vital stores and clearing away debris from the air raids.

Just after midday, following their aborted attempt to land at the Hook, General Heywood and his Military Mission No.10 arrived at Flushing on board HMS *Wivern*. Peter Cazalet introduced himself to Heywood and accompanied him to the Dutch HQ to meet Rear Adm Van der Stad. When they arrived, they found the French commander, Durand, was also present.[11] The Dutch admiral explained the current situation in Zeeland to both the Allied generals and agreed that the Dutch and French commands should co-ordinate their actions. However, it soon became apparent to the Dutch that co-ordination on equal terms and on a basis of mutual respect meant nothing to Durand. The French general complained about the Dutch forces he had witnessed on his way to the Dutch HQ, believing their strength and shape was far below minimum requirements. He was under instructions to organise the defences of Walcheren and Zuid-Beveland and he would completely abandon the Dutch defence plan for the area. Van der Stad reluctantly accepted the French general's authority, without confirmation from his own superiors, and transferred the command of all Dutch forces in Walcheren and Zuid-Beveland to Durand. [12]

With the conversation between the French and Dutch commanders becoming more acrimonious, Cazalet and Heywood excused themselves and returned to Flushing, where HMS *Wivern* was preparing to leave. At 16:00 the destroyer weighed anchor and sailed for Dover, leaving Heywood and his mission at Flushing. Later in the afternoon Heywood ordered two officers and two other ranks from his mission to embark on the Dutch mail steamer *Princess Juliana,* which was taking a company of Dutch troops to Ymuiden, with instructions to try to make their way to The Hague from there. The following day the Dutch ship was bombed and severely damaged. The four British servicemen survived the attack, and the ship was towed to the Hook of Holland, where they disembarked to await further instructions.[13]

Meanwhile, back at Flushing, four British trawlers and drifters arrived to assist with minesweeping duties. At the request of the Dutch naval authorities, Cazalet immediately ordered the two trawlers to move on to the Hook where magnetic mines were reported being laid between there and Rotterdam. A further two British trawlers arrived at Flushing later in the afternoon. At 17:00 the port was subjected to another heavy air raid, sinking one Dutch merchant vessel, and cutting off the town's water supply. Following the raid Cazalet ordered the four British minesweeping vessels to leave the harbour immediately and anchor in the roads for the night. This turned out to be a fortuitous move for, shortly after dark, German bombers retuned for yet another attack.[14]

While his XD party spent the night in the naval gymnasium, Cazalet took a room in Flushing's Grand Hotel, where he set up his HQ and proceeded to begin writing up his reports using the hotel's notepaper. Later in the evening he made his visit to the French HQ at Middelburg for his meeting with Durand. At the meeting they considered the possible demolition of the causeway joining Walcheren Island to South Beveland. It was agreed that Cazalet, together with Durand's senior engineer officer, would travel to Walcheren to inspect the causeway the following day. Cazalet then returned to his hotel to get some much-needed sleep, only to be woken at 03:00 by yet another German air raid.[15]

The morning of Sunday, 12 May saw Cazalet and Durand's engineer inspecting the causeway at Walcheren. Cazalet described it as an 'extremely well-built solid structure carrying both railway and road'. As it was so well-built it was decided that any permanent demolition was impossible, with the limited stores at their disposal. They estimated that at least 15 tons of explosives would be required to inflict any serious, long-term damage to the causeway.

With his inspection completed, Cazalet returned to Flushing just in time to witness another heavy German air raid. The raid lasted over forty minutes, during which time over 100 bombs were dropped causing considerable damage in the port area. A large pontoon was hit and a ferry disabled by a direct hit, which also destroyed the loading ramp onto the ferry. Storehouses and offices near the railway station were wrecked and a Dutch minelayer and hospital ship were sunk.[16]

Such had been the extent of the damage caused by the increasing intensity of the raids that much of the demolition work planned for Party C had already been achieved by the German aircraft. When Cazalet weighed up the situation at the port and concluded that any demolition operations were now only a remote possibility, he decided to move himself and his party to Middelburg. Once established there he could stay in close contact with the actions of the Dutch and French commanders, neither of whom inspired him with any confidence, and be prepared to act on his own initiative if the situation demanded.[17]

Earlier in the day, the destroyer HMS *Kimberley* arrived at Flushing where she embarked Heywood and his mission. As soon as the embarkation was completed, the destroyer left the port heading for Ymuiden. Heywood left one member of his mission, 2nd Lieutenant A.M. Balfour, behind to act as liaison officer with the local Dutch command.

Cazalet proceeded to move his XD party to Middleburg, only then to receive a request from Durand to send them back to Flushing to assist with the unloading of ammunition from the French supply ship *Pavon*. Due to long delays waiting for transport, it was already mid-evening by the time the party arrived back at the port. When they reached the *Pavon* they were dismayed to find that the ship's crane had been badly damaged in the bombing, and it was impossible to unload the ammunition from deep in the hold without it. Cazalet described the whole event as a 'fiasco' and ordered his men back to Middelburg.[18]

On the following day, Monday, 13 May, Cazalet found himself in a dispute with the Dutch authorities. During the night a request had been received from The Hague to send two minesweeping vessels to Ymuiden. Despite it having the backing of the British Naval Attaché at The Hague, Cazalet refused the request claiming it would leave inadequate minesweeping forces at Flushing. To reinforce his refusal, he instead ordered his remaining minesweeping vessels to sail to Zeebrugge, where they would be safer from German bombing but still close enough to provide an efficient minesweeping service for Flushing.[19]

That evening Party C was again sent to Flushing to unload the *Pavon*. The ship's crane had now been repaired, and all the ammunition was successfully unloaded by midnight with the men of Party C impressing the French with their hard work and efficiency. However, Cazalet was forced to order his men to remain at the port for the rest of the night as the situation in Middelburg had deteriorated with a considerable amount of shooting in the streets of the town. This later turned out to be just a case of various nervous Dutch sentries firing on each other, but with German forces now fast approaching Zeeland, Cazalet's concern was understandable.[20]

On the morning of Tuesday, 14 May the destroyer HMS *Whitley* arrived at Flushing. Cazalet immediately seized the opportunity to go on board to arrange with her captain for a line of secure signal communications with London. Although there was still excellent telephone communication between Flushing and London, the ship's radio was the only way to send and receive secure messages.

Cazalet was by now acutely aware of the rapidly deteriorating military situation. It was the fifth day of the German invasion and the Dutch main defences in the south front, known as 'Fortress Holland', had collapsed and it seemed that a Dutch capitulation could not now be far off. After leaving *Whitley*, he took himself off for a tour of the local coastal defence gun batteries to see if they had been prepared for demolition. To his surprise, Cazalet found that the Dutch were quite prepared to destroy their guns if it became necessary. However, as they refused to allow any direct help from his XD party, Cazalet had to be content with just explaining the method of exploding the charges to them but still left confident that they would 'rise to the occasion' if the situation demanded.

At 19:00, Cazalet returned to the *Whitley* to send situation reports to the Admiralty and the War Office and then, at 22:30, he heard news of the radio broadcast by the Dutch commander-in-chief, General Winkelman, announcing the surrender of all his forces in the Netherlands with the exception of those in Zeeland Province.[21] Winkelman had made a specific qualification in his armistice proposal to the German command, stating that Zeeland would remain out of the armistice terms, as the province was largely occupied by French troops over which he had no authority. The Germans reluctantly accepted this additional term. It meant that the territorial commander of Zeeland, Rear-Adm Van der Stadt, not only became acting C-in-C over the remnants of the Dutch forces that were excluded from the armistice, but was also now the highest-ranking Dutch Government official in the last non-German occupied part of the Netherlands.[22]

It was going to be a long night for Cazalet, whose thoughts now turned to preparing his XD party for evacuation and the means to achieve it. Shortly before midnight he was summoned to a conference at the French HQ in Middelburg. When he arrived, he found Durand and Van der Stadt had been joined by the commander of the French naval forces in Holland, Rear Admiral Charles Platon. Platon, an Anglophobe and anti-Semite, had already struck up a good mutual working relationship with Van der Stadt, in marked contrast to that between the Dutch admiral and Durand, which was now becoming increasingly frayed. It was clear to Cazalet that Platon had been sent to stiffen resistance in Zeeland. The French admiral dominated the conference, while Van der Stadt and Durand appeared to Cazalet to be 'incapable of clear thought' and 'in a state of near panic' during the meeting. Platon ended the conference insisting on resistance to the last man.[23]

By the morning, it had become clear to Cazalet that the morale of the Dutch forces was completely broken. The Germans had crossed the inundations in South Beveland and were approaching the *Zanddike-line* defences on Walcheren Island, but to Cazalet the French positions appeared to be strong and capable of holding off the German forces. However, his confidence took a blow when, later that morning, he made another visit to the French GHQ where it soon became apparent to him that there was a 'complete lack of liaison with other units and little determined direction'.[24]

That afternoon Cazalet returned to HMS *Whitely* at Flushing where he received a signal from the Admiralty to say that the destroyer HMS *Valentine* had been run aground off Terneuzen after being attacked by German bombers while patrolling the mouth of the Scheldt. Cazalet immediately requested the assistance of a Dutch tug to take a demolition team from *Whitely* out to the stricken vessel and embark survivors and then arranged for ambulances to be ready to receive them.[25]

That night Middelburg and Flushing were both heavily bombed but fortunately most of the civilian populations of both towns had already been evacuated to the western part of Walcheren, thus avoiding the raids. As dawn broke on 16 May it was obvious that the military situation had become critical. The *Zanddike-line* had been abandoned by its Dutch defenders, and the French had fallen back to the narrow and shallow canal that ran through South Beveland.[26] When he visited the French HQ Cazalet found Durand in 'a state bordering on panic'. A few German landing parties had crossed the canal on South Beveland, taking advantage of the void dividing the two French battalions that were defending it. These landings had now been reinforced, leaving the French defence plans in disarray. At last, the question of demolitions took on some importance and Cazalet ordered his XD party back to Flushing ready to carry out their operations.[27]

At 01:00 on Friday, 17 May all French forces were withdrawn from South Beveland to defend Walcheren. It was now obvious to Cazalet that the situation was very precarious and so at 05:30 he gave instructions for his team to place all their charges and to stay with them until orders came through to commence demolitions.

Late the previous night, Cazalet had been approached by the Dutch authorities with a request to destroy one of their naval vessels lying on the stocks at Flushing. The vessel was the HNLMS *Philips van Almonde*, an 1,800-ton destroyer which had been originally launched in 1939 but was now back in dock in the process of being fitted-out.

As soon as dawn broke, Cazalet went to inspect the vessel, which he found to be almost ready for sea. He then arranged a meeting with the shipyard's works manager. The manager agreed that, although the usual preparations would take another two weeks to complete, it might be possible that the vessel could be re-launched that same day. However, all the manager's workmen had now been evacuated, and he had no one left to perform the launch operation. Cazalet eventually obtained the services of 100 young sailors from the local naval training establishment to assist with the launch, while the works manager was able to persuade a few of his key men to return to the docks to help with the preparations. After several failed attempts to launch the destroyer, the operation was abandoned, and Cazalet, lacking sufficient demolition charges, placed two depth charges around the ship ready for the final authorisation to destroy her. [28]

Meanwhile, the military situation was deteriorating even further. Van der Stadt had already been instructed by the Dutch Government, now in exile in London, not to allow himself to be captured and had moved his command post from Middelburg to Breskens, leaving the French HQ to control the defence of the former. However, the French had their own concerns and were now looking at an exit strategy. As the day wore on, pressure grew for them to fall back to Flushing, their only possible route out of Holland.[29] The sense of panic at the French military HQ had been compounded by the sudden unexplained disappearance of Durand. Then, at 15:00 a message was received by Platon from the new French military commander, General Deslaurens, informing the admiral that he would soon be compelled to withdraw his troops from Walcheren Island and that it was his intention to evacuate Flushing that night. Platon immediately summoned Cazalet and ordered him to commence demolitions,[30] signing a hastily scribbled note for him:

To Command[er] Cazalet
You may demolish everything from now onwards, except boats.
Platon - Flushing - 1500, May 17.[31]

However, no sooner had Platon signed this note when French troops and transport began flooding back into Flushing. It soon became obvious to Cazalet that their presence would seriously hamper demolition operations. No boats could be sunk and now no bridges could be destroyed as it would disrupt the French evacuation operation. In addition, the proximity of the port's oil tanks to the roads and harbour meant that these could not be destroyed either, lest the smoke from their burning would also hinder the movements of the French troops.

With time fast running out, Cazalet and his team completed demolitions on the *Philips van Almonde* which was still lying on the stocks, and they also managed to destroy an oil refinery and pumping station, together with the main lock to the harbour basin. Cazalet also sent demolition charges to the Dutch gun crews manning the coastal batteries with instructions for them to destroy their guns. Cazalet received confirmation back that at least one battery carried out his instructions, and it was hoped that the others would follow suit before the Germans overran them.

At 18:10 on 17 May, their work done, Peter Cazalet's XD Party C boarded a French Navy chasseur at Flushing, which transported them across the Scheldt to Breskens. From there they made their way by foot to Zeebrugge, where they spent the night. They eventually reached Dunkirk late the following day where they spent another uncomfortable night sheltering from a heavy German air raid which also seriously damaged the train ferry they were hoping to sail on for England the following morning. The party were eventually put on board the destroyer HMS *Vimiera,* which left Dunkirk at 16:00 and reached Portsmouth at 01:00 on 20 May.[32]

In his report to the Admiralty on the operation, Cazalet was critical of the quantity of explosives he had been supplied with, claiming that they were insufficient to carry out the demolitions that had been planned for his party. However, Cazalet also found space in his report to praise the behaviour of his men:

> The behaviour of the party was on the whole excellent. Three younger men showed signs of nervousness after the first air raid, but this was at once nipped in the bud, and did not appear again. In every other respect, the men behaved as sailors always do under such circumstances.
>
> They easily adapted themselves to the changing situation, and were invariably cheerful throughout. A Dutch officer remarked to me as we were leaving Flushing – 'If only our men had the morale of yours, things would have been very different'.[33]

Chapter 15

ANTWERP (10-18 MAY)

The destroyer HMS *Brilliant* left Dover at 11:57 on the morning of Friday, 10 May, under the command of Lieutenant Commander Francis Brodrick RN. On board were XD Party D consisting of three naval officers and twenty-five ratings, together with one officer and twenty-four sappers of the KFRE.

In overall command of Party D was 35-year-old Commander Arthur Caerlyon Stanford RN. A tall, athletic, and highly regarded officer, Stanford had attended the Dragon Prep School in Oxford prior to joining the Royal Navy as a 13-year-old in 1918. He first served at sea as a midshipman on board the battleship HMS *Warspite* in 1922 and was promoted to sub lieutenant in 1925 after being noted for his good intelligence work for his report on Saint Thomas in the US Virgin Islands while serving on the West Indies Station, which also resulted in him being recommended for a staff course.[1] He gained further promotions over the following twelve years until eventually attaining the rank of commander in December 1938. After the outbreak of war, Stanford joined Admiral Binney's staff and became involved in the planning of the XD operations before being designated to command the proposed Antwerp XD Party in January 1940.

Leading the sappers of Party D was 2nd Lieutenant 'Shorty' Wells, who had only joined the KFRE from the Officer Cadet Training Unit in April. He was in command of two sections, D1 and D2, each section consisting of twelve men.[2]

As with those of the other XD missions, Stanford's orders were, on arrival at Antwerp, to contact the local authorities to explain his team's presence there and then to act in close cooperation with them to achieve his objectives. Another important task was to persuade all shipping in the port to leave as soon as possible. If, on arrival, he found the French in occupation of the port, he was to place himself completely at the disposal of the French military commander and work under his direction. However, if he found the enemy approaching and he was unable to communicate with the relevant authorities, he would be permitted to carry out the demolitions on his own initiative if he believed the situation warranted it.

Stanford was ordered to consider the safety of HMS *Brilliant* to be of 'paramount importance' and not to expect the destroyer to remain in port if her commander thought her to be in danger. Again, in common with the other XD parties, if Party D failed to rejoin *Brilliant* before she departed, then they would be expected to make their own way back to England.[3]

The objectives allocated to Stanford's RN demolition team included the destruction of twenty oil lighters, six dredgers, 200 barges, and some of the port's essential infrastructure. Meanwhile, Lieutenant Wells and his sappers would target the destruction of 150,000 tons of oil and petrol stored at the port. To assist them in this task the British Military Attaché would arrange for tugs or lighters capable of carrying Wells with his team and all their stores to be available on their arrival, ready to transport them to their objectives.[4]

At 14:41 *Brilliant* arrived at the Wandelaar light vessel, off the Belgian coast, where she took up station astern of HMS *Verity* on her way to Flushing with XD Party C. After picking up a pilot in the Wielingen Channel, Brodrick sailed his destroyer into the Flushing Roads, exchanging cheers in passing with the crew of Dutch cruiser HNLMS *Sumatra*.

As *Brilliant* proceeded at 25 knots up the River Scheldt, large crowds gathered at every village to cheer and wave as she passed them. No great difficulties were encountered in navigating the river, although Brodrick occasionally had to reduce speed to avoid damage to barges and ferries. Other than that, good progress was made and, apart from a solitary Junkers JU86 transport that overflew them without incident, no enemy aircraft were encountered.

Brilliant arrived off Doel at 18:30, where she halted briefly to await permission from the Belgian authorities to proceed on to Antwerp. By 18:45 Brodrick had brought his ship in sight of the port where he could see that a German dive-bombing attack was taking place and counted about twenty-four JU87 'Stuka' dive-bombers releasing their bombs over the port, targeting shipping, docks, and wharves. Belgian anti-aircraft fire was sporadic and inaccurate and no opposing fighter aircraft could be seen. The German aircraft broke-off their attack at 18:57, having caused only minor damage to the port, allowing Brodrick to proceed and by 19:42 he had *Brilliant* safely tied-up on the Canadian

Pacific Railway jetty. Stanford then went ashore to consult with the British Naval Control Officer at the port, Captain Arthur Henniker-Heaton RN (Retd).

Henniker-Heaton was a 57-year-old veteran of the First World War who had led a chequered naval career. The younger son of a Member of Parliament and Baronet, Arthur was born in Australia before the family returned to settle back in England when he was just 1 year old. He attended the Britannia Naval College at Dartmouth before joining his first ship at the age of 15. He was promoted to lieutenant in 1904 and appointed to command his first vessel, the torpedo boat TB20 in 1908. In 1912 he was promoted to lieutenant commander while serving on HMS *Torch* on the Australia Station, but a few months later he was removed from the ship by the commander-in-chief and sent back to England after appearing drunk on duty. He blamed his condition on a small amount of alcohol taken whilst he was on medication, which had 'greatly amplified its intoxicating effects'. Nevertheless, once back in England he was put on half-pay for six months. He then went on to serve on the battleship *Lord Nelson*, where he failed to impress her captain who recorded that his junior officer 'possessed no initiative and lacked executive ability'.

After the outbreak of the First World War, Hennicker-Heaton was appointed to command the destroyer *Ness* and later commended for his action in attacking German submarines. In December 1917 he was in command of the torpedo-boat destroyer *Mandate* when it was involved in a collision with the sloop *Anchusa*. At the following Court of Enquiry, Henniker-Heaton aroused the Admiralty's displeasure in the matter but was still promoted to the rank of commander on 31 December 1917. In March 1918 he was admitted to hospital with appendicitis and, following an operation, developed further health problems and was not passed fit again until 1919.

In 1921, a Court Martial charged Henniker-Heaton with navigating at excessive speed near the Isle of Wight while in command of the destroyer *Ursula*. He was sentenced to be reprimanded for 'negligent performance of duty'.

Henniker-Heaton was placed on the Retired List at his own request on 1 November 1922, but was allowed to apply for a step in rank when he reached his forty-fifth birthday, which he achieved to become captain in 1928. Although classed as 'Retired' he was retained on the Reserve List and attended a short course at the RN College Osborne in 1938. In August 1939, with the prospect of war looming in Europe, Henniker-Heaton joined the Naval Control Service and on 1 May 1940 was appointed Consular Shipping Advisor at Antwerp and was running the NCS office there when the Germans invaded Belgium just a few days later.[5] It was now his responsibility to ensure all British merchant shipping left the port safely and at the earliest opportunity. To his credit, Henniker-Heaton had the situation well under control, with all British and Allied vessels ready to leave within the next forty-eight hours, and he was now co-ordinating the evacuation of the consular staff and the hundreds of British subjects that had gathered at the port.

Following his NCS meeting, Stanford returned to *Brilliant* where he and the rest of his party spent a fraught night, disturbed by several air raid alarms but, to their relief, no bombs fell near the ship.[6]

As dawn broke on Saturday, 11 May several German reconnaissance aircraft were spotted flying over the port. Then, at 07:40 a single twin-engine bomber was sighted approaching *Brilliant* from the south-west, flying at an altitude of just 100 feet. Brodrick ordered his ship's port-side 'pom-pom' gun to open fire on the bomber, which was also engaged by anti-aircraft guns from the shore. The aircraft took several hits causing it to veer away into the clouds and it was later reported as having crashed the other side of the river with its destruction credited to *Brilliant* by the local authorities.[7]

The safe evacuation of civilians was fast becoming a priority for the port authorities, who requested Brodrick to move his ship from the Canadian Pacific jetty to make way for a civilian vessel that was to embark some of the refugees. Brodrick agreed to the request and at 08:45 *Brilliant* shifted about 800 yards downstream to take up her new berth at the old Red Star Line Wharf. Brodrick and Stanford then went to visit Henniker-Heaton at the NCS office where they were updated on the current shipping situation. Henniker-Heaton also emphasised the Belgian authorities being 'very touchy about others interfering with them' and he anticipated that Stanford would have great difficulties in persuading them to cooperate with his demolition operations. Brodrick then asked Henniker-Heaton for his assistance in obtaining the use of a small vessel to accommodate the demolition parties and to provide them with a means of escape in case *Brilliant* was forced to withdraw before their operations could be completed.

Stanford moved on to report to the British Consul General, Sir Godfrey Fisher, whose offices were by now packed with desperate British nationals seeking passage to safety in England. After consulting Fisher, Stanford then went to visit Antwerp's military and civilian governors to seek permission for his demolition parties to make a reconnaissance of their objectives. However, the Belgian governors had not been made aware of any agreed arrangements to accommodate

Stanford's mission and showed little enthusiasm for it. Although the Military Governor, General Van Rolleghelm, had been made responsible for the destruction of military installations, he did not consider the port facilities to fall within that category. The governors refused to allow Stanford to make any reconnaissance and insisted his men stay on board their ship. Stanford reluctantly agreed to comply with Van Rolleghelm's demands but took advantage of his journey back to *Brilliant* to make a brief covert reconnaissance of some of the port's lock gates concluding that they could easily be destroyed. However, he seriously doubted that he would have sufficient explosives to destroy many, if any, of the multitude of wharves, storehouses, dock cranes, and other ancillary structures that were involved in the efficient operation of a port like Antwerp.[8]

Meanwhile, Brodrick, accompanied by Lieutenant Commander Gonin RN of the NCS staff, called on the Captain of the Port, the Harbour Master, and the Water Bailiff to urge them to compel all vessels to leave Antwerp as soon as possible to avoid being captured or destroyed by the Germans.[9]

Back on *Brilliant*, 'Shorty' Wells and his sappers, having slept the night below deck fully clothed, kept themselves busy top side cleaning their weapons and checking their equipment. They also managed to find some time to relax and sunbathe around the ship's gun turret, watching the crowds of curious locals that gathered on the jetty in defiance of the air raid alarms that continued into the afternoon.[10]

During a break in the air raids that afternoon, Sir Godfrey Fisher, accompanied by Antwerp's Civil Governor, Georges Holvoet, visited *Brilliant*. Brodrick welcomed them aboard his ship but warned them that he may be compelled to leave the port at short notice if the bombing intensified. Although he was willing to take some refugees with him, he would be leaving the demolition parties behind to fend for themselves.

After six hours of bargaining and haggling, and with the assistance of a senior Belgian naval officer, a reasonable price was eventually agreed for the charter of two tugs to accommodate the demolition parties. The result of these successful negotiations was given to Stanford when he returned to the NCS office later in the afternoon. However, Henniker-Heaton tempered this welcome news with a warning to Stanford that word was filtering through from London that the Admiralty were considering ordering *Brilliant* to withdraw from the port within hours to avoid the danger from German bombing, and that he was expecting a telephone call soon confirming that instruction.[11]

Corporal Jack Mitten, one of the NCOs in the RE party, was keeping a diary in which he recorded details of the activity in the skies above *Brilliant* throughout the day:

> ... Last raid 1500. 7 bombers. 6 Bombers passing over now 1550. 5 more following 1620. 12 more bombers passing over. Plenty of gun fire from batteries. 1630 Bombers being chased by 7 pursuit aircraft.
>
> 1705. 6 aircraft having a fight. 1710. 2 bombers over ships: have to get below decks again. Saturday night can't go ashore too many raids. 2000 hours. Have just toured ship. More Air Raid Alarms. Plane that passed low over ship this morning was hit by boat's gun. It crashed outside town killing 35 people. Turned in again fully clothed more alarms.[12]

The two chartered Belgian tugs arrived alongside *Brilliant* at 06:30 the following morning, Sunday, 12 May. After their early morning parade, the RE party boarded one tug, while the RN party embarked on the other. Stanford and Brodrick then went to the NCS office where Henniker-Heaton told them that he had received the expected telephone call from the Admiralty ordering *Brilliant* to leave port. After some discussion with the Consul General, and in view of the rapid advances being made by the Germans, it was decided that the destroyer would leave that afternoon after taking on board the Naval Control staff and the British refugees that had been approved by the consulate. The Consul General himself elected to stay behind to care for any further refugees, while Stanford and his demolition parties would remain behind in their chartered tugs.

By 14:00 that afternoon, Brodrick and his crew were making their final preparations to leave Antwerp having safely embarked the NCS staff, along with about fifty British refugees. At 14:18 *Brilliant* embarked a pilot, slipped her moorings and proceeded down the Scheldt. By 15:50 she was in the Schaar van Waarde Channel, still 25 miles from Flushing, when she came under attack from a single Junkers JU88 aircraft. *Brilliant* increased speed to 5 knots and opened fire with her 'pom-poms'. The German bomber dropped six bombs, which fortunately all fell well astern of the destroyer without detonating.

Brilliant arrived off Flushing at 17:00 where she exchanged pilots for the final leg of her journey from Dutch waters. After dropping her pilot near the Wielengen Buoy, *Brilliant* proceeded on without incident to Dover, where she arrived at 21:20, securing at Admiralty Pier to disembark all her much-relieved refugees.[13]

Meanwhile, back at Antwerp, Stanford was now concentrating on organising transport for all the remaining British refugees and ensuring that all the smaller vessels left the port as soon as possible. He held discussions with the senior port officials, urging on them the necessity for all barges, lighters, and salvage vessels to leave the port, so denying their use to the Germans.[14]

Following *Brilliant*'s departure, the XD parties were trying to settle into their new temporary accommodation vessels while having to also come to terms with losing the protection of the destroyer's guns. Security around the tugs was stepped-up, lookouts stationed, and guards placed along the quayside to keep away unwanted visitors.

Having consumed the solitary sandwich that comprised his 'afternoon tea', Jack Mitten was trying to find a space on the deck of his tug to sleep. Having noted that the naval party had foregone the cramped conditions aboard their tug in favour of bedding down in a bombed-out shipping office along the quayside, many of Jack's sapper comrades decided to follow suit so he was eventually able to stake his claim to a place in the relative comfort of the tug's cabin.

As the evening drew on, parachutists were observed landing in the area, some equipped with bicycles. As a result, the guards ashore were doubled up, but thankfully the night passed without incident.

The dawn of Whit Monday, 13 May, saw more German aircraft in the skies above Antwerp, rudely awakening the XD parties from their slumbers. At 09:00, Commander Stanford addressed his men, updating them as best he could on their current situation. He also reported that Dutch troops were now being seen in Antwerp, bringing some much-needed reinforcements to its defences. After his briefing Stanford then authorised the welcome issuing of a 'beer ration' to boost his parties' morale.

At 11:00 Jack Mitten took up his first guard duties ashore. He was struck by how friendly all the Belgians were that approached him, vainly hoping that he was just part of the vanguard of thousands more British troops that would soon be arriving to help defend their beleaguered city against the approaching German forces. Mitten hoped to venture into the town after his guard duties were finished to see for himself what was happening, but was warned off, in case he was mistaken for a German.[15]

Meanwhile, Commander Stanford was busy arranging passage on board the Belgian liner *Ville de Bruges* for the last of the British refugees, and holding meetings with several of the barge, tug, and salvage operators, impressing on them the urgency of getting their remaining craft away. The operators hoped that, providing sufficient towage was available, all the port's dredgers, floating cranes and elevators would be gone at least by the end of the following day.[16]

Stanford was able to get through by telephone to Brussels for the first time since his arrival, and spoke to Lt Col Blake, the Military Attaché at the British Embassy, who gave him the location of the Belgian GHQ. Stanford then obtained the use of a car and driver and motored out to visit the GHQ at Fort Breendonk, midway between Brussels and Antwerp, where he met with the Head of the British Military Mission to the Belgians, Major General Needham, and with Admiral of the Fleet, Sir Roger Keyes who was there in his capacity as the British representative to King Leopold, Commander-in-Chief of the Belgian forces. Needham gave Stanford an outline of the current military situation which he was authorised to communicate to Gen Van Rolleghelm.

When he returned to Antwerp, Stanford immediately went to see Van Rolleghelm. The Military Governor was most grateful for the information that Stanford had for him and was now far more willing to listen to Stanford explain his mission in full. On the strict understanding that no action would be taken without his permission, Van Rolleghelm offered Stanford his full cooperation and lent him an officer from his staff to go around his objectives with him and to ensure the goodwill of the sentries. The general also placed a lorry at Stanford's disposal to provide transport for his parties. The tour around the objectives was completed and Stanford was now satisfied that he could carry out his orders successfully when the situation demanded it, and with the full agreement of the Belgian authorities.[17]

With their own homeland now almost overrun by the German forces, hundreds of Dutch refugees had begun flowing into Antwerp, most of them hoping to find vessels to take them to safety. However, this influx of refugees also provided an ideal cover for enemy infiltration. Fortunately, the Belgians were alert to this danger and had strengthened security around the port area, capturing two German spies on the neighbouring jetty to the one where the XD parties' tugs were moored. As an additional precaution against further infiltrations and following rumours that the main German advance could be reaching Antwerp by the morning, the two tugs moved their moorings that night to another jetty further downstream.[18]

When dawn broke on Tuesday, 14 May, the liner *Ville de Bruges* departed for England, carrying the last of the British refugees, together with Arthur Henniker-Heaton and his Naval Control Service staff. By 07:00 the liner had sailed about 10 miles along the Scheldt when she was attacked by German bombers just off Fort Lillo. One bomb fell into No. 4 Hold and exploded, killing four crew members and setting the vessel ablaze. Fortunately, all the sixty-four passengers were below deck and were protected from the worst effects of the explosion by a steel bulkhead that separated their quarters from the ship's hospital. The lifeboats were manned and all the passengers, including thirty-two British refugees, were rowed safely ashore. Meanwhile the crew continued to fight the blaze but, with her engines out of action, the liner drifted aground just off Doel and was eventually abandoned to her fate.[19]

After spending his fourth night afloat at Antwerp, Corporal Jack Mitten witnessed the unhappy scenes unfolding at the port that morning:

> At 0715 we heard an explosion. Jerry had dropped a bomb on the liner [...]. It is a lovely sunny morning and what Belgiams [*sic*] are left are just wandering about aimlessly.
>
> 10.15 Three lifeboats of refugees brought back from Liner, which caught fire and was beached. Machine gun fire can be heard nearer now. More refugees passing through town. [...] A launch loaded [with] some up alongside us. Everybody crying bar us. We were too hungry not having enough rations. It is a pitiful sight all these refugees going through the town, poor old women and little children.[20]

Meanwhile, through the good offices of Van Rolleghelm, Arthur Stanford had arranged to meet with the officer responsible for Antwerp's Fuel and Lubricants Control Service, Commandant Joseph Devalkaneer. Stanford, accompanied by Lt Wells from the sapper party, visited the commandant at his HQ that morning. They were shocked when Devalkaneer informed them that no plans for the destruction of the port's oil installations had been prepared. However, the Belgian was extremely helpful and happy to cooperate fully with the British mission. The three officers then got to work and outlined some brief plans for the operation. During their subsequent discussions, Devalkaneer revealed that there was approximately 150,000 tons of oil stored at Antwerp, of which 70,000 tons were 'heavy' oils such as diesel, and various lubricating oils. The remainder of the stocks comprised petrol, benzine and other light oils. Agreement was also reached for the Royal Engineers to go to the main oil depot to practise their demolitions, and for them to stay in position there ready to receive the executive order to proceed with their mission.[21]

Following this meeting, Stanford returned to the office he had set up on the quayside. In the afternoon he received a visit from a French naval captain, who explained that he had been charged with a similar mission to Stanford's. This was in accord with the Allied agreement that the French would provide a back-up demolition force for Antwerp in case the British mission hit any problems. The two officers discussed the current situation at Antwerp and agreed to divide up the objectives between their two forces and 'smooth-out' some contradictions in their respective orders.

Stanford appeared to be happy with the level of Anglo-French cooperation achieved at the meeting. However, by the following morning it soon became obvious that his confidence had been misplaced. Unbeknown to Stanford, the French officer had rushed out to reconnoitre his objectives without advising the Belgians and giving no thought to the consequences of his actions. The Belgian authorities, alarmed at what they regarded as possible precipitative and premature action by the Allied demolition teams, issued immediate orders that on no account should any of the locks suffer any damage, thus nullifying at a stroke Stanford's primary objective of denying the efficient operation of the port to the Germans. Despite his vigorous protests, Stanford was unable to have the order rescinded and was left to make the best job he could with his remaining objectives.[22]

Fortunately, the French officer's actions had not affected the Royal Engineers XD team's plans for the morning. Having spent much of the night on guard duty and with only a few hours' sleep, Jack Mitten woke on Wednesday, 15 May to the news that he and his comrades were to at last proceed to their main objective that morning. However, Mitten now viewed the mission with some apprehension: '0930. Just going up river to look at our job, at present it seems suicide. Antwerp full of spies. Refugees by the hundred passing through the town terrified. It's one continuous air raid. We left off seeking cover long ago.'[23]

While the sappers were on their way to their objective, Arthur Stanford paid another visit to the Belgian GHQ to consult with Sir Roger Keyes. When he arrived, Stanford gave a detailed report on his mission's objectives and the current military situation at Antwerp, as Keyes noted in his diary: 'He told me that everyone there was confident of being able to hold it'. The Belgian generals present therefore regarded any decision to order demolitions to be premature and raised several objections to any such proposals. However, Keyes knew that the XD mission had also attracted the attention of King Leopold, so he took Stanford to meet the king who interviewed Stanford personally. Stanford made a big impression on the Belgian monarch and C-in-C, who took a keen interest in the matter of destroying Antwerp's port facilities. Leopold sent orders to Van Rolleghelm to assist Stanford with his mission in 'every possible way'.[24] He also gave orders for the oil stocks to be rendered 'unusable' and for the destruction of the larger dock cranes, but no other demolitions would be allowed, including the lock gates, stating that such action would 'irreparably destroy the port for years and serve no military purpose.' Stanford then asked the king for permission to block the locks with sunken barges instead. The king agreed in principle but could not commit to authorising such a drastic measure at that time.[25]

Stanford returned to Antwerp and made his preparations, which included moving barges into the locks ready to be sunk as soon as he had received final authority to do so. He also gave Lieutenant Wells orders to commence his demolitions at the oil storage installation at 04:00 the following morning.

Stanford's thoughts then turned to ensuring their means of escape once the mission had been completed. The German troops were threatening the northern side of the Scheldt but were meeting stiff resistance from the Belgian forces. However, the situation was looking very bleak from the Allied point of view, and the XD parties were in danger of being left isolated if the Germans were able to break through the Belgian defences. Meanwhile, Stanford still had the use of one Belgian lorry but that was not enough to transport all his men. Thankfully, the French military came to the rescue and agreed to provide another four lorries with drivers. The four vehicles were duly stationed on the south side of the river, under camouflage up a quiet side street ready to carry the XD parties to France once their missions had been accomplished. However, their drivers appeared far from happy to be there and worried they could be cut off from their French comrades who were already withdrawing from the port. The nervousness of the French drivers raised concerns that they could suddenly drive off and leave the British parties stranded. To avoid such a situation, Lieutenant Wells ordered some of the sappers, including Jack Mitten, to cross the river that evening to form an armed guard around the vehicles. Mitten was far from impressed with facing another night without much sleep: '20.00. Halfway through a haircut, news not so good, have to go across river to guard four French Lorries. […] Bombing very consistent all night. Have one hour sleep which makes 5 in two days.'[26]

With all his preparations in place to commence operations at 04:30, Arthur Stanford was horrified to be woken at 03:00 on 16 May with the news that his orders to commence demolitions had been countermanded by the Belgian high command. He was also informed that the barges blocking the locks were not to be sunk. A furious Stanford went to see Van Rolleghelm, who could only confirm that the decision had been taken to delay any demolition operations. Stanford then asked if he could telephone the Belgian GHQ and speak to someone there directly, only to be informed that he could not contact them until later in the afternoon as the GHQ were in the process of moving from Fort Breendonk to Ghent, further to the south nearer the French border. Stanford waited in Van Rolleghelm's office until 15:00 when he was at last able to get through by phone to the new Belgian GHQ. He spoke to Sir Roger Keyes, who was stunned to hear that Stanford had not yet commenced his operations. Keyes immediately went to see King Leopold and got him to overrule his generals and gained permission for Stanford to commence the destruction of the larger dock cranes immediately, but to delay destruction of the oil stocks until 04:00 the following morning. At 16:00 Stanford, with the new orders in his hands, bade farewell to Van Rolleghelm and immediately proceeded to commence his operations.[27]

The first target for the RN team was an 80-ton crane mounted on rail tracks on the edge of one of the port's two dry docks. The base of the crane consisted of four steel-strutted legs on wheels. Large explosive charges were placed where the struts met at the base of the two legs nearest the dock. Two smaller charges were placed around the outer struts. All the charges were fired simultaneously causing the crane to topple into the dock, crushing the dock gates in the process.

The second objective was a 100-ton floating crane moored across the entrance to the other dry dock. Two large 45-lb charges were placed on the side of the crane nearest the dock, alongside the water-tight bulkheads. The charges were then fired causing all four water-tight compartments on the dock side of the crane to flood. The rest of the crane was similarly flooded by firing charges placed on its far side. Two smaller charges were then placed under the crane's training rack and fired. The crane toppled across the dock gates and successfully blocked the entrance.

The RN team then moved on to its final objectives: two more floating cranes located at the Royal Lock entrance to the port's main basin. The larger of the two was a 200-ton crane and the smaller a 100-ton crane. Both cranes were prepared for destruction in the same way, with small charges placed alongside their water-tight compartments and larger charges placed on their centre pivots. The idea being that both cranes would topple over and block the lock entrance. When the charges were fired the larger crane fell-over as planned, but the smaller crane righted itself and sank upright. Although the smaller crane had been rendered useless, it had failed to fall across the lock gates to complete the blocking of the entrance to the basin.[28]

Meanwhile, the REs were spending another nervous night back in their Belgian tug, facing constant bombing raids and waiting for the final go ahead to commence their tasks. Jack Mitten had been guarding the French lorries and drivers in the early hours of the morning when he received some unwelcome news about their XD operation:

> Friday 17th May
> Supposed to have started this morning at 04.00 but it has been cancelled once again. Tug crew ever so restless and we are frightened of them sneaking off ship. […] French drivers nervous so have sent them to a fort further round the river.
>
> 13.00 Not a soul to be seen in Antwerp and every Tug and Boat anchored on the other side of the river except ours and the Naval [XD Party's] Tug.[29]

Back in London, Lord Hankey had begun his working morning with a visit to the Cabinet War Rooms, the underground bunker labyrinth in Whitehall. The new Prime Minister, Winston Churchill, had retained Hankey as a Cabinet Minister with the sinecure office of Chancellor of the Duchy of Lancaster but without a place in the War Cabinet. However, Churchill had specifically requested Hankey to resume 'all special duties entrusted to him by the previous War Cabinet'.[30] These special duties included the overseeing of the XD operations. On his arrival at the war rooms, Hankey was informed that the Allied armies were withdrawing from Belgium and that Antwerp would shortly be isolated. Hankey, realising the consequences, immediately sprang into action. At 09:45 he met with the Chiefs of Staff Committee and suggested that the time had come to take every possible step to ensure the destruction of the Antwerp oil stocks. The Chiefs all agreed that the destruction operation should be put into action. Hankey then phoned Colonel Jacob at the War Cabinet office and ordered him to contact Captain Hermon-Hodge RN who was in overall charge of the Naval XD operations to see if his parties were still at Antwerp. Hankey then phoned Roger Makins at the Foreign Office and asked him to contact the British Ambassador in Brussels, Sir Lancelot Oliphant, to get him to speak to the Belgian Government and insist that they give the necessary orders to destroy the oil. Makins agreed to do this but explained that the Belgian Government had now moved to Ostend, as had the ambassador, and the only line of communication with them had to be made through the Belgian Embassy in London with the risk that any 'secret' conversations may be overheard. Hankey replied that secrecy was immaterial and what mattered was to ensure the destruction of the oil 'at all costs'.[31]

The round of hectic telephone calls continued through the morning. At 11:30 Colonel Jacob called Hankey to let him know that he had spoken to Captain Hermon-Hodge, who had assured him that the situation at Antwerp was satisfactory. Two companies of French engineers, as well as the RE XD Party, were ready to destroy the oil tanks which he was confident they would do at 'the right moment'. After he had finished speaking to Jacob, Hankey called Makins again who confirmed that he had asked the Belgian Ambassador to get a message to the Belgian Government at Ostend. The ambassador had assured him that the order to destroy the oil would be given. Makins also told Hankey that telephone communications with Oliphant at Ostend had at last been established with the British Ambassador, who would also now be putting pressure on the Belgians to act. Makins phoned Hankey again just over an hour later to advise that the Belgian Government had settled all the arrangements for the destruction of the Antwerp oil stocks the previous day, but were still unsure if the orders had yet been carried out.[32] As frustrated and anxious as he was, Hankey had done all he could and would now just have to await further news from Antwerp.

Hankey would have been relieved to know that the Belgian Government's assurances were well-founded. Back in Antwerp preparations were well in hand to deny the oil stocks to the enemy. However, the method had changed. Destroying the tanks using explosives risked starting a huge conflagration which could end up engulfing the whole port; a risk the local Belgian authorities were not prepared to take, especially with the Belgian army now retreating through the port, hence the delays in giving the final orders. Instead, Commandant Devalkaneer had arranged for oil company officials to intermix all the 'light' oils with sugar at a nearby refinery, thus rendering them 'useless'. The subsequent mixture would then be run-off from the refinery into neighbouring fields.

Cooperation with the oil companies had also ensured the removal of sections of piping entering the tanks at the 'heavy' oil storage depot. The valves adjacent to the tanks had all been 'eased' ready to be opened to release all the oil from the tanks. Devalkaneer's troops had cut trenches through the depot site connecting all the different oil company compounds, which would allow all the heavy oil stocks to be drained out onto adjacent low-lying lands.[33]

While they had been waiting, the KFRE team had been busy removing the plugs from over 2,000 barrels and drums of oil that were stacked along the wharf at the storage site. Then at 15:30 on 17

May, they at last received their final orders to commence operations. The sappers rushed into action, some rolling the unplugged barrels forward, so all their contents drained into the Scheldt, while others set about opening valves and removing blank ends of pipes on all the storage tanks to commence the huge 'drain-off'. After that had all been done the sappers went around all the various stores puncturing any remaining sealed oil barrels with pickaxes. Finally, five benzine tanks and three large lubricating oil storage tanks situated in other nearby sites were all drained off. By 18:00 the whole operation had been successfully completed without a single casualty, and the sappers were able to board their tug and return to the relative safety of the south bank.[34]

However, by now the German forces had already occupied part of the town and the sappers faced an anxious couple of hours while they waited for their RN comrades to join them.

The naval XD team had been continuing with minor demolitions around the port, and it was 20:00 before they boarded their tug. Despite the continuous bombing and shelling they were met with a loud cheer when they reached the south bank, and by 20:30 all equipment had been transferred from the tugs to the waiting French lorries.

Once all the equipment was loaded, the XD parties packed themselves onto the lorries, some of them far too exhausted to even sit down on the narrow bench seats. Instead, most just slumped on the floors of the trucks as they set off into the night.

After eventually escaping the chaos of Antwerp the trucks initially made good progress through Belgium thanks to the roads being relatively free of refugees. This was mostly a result of a proclamation from King Leopold forbidding civilians to leave their houses under pain of being shot, leaving the roads clear for the military traffic.[35]

The original plan had been for the XD parties to make their way through Ghent and Bruges to Ostend, where they hoped to find a vessel to take them back to England. However, as the night drew on there were frequent stops both for military checkpoints and to take cover from German air raids, so it was just before dawn when they eventually arrived at Ostend, only to find the port abandoned with not a ship in sight. Their only alternative now was to carry on along the coast roads into France.

At 05:30 on Saturday, 18 May, the small convoy arrived at the port of Dunkirk where Arthur Stanford managed to find a train ferry that was willing to take him and his men across to Dover. Most of them had not eaten or washed for two days so, even though the ferry was already packed with Belgian refugees, the crew still ensured the Brits had a good hot meal and access to all the necessary facilities to help recover from their ordeal. Within a few hours they were entering Dover Harbour where the two groups split up. The sailors headed off to the local naval barracks, while the Royal Navy provided transport back to Milton Barracks, Gravesend for the KFRE team.

In London, a much-relieved Lord Hankey had received the welcome news about the Antwerp oil stocks from Ian Jacob in a phone call at 10:45 that morning. He was now relying on the French and Belgian forces to do a similar job with the stocks at Ostend and Zeebrugge. But, with the German panzers now advancing fast through France, the time would soon come when his thoughts would also have to turn to the question of the fate of oil stocks in French ports.[36]

Chapter 16

AFTERMATH

After a short but devastating campaign, the Netherlands officially surrendered to the Germans on 15 May 1940. That same day, in a note to Captain Pritchard at the War Office Directorate of Military Operations, Lt Col Clifford Brazier was able to report:

1. [...] the return of all the "B" Group (B1, B2, B3, B4, B5, and B6) in Rotterdam without casualty. They have completed all objectives on the South Side of the Maas. From Captain Goodwin's report [...] they were precluded from the objectives on the North Side right up to the time of withdrawal.
2. I have also to report the return of A1, A2, and A3. [Ymuiden] All the objectives of this group were attained. Only one Sapper is missing, 2075944. Spr. Perryman. W.C.*
3. The organisation and special training appears to have worked, and the information supplied invaluable.

    The methods used were a combination of all means envisaged, i.e., breaching by various means, mixing of heavy and light oils and ignition by primer, blanket, or Very cartridge.

    No information has been received from the Group D1 and D2 [Antwerp].

    I should like to call attention to the initiative and resource of Capt. Keeble, R.E., and Capt. Goodwin, R.E. who, in the face of

* It is strange that there is no mention of the 'missing' Sapper Perryman in Captain Keeble's report, nor does Clifford Brazier make any mention of him, or anyone, being missing from the Ymuiden operation in his memoirs. Likewise, although not present himself at Ymuiden, Bernard Buxton knew the whole story of the operation but makes no mention in his memoirs of anyone going missing. Perryman was certainly listed as being a member of 'A2' Section of the Ymuiden XD party, but his disappearance remains a mystery.

> almost constant enemy air raids carried out their objectives and effected a safe withdrawal. The other section Officers all acted with determination and enthusiasm ...[1]

Despite the lack of any firm information, at that morning's meeting of the War Cabinet the First Lord of the Admiralty, A.V. Alexander, felt able to tell his colleagues 'that all oil stocks at Amsterdam had been destroyed and five-sixths of the total (460,000 tons) at Rotterdam'.[2] It was another ten days before Alexander could provide the War Cabinet with more detailed report of the demolition operations in Holland, the results of which had accounted for:

> AMSTERDAM
> 80,000 tons of oil
>
> ROTTERDAM
> (South Bank) 365,000 tons of oil.
> (North Bank) 41,000 tons of oil (Approx.) – tanks not destroyed by demolition parties but subsequently seen ablaze.
>
> YMUIDEN
> Coast defence guns destroyed.
> Main Power House for North and Middle Lock blown up.
> Two Machinery Houses to North Lock blown up.
> One Machinery House to Middle Lock blown up.
> Entrance to small lock blocked by two tugs and stone ballast emptied between double gates of lock.
> South Channel blocked by one merchant ship and [one] trawler.
> Main entrance to harbour between breakwaters blocked with one 11,000-ton merchant ship and one trawler.
> Main control board of Ironworks blown up and structural damage done.
> Merchant ship sunk alongside the ironwork quay.
> One small and one medium floating dock sunk in fish harbour.
>
> The following miscellaneous craft sunk :-
> Floating Crane
> 2 Harbour Launches
> 4 motor drifters
> 2 tugs
> I large coal lighter
> 1 dredger
> Several hoppers

The HOOK
Coast Defence Guns destroyed.
Railway station points and rolling stock blown up.

All charges placed for destruction of quays, cranes, etc. but order received by telephone on no account to fire them.
No ships available.
Northern arm of breakwater breached by torpedo.[3]

The combined RN/RE XD parties A and B had obviously achieved excellent results. However, the all-RN Party C had been far less successful with its mission at Flushing, although the results of German bombing there had achieved some of its targets for them.

The combined RN/RE Party D Antwerp mission had been the longest of the four XD operations. What had been planned as a twenty-four-hour operation had lasted for almost nine days, but it had achieved almost all its objectives. As well as the sinking of the four floating cranes and subsequent blocking of the lock gates, Commander Stanford was able to claim credit in his report, submitted on 20 May, for overseeing the evacuation of a large number of vessels from the port, including twenty-six ocean-going merchant ships, about fifty tugs, almost all the port's dredgers and floating salvage gear, most of the grain elevators, 90 per cent of the motorised oil barges and about 600 other barges. But probably, and most importantly, he was able to claim the successful destruction of approximately 150,000 tons of oil and fuel, thus denying its use to the Germans.[4]

Brazier was justly pleased with his men's efforts and in a note accompanying his report to Captain Pritchard at the War Office, he made clear that he was up for more: 'Am quite proud of the fact we were entrusted with the job and "holed-out". What about another?'[5] Little did he realise just how soon his wishes would be granted.

Chapter 17

EPILOGUE

Party D was the last of the KFRE XD parties to return from their missions. When they arrived back at Milton Barracks, they found that 140 of their comrades, led by Captain Bernard Buxton, had been rushed to Wellington Barracks, in London, the previous day to assist the Grenadier Guards with erecting defences around Westminster. For the next two days, the London detachment was engaged in building pillboxes in the area, including Admiralty Arch and Downing Street. They were joined on the evening of Saturday, 18 May by Captain 'Peter' Keeble, who had been resting after leading the KFRE Hook of Holland XD mission. As the senior captain, Keeble took over command of the KFRE London detachment from Buxton. He barely had time to take stock of his new responsibilities before the whole detachment was recalled to Milton Barracks on Sunday, 18 May.[1]

Earlier that week, command of the KFRE had been transferred from Lt Col Brazier to Captain Dawson. Brazier had now been tasked with forming a corps troop of Engineers which would eventually see the KFRE merge with other RE units. However, his work had taken on a new urgency as the military situation in France was deteriorating fast. Peter Keeble was immediately despatched across the Channel to reconnoitre XD objectives in northern France. Meanwhile, all those that had been trained for or taken part in the operations in Holland and Belgium were formed into a Field Company RE as part of Brazier's new Kent Corps Troop. The new company immediately began preparing for XD operations in France, while the rest of the KFRE continued with their more mundane but still very important duties manning searchlights and preparing defences around the Thames Estuary shorelines, until they, too, were merged into the new corps troop.

The XD operations in France and similar operations undertaken by some of the same men in other theatres later in the war, fall outside the scope of this book, but suffice to say they included many acts of bravery and adventure to which I hope to do full justice in the future.

Appendix I

LETTERS FROM SIR ALEC CADOGAN TO HM AMBASSADOR AT BRUSSELS AND HM MINISTER AT THE HAGUE, 12 OCTOBER 1939

Immediate
SECRET 12th October, 1939.
His Excellency, The Right Honourable
Sir R. Clive, G.C.M.G.

Although our attempts to start Staff conversations with the Belgian Government on purely military matters have not so far been successful, there is a cognate question which it is important that we should, if possible, discuss with them at the earliest opportunity, namely, the possibility of denying to the enemy, or obtaining for our own use, certain military and economic resources in Belgium in the event of Belgium being invaded and subsequently overrun by Germany.

2. We take it as axiomatic that Belgium would resist invasion by Germany and call for our assistance, and we assume that if the country were overrun the Belgian Government would, as in the last war, remove themselves and continue the struggle in company with their allies. That being so, it would be to the interest of the Belgian Government no less than of ourselves that they should leave behind as little as possible in the way of military and economic resources which would be of value to Germany in the conduct of the war.

3. It is clear that if such resources are to be either removed or destroyed, this cannot be effectively improvised at the last moment, and the ideal source would be for the two Governments to concert in advance such arrangements as might be necessary to ensure this end.

4. It is on the possibility of making an approach to the Belgian Government in this sense that we wish to consult you and to receive from you at the earliest possible date an expression of your view.

5. We are aware that the Belgian Government are anxious to avoid doing anything that might come to the ears of the German Government, and be regarded by them as a hostile act. We realise, therefore, that it is unlikely that the Belgian Government would agree to the joint preparation of plans for destruction. It might, however, be possible for you discreetly to draw their attention to the problem presented by the danger of these assets falling into German hands in event of a German attack. You could suggest that the Belgian Government might consider, if they had not already done so, the possibility of themselves preparing plans to destroy such assets, or to remove at short notice such of then as might be transportable to places of greater safety in the United Kingdom or France. You might add that His Majesty's Government would welcome such action on the part of the Belgian government, and would for their part gladly give all the assistance in their power to facilitate the removal, and, where removable is impossible, the destruction of such assets.

6. We should be glad to know what you think of this. In order that you may be in a position to judge of the character of the problem, I send you the following details of some of the chief items which we have in mind.

<u>**Gold Reserve and negotiable securities**</u>

7. We believe that the Belgian Government have already removed part of their gold reserve to a place of safety, but a substantial proportion still remains. The evacuation of this bullion would be a considerable problem if it had to be undertaken in a hurry when transport facilities were disorganized. Do you think you could suggest to the Belgian Government the desirability, as a measure of precaution, of getting the gold away in good time.

8. If the Belgian Government are prepared to discuss the matter of gold, perhaps you could take the opportunity to raise with them also the question of negotiable securities, e.g. foreign investments in the shape of bearer bonds and stocks, particularly dollar securities. It is important that these valuable assets should not fall into the hands of Germany, but we are given to understand that their number in Belgium

is not very large. They are for the most part not held in the Central Bank, but are probably scattered among banks and private institutions, a fact which may present difficulties. Even if the Belgian Government are to consider moving gold or securities out of the country in advance of the emergency, they should at any rate prepare a plan for doing so at the first possible moment when the German intention to invade becomes clear. We should be prepared to co-operate if desired. And if in the last resort they should be caught without a plan, we hope that you will use your utmost endeavour to induce them to send out of the country as much as possible of the gold and securities that still remain there.

9. We are in touch with the Treasury and Bank of England on the whole question, but we should be glad to receive your view.

Stocks of Raw Materials

10. The most important of these is oil. Other important commodities are copper, tin, zinc, cobalt, nickel, uranium, iron and steel and ferro alloys, manganese, molybdenum, wolfram, chrome, antimony, industrial diamonds, flax (including flax seeds).

11. We understand that action is already in hand to move stocks of copper and cobalt from Belgium, at the initiative of the Belgian Manager of the Union Minière. The Ministry of Economic Warfare are also proposing to make a discreet approach to certain other British firms having interests in Belgium, and to invite them to take what action they can to reduce stocks of raw materials in Belgium.

12. It is desirable that stocks should be reduced to a minimum since, except in the case of oil, little can be done at the last minute in the way of destruction. Stocks of oil could, however, be destroyed or run off, and it is most important that all possible steps should be taken to prevent them falling into the hands of the enemy. Do you think that the Belgian Government have this in mind, and that they have plans for the destruction of their oil stocks in event of their having to retreat before the enemy? Do you think that an approach could be made to the Belgian Government urging that they should prepare the necessary plans for destruction, if they have not already done so?

13. If no such approach proves to be possible in present circumstances, it is important that you should, in the event of an invasion of Belgium, take steps to ensure that the Belgian Government destroy or otherwise dispose of their stocks of oil to prevent their failing into German hands, and you should bear this in mind.

14. I would add for your own information that if the Belgians fail to destroy their own stocks of oil, we should have to take such steps as

were open to us to destroy them in our own interests, and alternative plans for this are being prepared.

Transportation

15. The most important item from this point of view is shipping, including oil tankers, cargo ships, salvage vessels, tugs, dredgers, and river barges.

16. We believe that the Belgians are fully alive to the need of removing what they can of their mobile shipping when the time comes, and it is of the greatest importance that sea-going ships, especially tankers, should be safely removed from Belgian ports to ports in the United Kingdom or France at an early stage of an emergency.

I7. It is doubtful whether anything can be done in way of salvage or demolition of tugs, barges or dredgers without the active co-operation of the Belgian Government; but we consider that their removal or destruction, preferably the former would be a matter of importance.

18. Do you think that these are matters which could be usefully raised with the Belgian Government now? If nothing can be said to them now, it would, of course, be essential, in the event of invasion, that you should at once press on them the vital necessity of taking action to remove to a safe place the vessels referred to above, and you should bear this in mind.

Locomotives and Rolling Stock.

19. The most important item here is the Belgian heavy locomotives. We think, however, that the question of the removal or destruction of rolling stock is a matter which could more conveniently be dealt with by the French and we are discussing the question with the French military representatives.

Mechanical Transport

20. The Belgian Government will no doubt be alive to the importance of destroying mechanical transport so as to prevent it falling into the hands of the enemy. You may think it possible to draw their attention to this now, but in any event the point should be strongly impressed upon them in the event of invasion. Your Military Attaché is being instructed accordingly.

Machine Tools

21. We are considering an approach to Belgian industrial interests with a view to the preparation of a plan for the removal or destruction of particular machine tools in the event of emergency. Should an

emergency arise you should urge the Belgian Government to take steps to secure their destruction.

Aerodrome facilities

22. The Air Ministry are instructing your Air Attaché, in the event of invasion, to impress on the Belgian air authorities the importance or preventing aerodrome facilities from falling into the hands of the enemy.

Aircraft and aircraft personnel

23. The Air Ministry will also arrange through your Air Attaché for Belgian civil aircraft and air personnel to be flown out in the event of invasion.

Military Aircraft

24. The Air Ministry are making arrangements through your Air Attaché; for the routing and reception of military aircraft which might leave Belgium in the event of invasion.

Dock and Harbour facilities

25. There remains the important and very delicate question of the denial to the enemy of dock and harbour facilities. So long as the Belgian forces, with their allies, were holding up the enemy, it would probably be desirable that such facilities should be kept open for the use of the former. If, however, the Belgians and the Allies were driven back the moment would come when it would be essential that the necessary demolitions should be undertaken so that the use of these dock and harbour facilities should be denied to the enemy.

26. Do you think that the Belgian Government have any plan for carrying out such demolitions and do you think that this is a matter on which any approach could be made to them now?

27. For your own information, the following are the chief operations which we should consider essential: -

(i) The blocking of Ostend and Zeebrugge and the carrying out of local demolitions.

(ii) The destruction of dock and port facilities at Ghent and Bruges.

(iii) The destruction of port facilities at Antwerp.

28. I would add, also for your own information, that if the Belgian Government failed to carry out such demolitions, we should be bound to take such steps as were open to us to carry them out ourselves, and the necessary plans have been prepared. See Kirkpatrick's secret letter to you of September 28th, 1939.

General

29. You will see that in some of the above cases it may be possible for us to take action now, or to lay plans in advance without the necessity of consultation with the Belgian Government, but in certain other cases the co-operation of the Belgian Government is essential if the best results are to be ensured.

30. The point on which we want your advice as soon as possible is whether you think any approach can be made to the Belgian Government at all at present, and if so in what form, and in respect of what subjects. Subject to the following sentence, you should not make any approach to the Belgian Government pending further instructions. Whether or not any approach can be made now, it is essential, however, that if any sudden emergency arises and Belgium is invaded, you should approach the Belgian Government immediately without waiting for instructions, and urge them to take every step in their power to deny to the enemy all the various facilities and resources referred to above. The removal of the gold reserve and negotiable securities, and the destruction of oil supplies are of especial importance. You should also inform them that we would be prepared to assist them to the best of our ability, and you should have in mind that, in the last resort, we should be bound to act in defence of our vital interests in the case of dock and harbour facilities and oil supplies. In that event the co-operation of the Belgian authorities would be of the utmost value. Your Service Attachés will receive more detailed information than can be given in this letter and more precise instructions as to the results we desire to secure.[1]

IMMEDIATE 12th October, 1939
SECRET

Sir N. Bland, K.C.V.O., C.M.G., etc., etc., etc.

As you will see from the enclosed copies of correspondence with Ismay of the Committee of Imperial Defence, the question of staff talks with the Dutch has been under consideration.

2. The problem of staff talks with the Belgians has also been carefully considered during the last few weeks, and Clive has had some secret conversations with Spaak. I enclose two telegrams from him which show how the matter stands. As we expected, the Belgian Government refused to take part in any kind of official staff conversations, though we still have some hope that part at any rate of our object may be achieved, either through the intermediary of the Military Attaché or by using some other less orthodox channel.

3. We assume that a request from us for the opening of official staff conversations with the Netherlands Government would not be favourably received. On the other hand, it may be that there is a chance something might be done discreetly through the Service Attachés or some other unobtrusive channel. We are in some doubt as to the best line of approach and we should be grateful to have your views.

4. Apart from the question of military conversations properly so-called, there is a cognate question which it is important that we should, if possible, discuss with the Netherlands authorities at the earliest opportunity, namely the possibility of denying to the enemy or obtaining for our own use, certain military and economic resources in Holland in the event of Holland being invaded and subsequently overrun by Germany.

5. We assume that the Netherlands would resist invasion by Germany. We should also suppose (though on this point we should be glad of your views) that if the country were overrun the Netherlands Government would remove themselves and continue the struggle from outside in company with the Allies. If that were so it would be to the interest of the Netherlands Government no less than of ourselves, that they should leave behind them as little as possible in the way of military and economic resources which would be of value to Germany in the conduct of the war.

6. It is clear that if such resources are to be either removed or destroyed, this cannot be effectively improvised at the last moment, and the ideal course would be for the two Governments to concert in advance such arrangements as might be necessary to secure this end.

7. It is on the possibility of making an approach to the Netherlands Government in this sense that we wish to consult you and to receive from you at the earliest possible date an expression of your views.

8. We are aware that the Netherlands Government are anxious to avoid doing anything that might come to the ears of the German Government, and be regarded by them as a hostile act. We realise, therefore, that it is unlikely that the Netherlands Government would agree to the joint preparation of plans for destruction. It might, however, be possible for you discreetly to draw their attention to the problem presented by the danger of these assets falling into German hands in the event of a German attack. You could suggest that the Netherlands Government might consider, if they had not already done so, the possibility of themselves preparing plans to destroy such assets, or to remove at short notice such of them as might be transportable to places of greater safety in the United Kingdom and France. You might add that His Majesty's Government would welcome such action on the

part of the Netherlands Government, and would for their part gladly give all assistance the in their power to facilitate the removal, and, where removal is impossible, the destruction of such assets.

9. We should be glad to know what you think of this suggestion. In order that you may be in a position to judge of the character of the problem I send you following details of some or the chief items which we have in mind.

Gold Reserve and negotiable securities

10. We believe the Netherlands Government have already removed part of their gold reserve to a place of safety, but a substantial proportion still remains. The evacuation of this bullion would be a considerable problem if it had to be undertaken in a hurry when transport facilities were dis-organised. Do you think you could suggest to the Netherlands Government the desirability, as a measure of precaution, of getting this gold away in good time?

11. If the Netherlands Government are prepared to discuss the matter of gold, perhaps you could take the opportunity to raise with them also the question of negotiable securities, e.g. foreign investments in the shape of bearer bonds and stocks, particularly dollar securities. It is important that these valuable assets, of which the Dutch are believed to have large holdings, should not fail into the hands of Germany. They are, for the most part, not held in the Central Bank, but are probably scattered among banks and private institutions, a fact which may present difficulties. Even if the Netherlands Government are unwilling to consider moving gold or securities out of the country in advance of the emergency, they should at any rate prepare a plan for doing at the first possible moment when the German intention to invade becomes clear. We should be prepared to cooperate if desired. And if in the last resort they should be caught without a plan, we hope that you will use your utmost endeavour to induce them to send out of the country as much as possible of the gold and securities that still remain there.

12. We are in touch with the Treasury and Bank of England on the whole question, but we should be glad to receive your views. For your own information, the Governor of the Bank of England is sending over an official on an informal visit to take soundings with his opposite number in Holland as to whether the Dutch will not take the necessary action. He is not optimistic as to the result of this overture. It may result in a rebuff, or the Governor of the Bank of Holland may at once approach his Government, in which case we might hear something from them. The Governor is not at all hopeful about getting the gold away before an emergency. This could not be done without

the fact being known, and he does not believe that the Netherlands Government would allow the Bank to take action. The point has been stressed to him that if the gold cannot be got away before an emergency, there should at least be an emergency plan, so that even if only a few hours were available the gold could be moved. This at least would be the second-best arrangement, but the best thing would be to get the gold away before an emergency arises. The securities, which are private property, would, of course, be harder to deal with than the gold which is Government property; and the Governor seems to think it unlikely that the Netherlands Government would be willing to move them until the last moment.

Stocks of Raw Materials

13. The most important of these is oil. Other important commodities are copper, tin, cobalt, nickel, iron and steel and ferro alloys, manganese, molybdenum, wolfram, antimony, industrial diamonds, and flax (including flax seeds).

14. So far as oil is concerned, of which very large stocks are held in Holland, the authorities here will do what they can, through various trade channels, to secure a decrease in the stocks held by the Royal Dutch Petroleum Company, by reducing future shipments. It is unlikely that the Dutch will agree to reduce stocks by sending oil out of the country.

15. So far as other commodities are concerned, the Ministry of Economic Warfare are proposing to make a discreet approach to certain British firms having commercial interests in Holland, and to invite them to take what action they can to reduce stocks of raw materials held in the Netherlands.

16. It is desirable that stocks should be reduced to a minimum since, except in the case of oil, little can be done at the last minute in the way of destruction. Stocks of oil could, however, be destroyed or run off, and it is most important that all possible steps should be taken to prevent them falling into the hands of the enemy. Do you think that the Netherlands Government have this in mind, and that they have plans for the destruction of their oil stocks in the event of their having to retreat before the enemy? Do you think that an approach could be made to the Netherlands Government urging that they should prepare the necessary plans for destruction, if they have not already done so?

17. If no such approach proves to be possible in present circumstances, it is important that you should, in the event of an invasion of Holland, take steps to secure that the Netherlands Government destroy or

otherwise dispose of their stocks of oil to prevent their falling into German hands, and you should bear this in mind.

18. I would add for your own information that if the Dutch should fail to destroy their own stocks of oil, we should have to take such steps as were open to us to destroy them in our own interests, and alternative plans for this are being prepared.

Transportation

19. The most important item from this point of view is shipping, including oil tankers, cargo ships, salvage vessels, tugs, dredgers, and river barges.

20. We believe that the Dutch are fully alive to the need of removing what they can of their mobile shipping when time comes, and the Board of Trade have already been approached by a representative of a Dutch shipowner who asked whether 30 ships could be placed in British ports. The Board of Trade will do anything that is possible, through the British Oil Companies, to reduce the number of tankers lying in Dutch ports, and to examine other possible methods of ensuring that tankers would not fall into the hands of the enemy. It is, of course, of the greatest importance that sea-going shipping, especially tankers, should be safely removed from Dutch ports to ports In the United Kingdom or France at an early stage of an emergency. But obviously little can be done except in collaboration with the Netherlands Government.

21. It is also doubtful whether anything can be done in the way of salvage or demolition of tugs, barges or dredgers without the active co-operation of the Dutch Government; but we consider that their removal or destruction, preferably the former, would be a matter of importance.

22. Do you think that these are matters which could be usefully raised with the Netherlands Government now? If nothing can be said to them now, it would, of course, be essential in the event of invasion that you should at once press on them the vital necessity of taking action to remove to a safe place the vessels referred to above, and you should bear this in mind.

Rolling Stock and Mechanical Transport

23. The Netherlands Government will no doubt be alive to the importance of removing or destroying railway rolling stock and mechanical transport so as to prevent it failing into the hands of the enemy. You may think It possible to draw their attention to this now, but in any event the point should be strongly impressed upon them

in the event of invasion. Your Military Attaché is being instructed accordingly.

Machine Tools

24. We are considering an approach to Dutch Industrial interests with a view to the preparation of a plan for the removal or destruction of machine tools in the event of emergency. Should an emergency arise, you should urge the Netherlands Government to take steps to secure their destruction.

Aerodrome Facilities

25. The Air Ministry are instructing your Air Attaché, in the event of invasion, to impress on the Netherlands air authorities the importance of preventing aerodrome facilities from failing into the hands of the enemy.

Aircraft and aircraft personnel

26. The Air Ministry will also arrange through your Air Attaché for Dutch civil aircraft and aircraft personnel to be flown out in the event of invasion.

Warships and Military Aircraft

27. The Admiralty and Air Ministry are making arrangements through the Service Attachés, for the routing and reception of warships and military aircraft which might leave in the event of invasion

Warships under construction

28. It is important that the submarines either completed or construction in Holland should be salved or destroyed. Your Naval Attaché is being instructed, in the event of invasion, to impress upon the Dutch Naval authorities the importance of denying to the enemy the possession of these submarines and the use of such naval dockyard facilities as exist.

Dock and Harbour facilities

29. There remains the important and very delicate question of the denial to the enemy of dock and harbour facilities. So long as the Dutch forces with their allies were holding up the enemy, it would probably be desirable that such facilities should be kept open for the use of the former. If, however, the Dutch and the Allies were driven back the moment would come when it would be essential that the necessary

demolitions should be undertaken so that the use of these dock and harbour facilities should be denied to the enemy.

30. Do you think the Netherlands Government have any plan for carrying out such demolitions or that they would be willing that we should co-operate with them in carrying them out? Do you think that these are matters on which any approach could be made to them now?

31. For your own information, the chief operation which we have in mind is the destruction of port facilities at Amsterdam, Ymuiden, Rotterdam, Hook of Holland and Flushing, and the demolition of naval and dockyard facilities. We also think it desirable that coast defences, if any such exist, should be demolished.

32. I would add, also for your own information, that if the Netherlands Government failed to carry out such demolitions, we be bound to take such steps as were open to us to carry them out ourselves, and the necessary plans are being prepared.

General

33. You will see that in some of the above cases it may be possible for us to take action now, or to lay plans in advance without the necessity of consultation with the Netherlands Government, but in certain other cases the co-operation of the Netherlands Government is essential if the best results are to be secured.

34. The point on which we want your advice as soon as possible is whether you think any approach can be made to the Netherlands Government at all at present, and if so in what form and in respect of what subjects? Subject to the following sentence, you should not make any approach to the Netherlands Government pending further instructions. Whether or not any approach can be made now, it is essential, however, that if any sudden emergency arises and Holland is invaded, you should approach the Netherlands Government immediately without waiting for instructions, and urge them to take every step in their power to deny to the enemy all the various facilities and resources referred to above. The removal of the Gold Reserve and negotiable securities, and the destruction of oil supplies are of especial importance. You should also inform them that we should be prepared to assist them to the best of our ability, and you should have in mind that, in the last resort, we should be bound to act in defence of our vital interests in the case of dock and harbour facilities and oil supplies. In that event the co-operation of the Netherlands authorities would be of the utmost value. Your Service Attachés will receive more detailed information than can be given in this letter and more precise instructions as to the results we desire to secure.[2]

Appendix II

MYSTERY DIAMONDS

In Chapter 4 of this book, I detailed the secret intelligence gathering missions undertaken by RN captains to ports in Holland and Belgium in the Autumn of 1939. The mission to Rotterdam was undertaken by Captain Moody RN over the three days 21-23 October.

On 22 October 1939 Moody, accompanied by the Naval Attaché Captain Schofield RN, paid an unaccounted-for visit by train to Amsterdam, where they spent the whole day. The reason for this visit remains a mystery, as Moody's report makes no further mention of it. It could be that they were just checking out the oil storage facilities, indeed that was one of Moody's prime mission objectives, although it is odd that he gives no details of these in his report. However, another possibility I have considered is that, with Amsterdam being the centre of the international diamond trade, Moody may also have been contacting some of the city's diamond merchants. Many of these merchants were Jewish and would have been present at their offices working on a Sunday.

The reader may recall that the Joint Intelligence Committee, in their report to the Chiefs of Staff on 4 October, had included industrial diamonds amongst the list of financial assets that they considered should not be allowed to fall into enemy hands. The report estimated that there were 10,000 carats of industrial diamonds in Holland, plus a large quantity of gem diamonds. Industrial diamonds have the necessary physical characteristics to be effective in the manufacturing processes of a range of military-related equipment including aero engines, artillery, gyroscopes, tanks, torpedoes, and prisms and lenses for gun and bombsights. Given the circumstances it would seem reasonable to take advantage of an already secret mission for it to include making some contact with Amsterdam's senior diamond merchants. Of course, this is just pure speculation on my part, and as yet I have not come across any official documentation to back up my theory. However, there are aspects of the affair that I believe are worthy of further consideration.

Any such contact with the diamond merchants would be considered very sensitive and good reason for it to be kept secret and not mentioned in Moody's official written report. As Moody was working on the orders of Vice Admiral Binney and reporting back to him, it is certainly strange that an entire day out of only three he spent in Holland, was allowed to be dismissed with just one sentence in his report. Could it be that Binney had been asked by MI6 to include contacting the Amsterdam diamond merchants as part of Moody's mission? We will never know the answer to that question as MI6 records are not available to the public. However, as we shall see, MI6 were certainly involved.

Since being listed as part of the JIC report of 4 October, an official 'cloak of secrecy' seems to have been thrown over the whole matter of the Dutch diamonds. No mention of diamonds was made in Sir Alec Cadogan's despatch to the British Ambassador at The Hague Sir Nevil Bland on 12 October (see Appendix I), in which he outlines the various Dutch assets that could not be allowed to fall into German hands. Also, there is no mention of diamonds in any of Lord Hankey's extensive collection of Cabinet papers relating to the denial of the Dutch assets to the enemy.

However, despite the dearth of official documentation relating to any plans or preparations to mount one, it is certain that an operation to secure Amsterdam's stock of diamonds did take place. The first clue can be found in the War Cabinet's *Weekly Resumé of the Naval, Military and Air Situation* for 9-16 May. Under the heading 'Operations off the Dutch and Belgian Coasts', para. 4 includes: 'Three Dutch merchant vessels with bullion were safely escorted to the United Kingdom, but a small Dutch pilot vessel with some bullion on board was sunk between Rotterdam and the Hook. **Diamond stocks were also transferred to the United Kingdom** [author's emphasis] ...'[1]

Unfortunately, no further information is given regarding the circumstances of the transfer or how it was achieved.

Another clue can be found in the transcripts of an interview given in 1983 by Rear Admiral Colin Madden RN as part of the Imperial War Museum's 'Oral History' series. Madden's gallant actions as a lieutenant in the Naval XD Party A at Ymuiden have been recorded in Chapter 12. In addition to his part in the demolitions, Madden recalls in his interview:

I have a recollection that the next day, which was, I think, the Sunday [12 May], Commander Goodenough told me to go to Amsterdam with one or two army officers to make conduct with some Dutch who had some diamonds which the British wanted to get out of Holland for use in England. I think we were meant to bring the Dutchmen too. Anyhow, we set off in a car to Amsterdam where we eventually arrived, and it was very eerie, because there was certainly nothing moving in Amsterdam [...] There was nothing there [...], it was really very disturbing and certainly nothing that a naval officer was used to, but the army officers seemed to understand it all.

We found the address and we went to the door. The door was shut but it wasn't locked, and we went in. There were certainly no Dutchmen about. It was all, as I say, I can think of no other word, it was all very eerie and rather deathlike really, and certainly very quiet. But there were doors closing and we had a feeling we were being watched and looked at. We opened all the drawers and we saw there were piles of papers but there were certainly no diamonds. We shouted and banged and walked around, and tried to look, and if we saw a door, I believe we broke it down, but there was nothing the other end really. And finally, with a little bit more noise going on outside, we had a feeling the Germans were very, very close, we really weren't doing any good, so we decided that rather than remain around rather pointlessly and being captured or possibly, killed, the best thing to do was go back to [Ymuiden] to see if we could help there, which was, of course, our main job.

So we jumped in our car again and set off, driving very wildly towards [Ymuiden]. [...] I got back to my headquarters, saw Commander Goodenough, and told him that I was very sorry, but we had failed.[2]

Although Madden's mission to recover the diamonds failed, his recollections are proof that it had been pre-planned. The puzzling aspect of it is that Commander Goodenough, who was in command of the XD A Party and was the senior RN officer in Ymuiden at the time, and who gave Madden orders to go to Amsterdam, makes no mention of it at all in his official report.[3] Nor does he make any mention of a diamond recovery mission in his diary.[4]

Another mystery is the identity of the two 'army officers' who accompanied Madden into Amsterdam. Apart from the Royal Engineers XD party, whose officers would have been busy with their own operation, the only other British Army personnel recorded as being at Ymuiden on that Sunday were the members of General Heywood's Military Mission to Holland. They had arrived that day but, according to Goodenough's report, they immediately set off to The Hague. Of course, it could be that the two mystery officers arrived as members of that mission and were detailed to go to Amsterdam with Madden, but that is just my speculation as there are no apparent records of Heywood's mission in The National Archives to verify that.

Remarkably, Colin Madden recalled another incident involving diamonds from that same Sunday at Ymuiden. Later that evening he had been helping prepare the steamer SS *Dotterel* for the boarding of over 100 British refugees who were on their way to the port, including the ambassador and his staff. After personally escorting the ambassador on board that night, Madden went back down the gangway to continue the loading of the ship:

> … we finished loading, and she was just about to go, when two Dutchmen came up to me and said they had a very important box which must get to England and could they give it to me if they couldn't get onboard, because they understood the ship was full. And I said, "What is in the box – what is this box?" and they showed me a box. It was really, I should say, about two or three cigar boxes. And they said "Well, it's full of diamonds, actually", so I said "Oh" and I felt to myself that diamonds, at this stage of the performance, were about the best passport anybody could have, so I said to them, "Look, you better come with me, we'll go and see the captain [*Dotterel*'s Master, Captain Green], and have a look at your box". And so, duly, I went to the captain who was rather amazed at what was going on. He was just an old tramp steamer captain, a very super chap, actually, as it turned out. And we went into his cabin. We locked the door. We opened the box, and indeed, it was full of diamonds. There were some lovely diamonds, blue diamonds, and super diamonds. I often rather wished I'd kept one. I'm sure I could, but I didn't. The rest were industrial diamonds, […]. The ship, we heard later, got safely home with the ambassador, the diamonds and the Dutchmen. And, in fact, the diamonds and the Dutchmen were met when the ship arrived in England, and it was those diamonds […], amongst the others that were rescued, that were used for the war effort …[5]

Madden's account of the diamonds being taken on board the *Dotterel* was being recalled from memories of events over forty years in the past and, like his expedition into Amsterdam, no other mention of it can be found in any of the official reports of the Ymuiden mission. However, research by a merchant navy historian, Roy Martin appears to confirm that diamonds were taken aboard the *Dotterel*:

> On reaching the Hook of Holland the Master received instructions to proceed to the port of Ijmuiden to evacuate the British citizens. They reached Ijmuiden late that evening and berthed close to the lock gates, where the ship was prepared to receive 150 refugees who were to be

> housed in the cargo holds. The ship had no food for this number. At 1800 the Dotterel moved to another berth to embark her passengers, where she was repeatedly attacked by aircraft. The last refugees boarded at 0130 on 18 May and the ship sailed for Harwich. She was escorted into the port by a destroyer. **The passengers were disembarked and Captain Green delivered several packages of diamonds to the naval authorities** [author's emphasis].[6]

Further investigation over the internet has resulted in finding posts to various on-line forums made by Netherlands-based military historian, Darron Wadey. Darron has taken a great interest in, and obviously undertaken a lot of research on, the mysteries surrounding the securing of Amsterdam's diamond stocks in 1940 and in one post to *shipsnostalgia.com* forum on 7 March 2021, he identifies one of the mystery 'Dutchmen' who presented themselves and the box of diamonds to Colin Madden on the steps of the *Dotterel*:

> As for what *Dotterel* helped evacuate, it also took a sizeable portion of the industrial diamond stock held by J.K. Smit & Zonen, probably the largest merchant of same in Amsterdam. They were delivered to Captain Green, master of the *Dotterel* by Mr. Johan Smit, owner of the company. He was given typed orders by the Dutch army to report to the (British) Royal Navy senior officer in the harbour, Commander Goodenough, who was actually there to supervise demolition work. From there, he was directed to the *Dotterel*.
>
> Mr. Johan Smit was also offered safe passage on the *Dotterel* by the Dutch authorities, given his knowledge and expertise, but declined. Unbeknownst to him, his son, plus two others, were travelling in the opposite direction at the same time in *HMS Walpole* to collect as much as Amsterdam's industrial diamond stock as possible They arrived at dawn on 13 MAY, returning in the evening of the same day, with the remainder of J.K. Smit's stock, plus stocks from two other diamond merchants.[7]

Wadey's mention of the HMS *Walpole* mission throws more light on a story which was the subject of a book written by the journalist, David E. Walker and published in 1955 under the title *Adventure in Diamonds*.[8] Written just ten years after the end of the war, when much about it was still considered 'Top Secret', the book gives an account of an episode that took place over the Whitsun weekend of May 1940. With access to very little in the way of official documentation, Walker had to rely on the personal recollections of the few individuals involved who were willing to talk about the operation, some of whom required their anonymity to be preserved.

The three main characters that feature in the story are two civilians and a mysterious British Intelligence officer. The two civilians were both British-based employees of the Dutch company 'J.K. Smit en Zonen', one of the largest diamond merchants in the world. One of them was Jan Kors Smit, the son of the company's chairman, Johan J. Smit. In his book, Walker assigns the other civilian a false name, 'Walter Keyser', to protect the man's true identity. Darron Wadey's research has revealed this individual to be Willem Woltman, a Dutchman who had been living in England for several years working in J.K. Smit's London office. He lived with his wife and son in leafy Surrey and, with all his close relatives in Holland now deceased, had eventually taken British nationality.

In Walker's book, following the German invasion of the Netherlands on Friday, 10 May 1940, Jan Smit and 'Keyser' raise their concerns with the British authorities regarding the vulnerability of the stocks lying in various diamond company safes in Amsterdam. They are then contacted by a 'Major Dillon' from British Intelligence, with whom they agree a plan to salvage the diamonds before they can be seized by the Germans.

The three men are given passage on the RN destroyer HMS *Walpole,* which sailed from Harwich on the night of Sunday, 12 May and arrived at Ymuiden at dawn the following day. From Ymuiden the party travelled by car into Amsterdam, where they meet with Johan Smit who had delivered his own company's diamonds to the *Dotterel* the previous evening. Smit had now arranged for two more of the city's diamond merchants to follow his example and surrender their stocks to the British. The party retrieved the diamonds and then made their way back to the port. When they reached Ymuiden, they re-embarked on *Walpole,* which took them back to Harwich.[9]

The Admiralty War Diary confirms that 'WALPOLE left Ymuiden 2200/13 with diamonds'.[10] The Nore Command War Diary similarly states: 'May 13th ... A ~~destroyer~~ WALPOLE brought Amsterdam diamonds from Ymuiden'.[11] Apart from the general mention in the War Cabinet *Weekly Resumé,* these appear to be the only 'official' British records of this operation from the time it took place.

Walker's book was also turned into a highly fictionalised film, *Operation Amsterdam,* released in 1959, starring Peter Finch as Jan Smit, Alexander Knox as 'Walter Keyser', and Tony Britton as 'Major Dillon'.[12]

The true identity of the mysterious 'Major Dillon' was eventually revealed in Keith Jeffery's 2010 book, *MI6 – the History of the Secret Intelligence Service 1909-1949*. For his book, Jeffrey was granted 'unprecedented full and unrestricted access to the closed archive of the Service'. On page 386 Jeffrey writes about events surrounding the German invasion of Holland in May 1940: 'During the invasion Major Monty Chidson, the fluent Dutch-speaker who had briefly headed The Hague station in 1937, in one of D Sections few real successes managed to seize the bulk of Amsterdam's industrial diamond stocks (essential for machine tools) and, with the help of two Dutchmen, to bring them safely to England.[13]

A search for Chidson's name in The National Archives resulted in finding his personnel file from his time serving with the Special Operations Executive (SOE) later in the Second World War.[14] This file reveals that he was born in London in 1893; educated at Clifton College and the Royal Military Academy, Woolwich, and commissioned into the Royal Artillery in 1912. After two years' service with the Royal Garrison Artillery, he was seconded to the Royal Flying Corps in August 1914, where he passed a course at the Central Flying School and became a pilot in October 1914. He was shot down over France in 1915 but survived and was captured by the Germans. He was a Prisoner of War in Germany until March 1918, when he appears to have escaped into Holland and been interned by the Dutch authorities until March 1919. During his time in Holland, he was employed as a 'confidential typist' to a Committee of Enquiry which was investigating enemy atrocities against British PoWs. He also acted as ADC to the Senior British Officer of interned British Troops in Holland. In recognition of his services during his internment, Chidson was awarded the MBE in 1920.

After repatriation he worked in the Demobilisation Directorate at the War Office, before rejoining the Royal Artillery as Adjutant. From 1921 to 1924 Chidson was attached to the Military Intelligence Directorate at the War Office and eventually transferred to M.I.1 (a) – a sub-Section of Military Intelligence dealing with the distribution of intelligence records and reports. His last year there was spent as Liaison Officer to the various foreign Attachés based in London.

From September 1924 until December 1930, Chidson was Royal Artillery Adjutant at Gibraltar. After returning to Britain, he commanded an anti-aircraft gun battery until 1931. He appears to have then joined the Secret Intelligence Service (MI6) and been appointed PCO at The Hague in 1935, where he served until his recall to London in 1937.

In 1938 Chidson was promoted to the rank of lieutenant colonel, and when war broke out in September 1939 he was in charge of 'D' Section of MI6, which dealt with 'subversive activities' and was the forerunner of the SOE. His personnel file records that: 'In May 1940, after Germany invaded the Low Countries, he was sent on a special mission to Amsterdam and in recognition of the success of this mission, which was naturally carried out at considerable personal risk, he was awarded the D.S.O. [Distinguished Service Order].'[15]

A further search of the National Archives resulted in finding the recommendation for Chidson's DSO:

> On May 12 information reached us that an extremely important collection of industrial diamonds were located in AMSTERDAM.
>
> Despite the fact that this Officer is on the German Black List, he insisted on going over himself.
>
> He proceeded to AMSTERDAM where he remained for some 24 hours, during which time there was considerable street fighting and Fifth Column activity in the town. He brought out the whole of the industrial Diamond stock and thus prevented the Germans from obtaining an extremely important source of industrial activity.
>
> His action would by itself have won a recommendation for an award but considered in the light of the certainty of his fate if caught by the Gestapo, he displayed courage of a very high order.[16]

Chidson's DSO award was announced in the *London Gazette* on 20 December 1940.[17]

It is interesting to note that no mention of Chidson's civilian accomplices is made in any of the official records, and Montague Chidson himself passed away in 1957 without ever publicly revealing either his role or theirs in this extraordinary operation. Indeed, although his identity was known to David Walker (probably from his contacts in the War Office), he refused to offer the journalist any information for his book and demanded that his name be kept secret.

Pre-owned copies of David Walker's book *Adventure in Diamonds* can still be found for sale on various internet sites, as can DVD copies of the film *Operation Amsterdam*, both of which I can recommend for any readers interested. Although the latter, as I have said, is a highly fictionalised account of the story, it is still an entertaining watch. Also worth a look is the following website, which includes a major contribution about the Amsterdam diamond saga from Darron Wadey: http://vandwdestroyerassociation.org.uk/HMS_Walpole/diamonds.html.

Appendix III

DECORATIONS AND AWARDS

Many of the Royal Navy and Army personnel involved in the various 'XD' missions were later recognised for their actions during the operations.

Royal Navy[1,2]

Party A – Ymuiden and Amsterdam

'This was a very important Operation carried out with complete efficiency.'

Distinguished Service Order DSO

Commander M.G. Goodenough RN

Distinguished Service Cross (DSC)

Lieutenant C. Madden R.N.

Distinguished Service Medal (DSM)

Chief Petty Officer F. Parry
Petty Officer R.J. Fleming
Leading Seaman W.C. Sutton
Able Seaman T.E. Clery
Able Seaman S. Pendleton
Signalman G.H.J. Gill

Mention in Dispatches

Lieutenant C.R.G. Wilkinson RN
Petty Officer J.C. Blackwell
Able Seaman O. Keegan
Able Seaman W. Collins

Party B – Hook of Holland

'A small party. Whittle was himself badly bombed. The work was well carried out in considerable danger and difficulty.'

Distinguished Service Cross (DSC)

Lieutenant J.W. Whittle RNVR

Distinguished Service Medal (DSM)

Petty Officer A.E. Evans

Leading Seaman R. Lea

Mention in Dispatches

Midshipman C.B.R. Osbourne RNVR

Mention in Dispatches (Posthumous)

Commander J.A. Corrie Hill

Party C – Flushing

'A fairly small party, frequently and heavily bombed. They had not a great deal to do but they did everything required with great thoroughness and despatch in a very difficult and dangerous situation.'

Distinguished Service Cross (DSC)

Commander P.G.L. Cazalet RN

Distinguished Service Medal (DSM)

Petty Officer W.E. Sampson

Mention in Dispatches

Sub-Lieutenant J.W. Patterson RNVR

Ordinary Signalman F. Inman

Party D – Antwerp

'This was a small party and not bombed. It was entirely successful in its task, which was carried out with much tact in a very delicate diplomatic situation.'

Distinguished Service Cross (DSC)

Commander A.C. Stanford RN

Distinguished Service Medal (DSM)

Chief Petty Officer S.C. Cooke

Mention in Dispatches
Lieutenant N.J.K. Cadzow RNVR
Leading Seaman R.R.W. Morris
Able Seaman F. Lawson

Army (Royal Engineers)

The question of awards and decorations to the sappers of the Kent (Fortress) Royal Engineers who took part in their three 'XD' operations appears to have been quite contentious for some inexplicable reason. Whilst the awards recommended to the RN personnel on the same missions were promptly approved by the Admiralty and then announced on 27 July 1940, the comparatively small number of recommendations made by Lt Col Brazier for his men were still under scrutiny by the War Office at that time.

Brazier's recommendations (which included those for the XD operations in France in June) concerned awards to just six individuals (three officers for Military Crosses and three other ranks for Military Medals). By October 1940, his recommendations had still not been approved, and the situation was causing great resentment amongst his men. On 17 October Brazier wrote to Lt Col Richard Gale at the Planning Section of the General Staff at the War Office, to whom he had submitted his recommendations back on 2 July, expressing his frustrations:

> At the conclusion of our X.D. Operations (Amsterdam to Bay of Biscay) I submitted recommendations for the reward of 3 Officers and 4 Other Ranks, can you tell me whether they are likely to receive recognition?
>
> A small band of men destroyed 2 million tons of oil, the success of which was entirely due to the courage and initiative of the young men who carried out the tasks.
>
> Since then many awards have been published for the Naval personnel who took them across and did similar demolition at the ports. The oil destruction was exclusively a Sapper affair, led by R.E. Officers and carried out by Sappers. This has been noted and commented upon with the result that those who took part regard themselves as a sort of Cinderella of the project.
>
> It seems a great pity that some recognition was not given at the time – as matters stand, they probably think they have a poor C.O. who is slow to recognise a job well done.
>
> When you get to my time of life medals do not mean much, but to a young soldier, and the rest of the Regiment, they count for a lot. Never overlook the fact that they may have the same job again.

> I am aware that the distribution of awards must be strictly limited, but why give them all to the Naval personnel?
>
> Presumably the destruction of 2 million tons of oil, many extensive refineries and kindred plants was an important contribution to our war effort and was carried out with little loss to the state.[3]

Little blame could be placed on Lt Col Gale's shoulders for the delays as he had forwarded on Brazier's recommendations to his superiors at the Directorate of Military Operations and Plans as early as 5 July with this accompanying note:

> Attached are recommendations for awards put forward by the Officer Commanding the "X.D." R.E. demolition parties.
>
> As you are aware these parties have had to act independently sometimes carrying out their work when everybody else is either being evacuated or has actually left […]. The Officers and N.C.Os. knew that the arrangements for their own withdrawal had to be left to chance; sometimes it was possible to get them away in Naval ships but as often as not they were thrown on their own resources and had to make their way back to England as best they could. There is, I understand, an agreed scale of awards based on so many per 100 or 200. For the above reasons I think these parties should be considered on a different basis and each case judged on its own merits. It is difficult to write up their exploits because there is rarely anybody present to see their work but the Admiralty have spoken very highly of these Engineer units of ours and Captain Hermon-Hodge [RN] has on more than one occasion mentioned particular individuals by name.
>
> I have not included Lt.-Colonel Brazier's name in this list, but I think some form of award should be given to him for it is unquestionably due to his organisation and to the spirit he has infused into his units that the exploits for which the company has become famous have been possible.[4]

From the myriad of correspondence relating to the matter, Brazier's recommendations appear to 'bounce' back and forth between various military commands and War Office departments and even involved one of the Army's most senior officers in the person of the Vice Chief of the Imperial General Staff, Lt Gen Sir Robert Haining, who took the matter up with the Military Secretary at the War Office, Maj Gen Andrew Floyer-Acland, in a note written on 22 October:

> […] My attention has been drawn to the fact that many citations have appeared in "The Times" for the Royal Naval personnel, who took these Royal Engineers over, "for saving valuable fuel stocks falling into enemy

> hands", etc. The R.E. sections went from ten to sixty miles inland to carry out their objectives in the face of the enemy and rarely saw any R.N. personnel after they had been dumped on the quay.[5]

Floyer-Acland's response was typically bureaucratic:

> I will, of course, do all I can to fit these nominees into our very small balances of available awards. But I am afraid I must ask for some more detailed account of the actions for which they are under recommendation – i.e. dates, places, and nature of meritorious work done - & an explanation of the award proposal eg. D.S.O., MC, DCM or MM, or OBE, MBE or Promotion. Would you get someone to do this.[6]

Floyer-Acland seemed to be completely unaware that the information he was requesting had already been reported in Clifford Brazier's initial submission back in early July, and which Lt Gen Haining pointed out was still being held under consideration by the War Office Branch M.S.3. This was the Section responsible for medals and gallantry awards, for which the Military Secretary was himself responsible.[7]

The continued delay did have one redeeming factor: it allowed time for some further scrutiny of the KFRE XD operations, which resulted in Brazier's recommendation for Military Crosses for three of his officers being upgraded to the Distinguished Service Order (DSO).

In an appendix to his father's book, Jock Brazier claims that this upgrade was down to Winston Churchill who, having read all the reports on the XD operations, 'put a pen through' the award citations, 'deleted MC, and wrote DSO through them'.[8] Although Jock Brazier cites The National Archives as evidence for this claim he does not quote any file reference for it, and I have been unable to find it myself. However, I have found a document in The National Archives, annotated on 31 October by Maj Gen Floyer-Acland, in which it appears that the Military Secretary has crossed out the MCs, written in 'DSO' in their place: 'I spoke to CIGS [Chief of the Imperial General Staff – General Sir John Dill] re: above [Award recommendations]. He agrees with me that all these recommendations are outstanding & that awards should be made in accordance with **my** [author's emphasis] amendments.'[9]

On 5 November the recommendations for the KFRE awards were finally submitted to the king, to which His Majesty assigned his approval two days later.[10]

The awards approved included (there were other KFRE awards approved that related solely to their later operations in France which fall outside the scope of this book, hence the actions quoted below also omit those references pertaining solely to those French operations):

An Additional Officer of the Military Division of the Most Excellent Order of the British Empire (O.B.E.)

Major (Brevet Lieutenant-Colonel) Clifford Claude Hendy Brazier, M.B.E., M.I.Mech.E., A.M.I.E.E., Royal Engineers.[11]

'As Commanding Officer of the Kent (Fortress) Royal Engineers, Lt.-Colonel C.C.H. Brazier, M.B.E., R.E., was responsible for the extensive demolitions of oil supplies in Holland and Northern France. The success of all these operations was unquestionably due to his organising ability, resource and skill. In all cases his men had to have access to installations beforehand which the local authorities were very loath to allow. So complete and well thought out were his plans that [even] when the Germans were actually in occupation of the areas in question his schemes were carried through in every detail resulting in the destruction of installations containing approximately two million tons of fuel, [...]

The unit under his command has had to work under extremely hazardous conditions, nearly always isolated in small parties, in areas occupied by the enemy and unsupported by any other troops. The high standard of both discipline and training which has enabled them to achieve success is due to the exceptional qualities both as leader and trainer that Lt.-Colonel Brazier has consistently displayed.'[12]

The Distinguished Service Order (D.S.O.)

Captain Robert Keeble, Royal Engineers.

'Captain Keeble commanded a Royal Engineer demolition party consisting of two officers and thirty other ranks unsupported by other troops, who carried out large scale demolitions during the period 8th – 12th May, in the Amsterdam area. He proceeded to the eastern extremity of the installations and in the face of the enemy personally fired the most difficult plant. He then withdrew his party through ten miles of country in German occupation, succeeded in making his way across the greater part of the North Sea in a small boat, and effected a rendezvous with one of H.M. ships without loss.

[...].'[13]

Captain Thomas Frederick Goodwin, Royal Engineers.

'Captain Goodwin commanded a Royal Engineer demolition party consisting of 6 officers and 70 other ranks unsupported by other troops who on 13th May carried out the destruction of oil plants in and near Rotterdam when that town and part of the oil installations were in German occupation. The execution of the demolitions entailed opening oil tanks, firing the petrol and oil contained therein, and destroying plant with high explosives. The success of the demolition was very largely due to the initiative, courage, and leadership of Captain Goodwin.

Having completed the demolition, Captain Goodwin successfully withdrew his party through twenty miles of country in German occupation, and succeeded in effecting a rendezvous with one of H.M. ships without loss. […].'[14]

The Military Medal (M.M.)

Lance-Corporal Alfred Richard Blake, Royal Engineers.

'Lance-Corporal Blake was in charge of one of the demolition parties which, during the period between 10th May and 14th May 1940 was charged with destroying Dutch oil installations at Rotterdam. He showed great courage and calm leadership during the frequent bombing attacks and in the street fighting he set an excellent example to the younger members of the party. […].'[15]

All the KFRE awards were officially announced in *The London Gazette* on 29 November 1940.[16]

NOTES

Chapter 1

1 https://en.wikipedia.org/wiki/Northfleet
2 K. McCoverin, 'Thomas Bevan: Cement Giant', *Northfleet History Group Magazine*, no. 15 (Winter), 2016
3 www.iwm.org.uk/memorials/item/memorial/151
4 www.cementkilns.co.uk/cement_kiln_bevans.html
5 Brazier, *Operation XD* (jacket notes)
6 Families in British India Society – Military Records (https://fibis.ourarchives.online/bin/aps_detail.php?id=1870343)
7 *The London Gazette*, Dec. 1916, p. 11748
8 British Library (link to), *Indian Army Reserve of Officers Applications*, (www.researchingww1.co.uk/indian-army-reserve-of-officers-application)
9 https://astreetnearyou.org/regiment/287/Indian-Army-Reserve-of-Officers
10 *The London Gazette*, March 1918, p. 2998
11 *The Quarterly Indian Army List*, April 1919, pp. 31 & 525
12 Ibid., April 1922, p. 525
13 Brazier, *Operation XD* (jacket notes)
14 *Hansard*, Vol. 262, 8 Mar. 1932
15 Ibid., Vol. 275, 9 Mar. 1933
16 Brazier, *Operation XD*, p. 2
17 *The London Gazette*, 8 Nov 1932, p. 7087
18 *Supplement to the London Gazette*, 9 Jun. 1938, p. 3694
19 *The London Gazette*, 3 Jan. 1939, p. 61
20 J. Skellorn, 'Grove House: Kent Fortress', *Northfleet History Group Magazine*, no. 15 (Winter), 2016
21 Buxton, *XD Operations1940 by Kent Fortress Engineers*, p. 6
22 Brazier, *Operation XD*, p. 5

Chapter 2

1 TNA, WO 166 / 3549 (1939, Aug 22-25)
2 Macdougall, *The Isle of Grain Defences*, pp. 7-8
3 Smith, *Isle of Grain: Hoo Peninsula, Kent (EH 1-2014)*, pp. 18-19

4 Macdougall, *The Isle of Grain Defences*, p. 9
5 Smith, *Isle of Grain: Hoo Peninsula, Kent (EH 1-2014)*, p. 19
6 Brazier, *XD Operations*, pp. 8-9
7 TNA, WO 166/3549 (1939, Sept 3)
8 Ibid. (1939, Sept 23)
9 Ibid. (1939, Nov 13)
10 Ibid. (1939, Nov 14)
11 Ibid. (1939, Nov 20)
12 Ibid. (1939, Nov 22-24)
13 Brazier, *XD Operations*, p. 11
14 TNA, WO 166/3549 (1939, Dec 13)
15 Ibid. (1939, Dec 27)
16 Ibid. (1940, Jan, Appendix 'A')

Chapter 3

1 Schonland - *Maurice Pascal Alers Hankey, First Baron Hankey of the Chart, 1877-1963* (https://doi.org/10.1098/rsbm.1964.0009)
2 The National Archives 'Blog' (WJR Gardner), 19 Oct 2016 - *Sir Maurice Hankey and the birth of modern government* https://blog.nationalarchives.gov.uk/sir-maurice-hankey-birth-modern-government/
3 *The Edinburgh Gazette*, 18 Jun. 1912, p. 628
4 The Oxford Companion to Military History – *Committee of Imperial Defence* (https://www.oxfordreference.com/display/10.1093/acref/9780198606963.001.0001/acref-9780198606963-e-300)
5 *The Edinburgh Gazette*, 11 Feb. 1916, p. 260
6 David Lloyd George, *War Memoirs*, Vol.II, p. 369
7 The National Archives 'Blog' (WJR Gardner), 19 Oct 2016 - *Sir Maurice Hankey and the birth of modern government* https://blog.nationalarchives.gov.uk/sir-maurice-hankey-birth-modern-government/
8 Ibid.
9 Schonland - *Maurice Pascal Alers Hankey, First Baron Hankey of the Chart, 1877-1963* (https://doi.org/10.1098/rsbm.1964.0009)
10 The National Archives 'Blog' (WJR Gardner), 19 Oct 2016 - *Sir Maurice Hankey and the birth of modern government* https://blog.nationalarchives.gov.uk/sir-maurice-hankey-birth-modern-government/
11 Ibid.
12 Peter Hennessy, *Cabinet* (Basil Blackwell, 1986)
13 https://discovery.nationalarchives.gov.uk/details/r/f5869342-c5c2-4f6c-95da-687634dae2ab
14 Stephen Roskill – *Hankey: Man of Secrets*, Vol. 3, p. 419
15 Ibid., p. 424
16 TNA, CAB 63/129 -Lord Hankey Papers – Contingency plans for action in the eventuality of a German invasion of Holland, pps. 2-7
17 TNA, CAB 65/1 - War Cabinet Conclusions, 23 Sept. 1939, WM (39) 24 5
18 Ibid. (WM 39-24-6)
19 TNA, CAB 63/129 - Lord Hankey Papers - Contingency plans for action in the eventuality of a German invasion of Holland, pps. 2-7

20 Ibid.
21 Ibid.
22 TNA, CAB 80/3/2 – Chiefs of Staff Committee Memoranda COS (39) 53
23 TNA, CAB 79/1/32 – Chiefs of Staff Committee Minutes COS (39) 32
24 TNA, CAB 80/3/3 – Chiefs of Staff Committee Memoranda COS (39) 64
25 Ibid. Para. 23
26 Ibid. Paras. 10 & 11
27 Ibid. Appendix. 3
28 Ibid. Para. 22
29 TNA, CAB 66/2/22 – War Cabinet Memoranda 1939, WP (39) 72
30 TNA, CAB 65/3 – War Cabinet Conclusions – Annexes, WM (39) 40 6
31 TNA, CAB 63/129 – Lord Hankey Papers - Contingency plans for action in the eventuality of a German invasion of Holland, p. 8
32 TNA, CAB 63/129 – Lord Hankey Papers - Contingency plans for action in the eventuality of a German invasion of Holland, pp. 9-15
33 Ibid., p.13
34 'Naval & Military Intelligence', *The Times* (London, England), Friday, Aug 13, 1897; p. 8; Issue 35281
35 TNA, ADM 196/48/9 – Admiralty Executive Officers Service Records – Thomas Hugh Binney
36 TNA, WO 106/1669 – Binney Project – Notes of meeting 9/10/1939 (1A)
37 TNA, CAB 66/2/22 (WP (39) 72) – War Cabinet Memoranda – Chiefs of Staff Paper COS (39) 65, 6 Oct. 1939

Chapter 4

1 Wim Klinkert - Journal of Modern European History - 2019, Vol. 17(1) - *The military and strategic role of Dutch neutrality, 1890-1940*
2 Ibid.
3 Ibid.
4 TNA, CAB 63/129, Lord Hankey Papers – Contingency plans for action in the eventuality of a German invasion of Holland, p. 59
5 Ibid., p. 60
6 Ibid., p. 61
7 Ibid., pps. 62 & 62A
8 TNA, CAB 65/1 – War Cabinet Conclusions WM 32 (39) 11, 30 Sept. 1939
9 Ibid., WM 33 (39) 7. 1 Oct 1939
10 TNA, 65/3 – War Cabinet Conclusions WM 38 (39) 5 – Confidential Annex, 5 Oct. 1939
11 Ibid.
12 Ibid. WM 39 (39) 4 – Confidential Annex, 6 Oct. 1939
13 Ibid.
14 TNA, CAB 63/129, Lord Hankey Papers - Contingency plans for action in the eventuality of a German invasion of Holland, pps. 18 - 21
15 Ibid., pp. 28-28A
16 Ibid.., pp. 34-58, Sir A Cadogan to Sir R. Clive & to Sir N, Bland, 12 Oct 1939.

17 Ibid., p.102
18 Ibid.
19 Ibid., pp. 30-31
20 Ibid., p.32
21 Ibid., pp. 81-84
22 Ibid., pp. 104-105
23 Ibid., pp. 23-24
24 Ibid., pp. 64-66
25 Ibid., p. 77

Chapter 5

1 TNA, ADM 196/92/145; ADM 196/53/67; ADM 196/45/62; ADM 196/127/296, Service Records - Moody, Clement
2 TNA, ADM 1/9793 – Vice-Admiral Binney's Committee 1939 - Report on visit to Rotterdam and The Hook of Holland 21 – 24 Oct 1939
3 TNA, ADM 196/55/195; ADM 196/93/2; ADM 196/127/376; ADM 196/145/352, Service Records – Hickling, Harold.
4 Jeffrey, Keith: *MI6 – The History of the Secret Intelligence Service 1909-1949*, pp. 153, 154, 387 (Bloomsbury Publishing, 2010)
5 https://www.hangarflying.eu/erfgoedsites/gedenkplaat-voor-p-o-reginald-william-newman/ . As a Pilot Officer in the RAF Reserve, Newman went on to be part of No.3 Air Mission operating in Belgium after the Germans invaded.
6 TNA, ADM 1/9793 – Vice-Admiral Binney's Committee – Report on visit to Brussels and Antwerp 21 – 25 Oct 1939
7 TNA, ADM 196/54/63; ADM 196/92/96; ADM 196/127/365; ADM 196/145/321, Service Records – Aylmer, Edward
8 TNA, ADM 1/9793 – Vice-Admiral Binney's Committee 1939 – Report on visit to Flushing and The Hague, 1 - 4 Nov 1939

Chapter 6

1 TNA, ADM 1/9793, Vice-Admiral Binney's Committee – C.N.S.'s Verbal orders – Vice-Admiral Binney's minute 12 Oct 1939
2 Ibid., D.O.D. (H)'s note, 14 Oct 1939
3 TNA, ADM 1/9793, Admiralty – Vice Admiral Binney's Committee 1939 – Note Binney to D.C.N.S. 4 Nov 1939
4 TNA, WO 106/1669 (2B) War Office - Binney Project - Holland and Belgium – Measures to be taken in the event of an invasion by Germany, Draft Plan for Land Demolition Parties. 15 Oct 1939
5 Ibid. (2B), Appendix A
6 Ibid. (48A) Minute – DDMO to Maj-Gen Newing & responses 16 Oct 1939
7 TNA, WO 106/1669, (3A) War Office – Binney Project – WO telegram to Aldershot Command & 55 Field Coy. R.E., 20 Oct 1939
8 Ibid. (9B & 9C) DMO memorandum to OC 55 Field Coy. R.E., Oct 1939
9 Ibid. (8A) Operation XD
10 Ibid.

11 TNA, WO 166/3572, 55 Field Coy. R.E. War Diary, 22 Oct 1939
12 TNA, WO 106/1669, (5A) War Office – Binney Project – Draft Appreciation by OC 55 Field Coy. R.E., 22 Oct 1939
13 TNA, WO 166/3572, 55 Field Coy. R.E. War Diary, 23 – 25 Oct 1939
14 TNA, CAB 66/2/45 (WP (39) 95) – War Cabinet – Lord Hankey - Holland and Belgium – Memorandum & Progress Report, 23 Oct 1939
15 TNA, CAB 63/129, (103) War Cabinet - Lord Hankey Papers – Belgium and Holland – Col Ian Jacob to Lord Hankey, Ref. 14/31/116, 22 Oct 1939
16 TNA, WO 106/1671, (3A) War Office – MO4 Papers – Holland & Belgium – Measures to be taken in the event of an invasion – Briefing for War Cabinet Meeting, 25 Oct 1939
17 Ibid.
18 TNA, CAB 65/1, (WM (39) 61) War Cabinet Conclusions, 26 Oct 1939
19 Ibid.
20 TNA, WO 106/1669, (7A) War Office – Binney Plan – Jacob to Lord Hankey, 26 Oct 1939
21 TNA, WO 166/3572, 55 Field Coy. R.E. War Diary, 26 Oct 1939
22 TNA, WO 106/1669, (10B) War Office – Binney Plan – 55 Field Coy. R.E. Operation Order No. 1, 30 Oct 1939
23 Ibid. (11B) 55 Field Coy. R.E. Operation Order No. 2, 1 Nov 1939
24 Ibid. 55 Field Coy. R.E. O – Binney Plan Operation Order No. 3, 1 Nov 1939
25 TNA, WO 106/1671, (9A) War Office – MO4 Papers – Holland & Belgium – Measures to be taken in the event of an invasion – Special Instructions for M.O.4 Duty Officer, 28 Oct 1939
26 TNA, ADM 1/9793, Admiralty – Vice-Admiral Binney's Committee 1939 – Minute to D.C.N.S & C.N.S, Despatch of destroyers and R.E. personnel to assist Holland and Belgium., 28 Oct 1939
27 TNA, CAB 63/129, (147-147A) War Cabinet – Lord Hankey Papers – Belgium and Holland – Lt. Col. Blake to Brig. van Custem, 28 Oct 1939
28 Ibid. (154-155) – Naval Attaché, Brussels and The Hague to Director of Naval Intelligence, 29 Oct 1939
29 Ibid. (148) - Hankey to Jacob, 2 Nov 1939
30 Ibid. (133) – Sir N. Bland to Sir A Cadogan, 29 Oct 1939
31 Ibid. (131) – Sir N. Bland to Sir A Cadogan, 29 Oct 1939
32 TNA, FO 371/23095/12097, (336-337) Foreign Office – General Correspondence. – Holland and Belgium – M.G. Christie to Sir Robert Vansittart, 3 Nov 1939
33 TNA, CAB 63/129 (151-153) War Cabinet - Lord Hankey Papers – Belgium and Holland - Sir R. Clive to Sir A. Cadogan, 2 Nov 1939
34 TNA, WO 106/1669 (10A) War Office – Binney Plan – War Cabinet – Holland and Belgium – Summary of the action to be taken if and when the invasion occurs, 30 Oct 1939
35 TNA, CAB 63/129 (143 – 144) War Cabinet – Lord Hankey Papers – Belgium and Holland – Sir A Cadogan to Sir R. Clive and Sir N. Bland, 1 Nov 1939
36 TNA, FO 371/23095/12097 (338) Foreign Office – General Correspondence – Holland and Belgium – Sir A. Cadogan to Sir N. Bland, 4 Nov 1939

Chapter 7

1 TNA, FO 371/23095/12097 (339-341), Foreign Office – General Correspondence – Holland and Belgium – Sir N. Bland to Sir A. Cadogan, 5 Nov 1939
2 TNA, FO 371/23096/12907 (355-356) Foreign Office – General Correspondence – Germany – Sir R Clive to F.O (Special Distribution) and War Cabinet, 7 Nov 1939
3 Ibid. (363) Sir R. Clive to F.O. (Special Distribution) and War Cabinet 7 Nov 1939
4 *The Advocate*, 9 Nov 1939 (https://trove.nla.gov.au/newspaper/article/68333474#)
5 TNA, CAB 63/129 (211-213) War Cabinet – Lord Hankey Papers – Belgium and Holland – Captain Schofield to Admiral Godfrey 10 Nov 1939
6 TNA, FO 371/23096/12097 (379) Foreign Office – General Correspondence – Germany – Sir R. Clive to F.O. (Special Distribution) and War Cabinet, 9 Nov 1939
7 Ibid. (378) comments by F Roberts and G. Jebb, 10 Nov 1939
8 TNA, CAB 63/129 (167-171) War Cabinet – Lord Hankey Papers - Belgium and Holland – Measures to be taken in the event of an invasion by Germany, 9 Nov 1939
9 Ibid. (172-174) Hankey to Churchill, 9 Nov 1939
10 TNA, CAB 65/4 (64-69) War Cabinet (WM 39 79) – Confidential Annexes – The Netherlands and Belgium, 11 Nov 1939
11 Ibid.
12 Ibid
13 TNA, WO 166/3572, 55 Field Coy. R.E War Diary, 10 Nov 1939
14 TNA, WO 106/1669, (21A) War Office – Binney Project – DDMO [Brig. Lund] to Lt. Col. Jacob, 11 Nov 1939
15 Ibid. (22A) Jacob to Lt. Col. Hayman-Joyce [for Lund], 12 Nov 1939
16 TNA, CAB 63/129, (202) War Cabinet – Lord Hankey Papers – Belgium and Holland – Jacob to Hankey, 13 Nov 1939
17 Ibid. (214), Schofield to D.N.I., 12 Nov 1939
18 Ibid. (215-216), Schofield to Admiral Godfrey, 15 Nov 1939
19 *Hansard*, (HC Deb 16 November 1939 vol 353 cc873) – 'The War Situation', statement by Chancellor of the Exchequer, Sir John Simon)
20 TNA, FO 371/23096/12097 (398) Foreign Office – General Correspondence – Germany – Sir N. Charles to Foreign Office, 18 Nov 1939
21 TNA, WO 166/3572, 55 Field Coy. R.E. War Diary, 14-30 Nov 1939
22 TNA, WO 106.1669 (31A) War Office – Binney Project – Jacob to Hankey, 21 Nov 1939
23 Ibid.
24 Ibid.
25 TNA, ADM 1/9793, Admiralty – Preparations for War – Admiral Binney's Committee – D.O.P., 25 Nov 1939
26 TNA, CAB 63/129 (217), War Cabinet – Lord Hankey Papers – Belgium and Holland – Jacob to Hankey, 30 Nov 1939

27 TNA, WO 106/1669 (19A), War Office - Binney Project – Jacob to War Cabinet, 20 Dec 1939
28 TNA, ADM 196/48/9, Admiralty – Binney, Thomas Hugh – Service Record

Chapter 8

1 TNA, WO 106/2014B, War Office – Directorate of Military Operations & Military Intelligence – Finland - Massy to Commander in Chief Home Forces, Northern Command, Eastern Command, Aldershot Command & Southern Command, 6 Jan 1940
2 TNA, WO 166/3572, 55 Field Coy. R.E. War Diary, 8 Jan 1940
3 TNA, WO 106/1669 (35A) War Office – Binney Project – D.M.O. to C.R.E. 12 Division, 12 Jan 1940
4 TNA, WO 166/443, 12th Division, Commander Royal Engineers War Diary, 14 Jan 1940
5 TNA, WO 166/3572, 55 Field Coy. R.E. War Diary, 11, 12, & 14 Jan 1940
6 TNA, WO 106/1669 (36A), M.O.4 to 55 Field Coy. R.E. 14 Jan 1940
7 Sebag-Montefiore, Hugh – *Dunkirk* (Penguin Viking, 2006), p. 34
8 Keyes, Roger – *Outrageous Fortune* (Secker & Warburg, 1984), p. 134
9 Ibid.
10 West, Nigel – *MI6*, p.116
11 Keyes, Roger – *Outrageous Fortune,* p.136
12 TNA, CAB 65/5/11, War Cabinet - Conclusions - WM (40) 11 – Minute 5 – Western Front, 13 Jan 1940
13 TNA, CAB 65/11/11, War Cabinet - Confidential Annexes - WM (40) 11 – Minute 5 – Western Front, 13 Jan 1940
14 Ibid.
15 TNA, FO 371/23096/12097, Foreign Office – General Correspondence – Holland & Belgium – R. Makins to Sir L. Oliphant, 13 Jan 1940
16 TNA, CAB 63/129 (221-226) War Cabinet – Lord Hankey Papers – Holland & Belgium – Jacob to Hankey, 14 Jan 1940
17 Ibid.
18 Ibid.
19 Ibid. (227-227a), Jacob to Hankey, 15 Jan 1940
20 Ibid. (228-231), Jacob to Hankey, 18 Jan 1940
21 Ibid. (232-233), Jacob to Hankey, 31 Jan 1940
22 Ibid, (234), Jacob to Hankey, 16 Mar 1940
23 Keyes, Roger – *Outrageous Fortune*, p. 137
24 Wooward, Sir Llewellyn – *British Foreign Policy in the Second World War,* (HMSO, 1962), p. 34
25 TNA, CAB 65/11/12, War Cabinet – Confidential Annex – WM (40) 12 – Minute 1 - Western Front, 14 Jan 1940
26 TNA, CAB 65/56/81, War Cabinet – Confidential Annexes and Notes to Conclusions – WM (40) 12 – Western Front, 14 Jan 1940
27 TNA, CAB 65/5/13, War Cabinet – Conclusions – WM (40) 13 – Minute 1, Western Front, 14 Jan 1940

28 TNA, CAB 65/11/13, War Cabinet – Confidential Annexes – WM (40) 13 – Minute 1, Western Front, 14 Jan 1940
29 Ibid.
30 Ibid.
31 Ibid.
32 Ibid.
33 Keyes, Roger – *Outrageous Fortune*, p. 139
34 Sebag-Montefiore, Hugh – *Dunkirk*, pp. 34-35
35 Keyes, Roger – *Outrageous Fortune*, p. 141
36 TNA, CAB 65/11/14, War Cabinet – Confidential Annexes – WM (40) 14 – Minute 7, Western Front, 15 Jan 1940
37 Ibid.
38 TNA, CAB 65/56/83, War Cabinet – Confidential Annexes and Notes to Conclusions – WM (40) 14 – Minute 7, Western Front, 15 Jan 1940
39 TNA, CAB 65/11/15, War Cabinet – Confidential Annexes – WM (40) 15 – Minute 7, Western Front, 16 Jan 1940
40 TNA, CAB 65/56/84, War Cabinet – Confidential Annexes and Notes to Conclusions – WM (40) 15 – Minute 7, Western Front, 16 Jan 1940
41 Sebag-Montefiore, Hugh – Dunkirk, pp. 36-37
42 TNA, WO 106/1669, M.A. Brussels to M.I.3. Colonel. Summary of Items of General Interest, 17 Jan 1940
43 TNA, WO 166/3572, 55 Field Coy. R.E. War Diary, 16 & 17 Jan 1940
44 TNA, WO 106/1669, D.M.O. to C.R.E. 12th Division and D.M.O. to Officer Commanding 55 Field Coy, 17 Jan 1939
45 TNA, WO 166/3572, War Diary, 19 Jan 1940.
46 Ibid., 8 Feb 1940

Chapter 9

1 TNA, WO 166/3549, Kent (Fortress) Royal Engineers – War Diary, Jan 1940
2 Ibid., 14 Feb 1940
3 Ibid., 19 Feb 1940
4 Buxton, Bernard - *XD Operations1940 by Kent Fortress Engineers*, p. 7
5 TNA, WO 106/1669 – War Office – Binney Project – Hayman-Joyce to Dewdney, 11 Mar 1940
6 Buxton, p. 8
7 TNA, WO 166/3549, - Lieut, Col C.C.H. Brazier, Operation Order No,3. 16 Mar 1940
8 Buxton – pp. 16-17.
9 TNA, WO 166/3549, - War Diary, March 1940
10 Buxton, p 18
11 Brazier, C.C.H. – *XD Operations*, p. 13
12 Buxton, p. 12
13 Ibid.
14 Ibid., p. 16
15 Ibid., p. 18
16 Ibid., p. 19

17 TNA, WO 166/3549, War Diary, 17 Apr 1940
18 Ibid., 30 Apr & 9 May 1940
19 Buxton, p. 20
20 Ibid.

Chapter 10

1 TNA, CAB 66/6. War Cabinet – Memoranda, WP (40) 98, The Question of Allied assistance to Belgium in the event of a German attack, 12 Mar 1940
2 TNA, CAB 63/129 (pp. 234-236), War Cabinet – Lord Hankey Papers – Holland & Belgium, Jacob to Lord Hankey, 16 Mar 1940
3 TNA, CAB 65/12, War Cabinet, WM (40) 71 – Confidential Annexes, 18 Mar 1940
4 Ibid.
5 Ibid.
6 TNA, CAB 79/3, War Cabinet – Chiefs of Staff Committee Minutes, COS (40) 56, German invasion of Holland, 18 Mar 1939
7 TNA, WO 106/1671, War Office – Directorate of Military Operations and Military Intelligence – Holland & Belgium; measures to be taken on invasion by Germany, Notes for War Cabinet, Assistance to Belgium, 19 Mar 1940
8 TNA, CAB 66/6, War Cabinet – Memoranda, WP (40) 101, Assistance to Belgium, Lord Halifax, draft telegram to Sir N. Bland, The Hague, 18 Mar 1940
9 TNA, CAB 65/6, War Cabinet – Conclusions, WM 72 (40), Minute 1, Western Front, 19 Mar 1940.
10 Ibid. WM 83 (40), Minute 3, The Military Situation, 6 Apr 1940
11 Ibid, WM 87 (40), Minute 4. The Supreme War Council, 10 Apr 1940
12 Ibid. Minute 10, Western Front - Attitude of Belgium, 10 Apr 1940
13 Ibid. WM 88 (40), Minute 10, Western Front – Attitude of Belgium, 11 Apr 1940
14 TNA, CAB 66/7, War Cabinet – Memoranda, WP (40) 126, Note by Chairman of the Military Co-ordination Committee [W. Churchill], Action to be taken if Germany invades Holland or Belgium, 11 Apr 1940
15 TNA, CAB 65/12, War Cabinet, WM (40) 90 – Confidential Annexes, 12 Apr 1940
16 Dilks, *The Diaries of Sir Alec Cadogan*, p.270
17 TNA, CAB 65/6, WM 92 (40), Minute 6, Western Front, 14 Apr 1940
18 Ibid.
19 TNA, CAB 63/129, (p.250- 253), Hankey to Oliphant [and Bland], 15 Apr 1940
20 Ibid., (pp. 256-259), Bland to Hankey, 19 Apr 1940
21 Ibid., (pp. 262-264), Oliphant to Hankey, 24 Apr 1940
22 Ibid., (pp. 268-271), G.H. Villiers - Anglo French Mixed Commission 1st Meeting Paris April 17-20, 22 Apr 1940
23 Ibid.
24 Ibid.
25 Ibid.

26 Ibid., (p. 272), Hankey to Oliphant, 7 May 1940
27 Ibid., (p. 274), Hankey to Jacob, 7 May 1940
28 Ibid., (p. 275), Jacob to Hankey, 7 May 1940
29 TNA, WO 106/1671, (22A & 23A), Operation XD – Revised Idea and Instructions, 6 May 1940
30 Ibid., (27A), Flag Officer Commanding Dover – Operation XD, 7 May 1940
31 TNA CAB 65/7, War Cabinet, WM 115 (40) – Conclusions, Minute 6, Netherlands and Belgium – possible German attack, 8 May 1940
32 TNA CAB 65/13, War Cabinet – WM 115 (40), Confidential Annexes, Minute 6, Netherlands and Belgium – possible German attack, 8 May 1940
33 The National Archives Blog - *10 May 1940: A day to remember*, 9 May 2020 (https://blog.nationalarchives.gov.uk/10-may-1940-a-day-to-remember/)

Chapter 11

1 Forczyk, Robert, *Case Red – The Collapse of France*, pp. 151-153
2 *Utrechts Nieuwsblad*, 10 May 1940. (https://www.grebbeberg.nl/bibliotheek/data/rapport.php?rap_id=9).
3 Read, Anthony & Fisher, David, *Colonel Z – The Secret Life of a Master of Spies*, p. 188
4 Keyes, Roger, *Outrageous Fortune – The Tragedy of Leopold III of the Belgians*, p. 175
5 Ibid., p. 174
6 TNA, CAB 63/132, (p.450), Lord Hankey Papers – Francis Aveling to Lord Halifax, Account of events connected with the German Invasion of Belgium, 17 Jul 1940
7 Dilks, David, *The Diaries Sir Alexander Cadogan, 1938-1945*, p. 280
8 TNA, CAB 65/7, War Cabinet – Conclusions, WM 117 (40), The Netherlands and Belgium – Invasion by Germany
9 Ibid., Denial of Dutch and Belgian Resources to Germany
10 Ibid.
11 Ibid.
12 CRE Library, A231.53 - Buxton, Bernard, *XD Operations – 1940*, p. 20
13 TNA, WO 166/3549, Kent (Fortress) Royal Engineers – War Diary – Appendix No.1, Operation Order No.1, 10 May 1940
14 TNA, WO 106/1671, War Office– Directorate of Military Operations and Military Intelligence – Holland & Belgium; measures to be taken on invasion by Germany, Vice Admiral Ramsay – Operation XD, Addendum No.1, 9 May 1940
15 TNA, WO 166/3549, Operation Order No.2
16 Buxton, p. 21
17 Ibid., p. 22
18 Report on Operation XD.A (Ijmuiden), Commander M.G. Goodenough R.N., 17 May 1940(http://www.holywellhousepublishing.co.uk/PDF/XDA-Ijmuidencompressed.pdf)
19 TNA, WO 106/1671 (28A), C.I.G.S to S. of S., 10 May 1940

20 TNA, CAB 65/7 – War Cabinet – Conclusions, WM 118 (40), The Netherlands and Belgium, 10 May 1940
21 Ibid.
22 Ibid.
23 TNA, CAB 65/7 – WM 119 (40), The Netherlands and Belgium, 10 May 1940
24 Ibid, The War Cabinet – resignation of the Prime Minister, 10 May 1940
25 Ibid.
26 TNA, WO 106/1669, (47A), War Office – Directorate of Military Operations and Intelligence – Binney Project – Holland and Belgium, measures to be taken in the event of an invasion by Germany, 10 May 1940

Chapter 12

1 TNA, ADM 196/194/367, Admiralty – Service Records – Michael Grant Goodenough
2 CAC, MISC 117 - Admiralty diary of Commander Michael G. Goodenough, 1939-1941 (https://archivesearch.lib.cam.ac.uk/repositories/9/archival_objects/1724425)
3 TNA, WO 106/1671 (26A), War Office – Directorate of Military Operations and Intelligence – Binney Project – Holland and Belgium, measures to be taken in the event of an invasion by Germany – Orders for Officer-in-Charge of Party proceeding to IJmuiden, 10 May 1940
4 CAC, MISC 117, Ibid.
5 TNA, WO 106/1671, Ibid.
6 Ibid.
7 Ibid.
8 Institution of Royal Engineers, *Journal* (Vol.119, No.1, p.65), Memoirs, Major Robert Keeble DSO MC TD, 9April 2005
9 TNA, WO 166/3549, War Office – Home Forces – Royal Engineers - Kent (Fortress) Royal Engineers – War Diary, May 1940, Appendix No.3, Lt. Col. Brazier, Operation Order No.3
10 CRE Library, A231.53, Buxton, Bernard, *XD Operations – 1940*, Appendix 7 (i), L/Cpl W. Twocock's Eyewitness Account, 10 May 1940
11 Commander M.G. Goodenough R.N, Report on Operation XD.A (Ijmuiden),17 May 1940 (http://www.holywellhousepublishing.co.uk/PDF/XDA-Ijmuidencompressed)
12 CRE Library, A231.53, Ibid.
13 IWM, Documents.1676 - Private Papers of Major B Buxton DSO TD, Appendix (iii), HMS Whitshed's Report – Amsterdam (Cdr E. R. Conder R.N. to Flag Officer Dover). 12 May 1940
14 Commander M.G. Goodenough R.N. Report, Ibid
15 IWM, 007287 – Madden, Colin Duncan (Oral history), British officer served with Royal Navy Demolition Party A during Operation XD to Ijmuiden Harbour, Netherlands, 5/1940 [Transcription], 8 Dec 1983
16 Commander M.G. Goodenough R.N., Report, Ibid.
17 Ibid

18 Ibid.
19 IWM, 007287, Ibid.
20 Commander M.G. Goodenough R.N., Report, Ibid.
21 TNA, WO 166/3549, Ibid, Appendix No.5, report from Capt. R. Keeble R.E., i/c "A" Group
22 Commander M.G. Goodenough R.N., Report, Ibid.
23 TNA, WO 166/3549, Ibid.
24 Commander M.G. Goodenough R.N., Report, Ibid.
25 Ibid.
26 The Defense Line of Amsterdam, - The Buiten-IJ and Durgerdam in May 1940, (https://www.stelling-amsterdam.nl/stelling/extra/durgerdam-1940/index.php)
27 TNA, WO 166/3549, Ibid.
28 Kindell, Don - *British and Other Navies in World War 2 Day-by-Day, NAVAL EVENTS, MAY 1940 Wednesday 8th – Tuesday 14th*. (https://www.naval-history.net/xDKWW2-4005-14MAY02.htm)
29 Commander M.G. Goodenough R.N., Report, Ibid.
30 IWM, 007287, Ibid.
31 Commander M.G. Goodenough R.N., Report, Ibid.
32 Kindell, Don, Ibid.
33 Commander M.G. Goodenough R.N., Report, Ibid.
34 TNA, WO 166/3549, Ibid.
35 IWM, 007287, Ibid.
36 Commander M.G. Goodenough R.N., Report, Ibid.
37 Ibid.
38 Ibid.
39 TNA, WO 166/3549, Ibid.
40 Ibid.
41 Brazier, C.C.H & P.H. – *XD Operations*, p. 21
42 Commander M.G. Goodenough R.N., Report, Ibid.
43 TNA, CAB 63/132, (p.37-41), Lord Hankey Papers - Reports of Demolition Parties in Holland, Belgium & France, Captain Davies report on visit to Amsterdam, 16 May 1940
44 TNA, WO 166/3549, Ibid.
45 Commander M.G. Goodenough R.N., Report, Ibid.
46 IWM, 007287, Ibid.
47 Commander M.G. Goodenough R.N., Report, Ibid.
48 TNA, WO 166/3549, Ibid.
49 IWM, 007287, Ibid.
50 Commander M.G. Goodenough, Report, Ibid.
51 IWM, 007287, Ibid.
52 Ibid.
53 Ibid.
54 CRE Library, A231.53, Ibid.
55 TNA, WO 166/3549. Ibid.
56 IWM, 007287, Ibid.
57 Forster, Bill – A Hard Fought Ship (http://www.holywellhousepublishing.co.uk/Atjeh.html)

Chapter 13

1 TNA, ADM 196/147/161, Admiralty – Officers Service Records – Younghusband, John Leslie
2 Oxford University Press - *WHO'S WHO & WHO WAS WHO*, Goodwin, Lt.Col. Thomas Frederick, 1 Dec 2007. (https://doi.org/10.1093/ww/9780199540884.013.U51644)
3 TNA, ADM 196/148/263, Admiralty – Officers Service Records – Hill, James Alexander Corrie
4 TNA, WO 106/1671, (4A), War Office – Directorate of Military Operations and Military Intelligence – Holland & Belgium: measures to be taken on invasion by Germany, Operation XD – Party B
5 TNA, CAB 65/7, War Cabinet – Conclusions, WM 118 (40), Minute 4, Netherlands and Belgium – Operation XD, 10 May 1940
6 NMM, HSR/D/11 – Wild Swan: 'Operation XD'
7 Ibid.
8 TNA, WO 106/1671, (26A), Ibid, XD (B)
9 NMM, HSR/D/11, Ibid.
10 Kimenai, Peter – 'Traces of War - Lost gold on the Nieuwe Waterweg' (https://www.tracesofwar.com/articles/5315/Lost-gold-on-the-Nieuwe-Waterweg.htm).
11 NMM, HSR/D/11, Ibid.
12 TNA, ADM 1/10763, Admiralty – Foreign Countries – German Invasion of Holland – Report by Commander F.C. Hartley, R.N.R., May 1940
13 Ibid.
14 Ibid.
15 Ibid.
16 NMM, HSR/D/11, Ibid.
17 Brazier, C.C.H & P.H. – *XD Operations*, p. 26
18 TNA, WO 166/3549, Kent (Fortress) Royal Engineers – War Diary, May 1940, Appendix 4, Capt. T. Goodwin R.E. to Officer Commanding Kent (Fortress) Royal Engineers – Report on 'B' Party at Rotterdam, 15 May 1940
19 Kimenai, Peter, Ibid.
20 Ibid.
21 NMM, HSR/D/11, Ibid.
22 TNA, WO 166/3549, Ibid.
23 NMM, HSR/D/11, Ibid.
24 Ibid.
25 Brazier, C.C.H. & P.H., Ibid., p. 27
26 NMM, HSR/D/11, Ibid.
27 TNA, WO 106/1733, (1), War Office - Directorate of Military Operations and Intelligence – Special operations; demolitions in Holland and Belgium, Letter from T.F. Goodwin to Colonel [Brazier], 11 May 1940
28 NMM, HSR/D/11, Ibid.
29 TNA, ADM 1/10763, Ibid.
30 TNA, ADM 2/202, Admiralty – Royal Marines – War Diaries – 'Harpoon': Defensive action covering withdrawal from Hook of

Holland, 'A Whitsun Week-End at the Hook of Holland', Major B.G.B. Mitchell for the Ministry of Information daily talk to the Press
31 TNA, WO 106/1667, (5A), War Office – Directorate of Military Operations and Intelligence – Operation 'Harpoon', Holland, Inter Service Planning Staff, 45th Meeting, 11 May 1940
32 TNA, ADM 2/202, Ibid – Maj. Mitchell, Report on operations carried out by Mitchell Force at the Hook of Holland, 17 May 1940
33 NMM, HSR/D/11, Ibid.
34 TNA, ADM 2/202, Ibid.
35 NMM, HSR/D/11, Ibid.
36 TNA, ADM 2/202, Ibid.
37 TNA, WO 106/1667, (11A) – Admiralty to HMS HYPERION, 12 May 1940.
38 TNA, CAB 79/4, War Cabinet – Chiefs of Staff Committee - 125 (40), Situation on the Dutch Coast, 12 May 1940.
39 TNA, WO 106/1667, (7A) – War Office to Home Forces, Emergency Operations – Warning Order, 12 May 1940.
40 Ibid., (6A) – War Office to Guards Commander, Hounslow, 12 May 1940
41 Ibid., (15A) – Maintenance Project for Special Force, 12 May 1940
42 Ibid., (20A) – Instructions to R.A.S.C. Commander accompanying "HARPOON"
43 Ibid., (21A) – Instructions to Lieutenant Colonel J. C. Haydon, O.B.E.
44 Ibid., (13A) – HMS HYPERION to Admiralty, 12 May 1940
45 Ibid., (14A) – Admiralty to Vice-Admiral Dover, 12 May 1940
46 TNA, CAB 79/4, 126 (40), Reinforcements for Fortress Holland, 12 May 1940
47 TNA, WO 166/1667, (16A) – Flag Officer Commanding Dover to Ships and Authorities in Nore and Dover Command Area, 12 May 1940
48 Ibid, (19A) – War Office to Home Forces, 12 May 1940
49 NMM, HSR/D/11, Ibid.
50 TNA, ADM 2/202, Ibid.
51 TNA, WO 166/3549, Ibid.
52 NMM, HSR/D/11, Ibid.
53 TNA, ADM 2/202, Ibid.
54 NMM, HSR/D/11, Ibid.
55 TNA, WO 166/3549, Ibid.
56 TNA, WO 106/1667 (17A) – Vice Admiral, Dover to Admiralty, 12 May 1940
57 TNA, ADM 2/202, Ibid.
58 TNA, ADM 2/202, Ibid.
59 TNA, WO 106/1667 (27A), War Office to V.A. Dover for HARPOON, 13 May 1940
60 TNA, ADM 199/795, Admiralty – Operations off Dutch, Belgian and French Coasts – Operations conducted by Vice Admiral, Dover in North Sea (South), May 10th – May 19th, 1940
61 TNA, WO 106/1667 (30A), Capt. (D16) to Naval Officer i/c Dover, 13 May 1940

62 Ibid, (31A), Capt. (D), 19th D.F. to F.O.C. Dover, 13 May 1940
63 TNA, ADM 199/795, Ibid.
64 Ibid.
65 TNA, ADM 1/10763, Ibid.
66 TNA, ADM 199/795, Ibid.
67 TNA, WO 106/1667 (32A-33A), Admiralty to War Office from HARPOON, 13 May 1940
68 TNA, WO 167/695, War Office – 2 Irish Guards, War Diary, May – June 1940
69 TNA, WO 106/1667 (34A), Admiralty to MALCOLM, 13 May 1940
70 TNA, WO 166/3549, Ibid.
71 Brazier, C.C.H. & P.H., Ibid., p. 29
72 CRE Library, A231.53, Buxton, Bernard, XD Operations – 1940, Appendix 8 (ii), Eyewitness account – Corporal A. Blake
73 Brazier, C.C.H. & P.H., Ibid., p. 31
74 TNA, ADM 199/795, Ibid.
75 Ibid, Commander T.A. Hussey – HMS 'Versatile', Report of Proceedings, 13-14 May 1940
76 TNA, ADM 2/202, Ibid.
77 Brazier, C.C.H. & P.H., Ibid.
78 TNA, ADM 2/202, Ibid.
79 TNA, WO 106/1667 (38A), HARPOON to War Office
80 Ibid. (36A), War Office to HARPOON, 13 May 1940
81 TNA, ADM 199/795, Ibid.
82 TNA, WO 106/1667, (39A), HARPOON to War Office, 14 May 1940.
83 Ibid, (40A), No.10 (Heywood) Mission to War Office, Air Ministry, Admiralty, 14 May 1940.
84 TNA, WO 167/695, Ibid.
85 TNA, ADM 199/795, Ibid.
86 TNA, WO 106/1667 (43A), Capt. (D) 16 to V.A. Dover, 14 May 1940.
87 Ibid. (47A), D. 16 to V.A. Dover, 14 May 1940
88 Ibid. (49A), Inter Service Planning Staff meeting minutes, 14 May 1940
89 Ibid. (50A), Admiralty to V.A. Dover, 14 May 1940
90 TNA, ADM 199/795, Ibid.
91 TNA, CAB 65/7, War Cabinet – Conclusions – Minute No.3, The Netherlands, 14 May 1940
92 TNA, WO 106/1667, (51A & 52A), Admiralty to V.A. Dover, & V.A. Dover to Capt. (D) 16, 14 May 1940
93 TNA, ADM 199/795, Ibid.
94 TNA, WO 106/1667 (55A), HMS WHITSHED for Maj. Gen Heywood to F.O.C. Dover, & Capt (D) 16
95 Ibid. (53A & 54A), Capt. (D) 16 to N.O..i/c Dover, 14 May 1940
96 Ibid. (56A), D. 16 to V.A. Dover, 14 May 1940
97 Ibid. (44A), D.M.O. & P. to V.C.I.G.S., 14 May 1940
98 Ibid. (57A), V.A. Dover to WHITSHED D1 D19 D16
99 Ibid. (59A), Admiralty to D. 16, 14 May 1940
100 TNA, ADM 199/795, Ibid.

101 TNA, WO 166/3549, Ibid.
102 TNA, ADM 202/401, Ibid.
103 TNA, ADM 199/795 Ibid.
104 Ibid.
105 TNA, ADM 202/401, Ibid.
106 TNA, ADM, 199/795 – The Commanding Officer H.M.M.T.B, No.16's report, 15 May 1940

Chapter 14

1 TNA, ADM 199/667, Admiralty – Operations off French, Belgian and Dutch coasts, Report of Proceedings of HMS Verity, 10 May 1940
2 TNA, ADM 196/148/77, Admiralty – Officers Service Records, Peter Grenville Lyon Cazalet
3 TNA, ADM 199/795, Admiralty – Operations off Dutch, Belgian and French coasts – Operation XD, Appendix I, Party 'C' to Flushing, 7 May 1940
4 TNA, WO 106/1671, War Office - Directorate of Military Operations and Military Intelligence – Holland & Belgium: measures to be taken on invasion by Germany, Operation XD, Orders for Officer-in-Charge of Party proceeding to Flushing, 10 May 1940
5 IWM, Documents.11491 (PGC1), Private papers of Vice Admiral Sir Peter Cazalet – Demolitions in Holland 1940
6 TNA, ADM 199/667, Ibid.
7 IWM, Documents.11491 (PGC1), Ibid.
8 TNA, ADM 199/795, Ibid, Commander Peter Cazalet - Report of Proceedings of Party 'C', 22 May 1940
9 TNA, ADM 199/667, Ibid.
10 TNA, ADM 199/795, Ibid.
11 IWM, Documents.11491 (PGC1), Ibid.
12 Goossens, Allert - 'War Over Holland – Zeeland – French-Dutch Command' (*http://www.waroverholland.nl/index.php?page=french-dutch-command*)
13 IWM, Documents 11491 (PGC1), Ibid.
14 Ibid.
15 Ibid.
16 TNA, ADM 199/795, Ibid.
17 Ibid.
18 Ibid.
19 Ibid.
20 Ibid.
21 Ibid.
22 Goossens, Allert - 'War Over Holland – Zeeland - Capitulation of The Netherlands' (*http://www.waroverholland.nl/index.php?page=capitulation-of-the-netherlands*)
23 IWM, Documents.11491 (PGC1), Ibid.
24 TNA, ADM 199/795, Ibid.
25 Ibid.

26 Goossens, Allert - 'War Over Holland – Zeeland – Bath and Zanddijkeline' (*http://www.waroverholland.nl/index.php?page=bath--and-zanddijkline*)
27 TNA, ADM 199/795, Ibid.
28 Ibid.
29 Goossens, Allert - 'War Over Holland – Zeeland – Middelburg' (*http://www.waroverholland.nl/index.php?page=middelburg*).
30 TNA. ADM 199/795, Ibid.
31 IWM, Documents.11941 (PGC1), Ibid.
32 TNA, ADM 199/795, Ibid.
33 Ibid.

Chapter 15

1 TNA, ADM 196/149/121, Admiralty – Service Records - Arthur Caerlyon Stanford
2 TNA, WO 166/3549, War Office – Home Forces – Royal Engineers - Kent (Fortress) Royal Engineers – War Diary, May 1940, Appendix No.1, Lt. Col. Brazier, Operation Order No.1. (Appendix A), 9 May 1940
3 TNA, WO 106/1671, War Office – Directorate of Military Operations and Military Intelligence – Holland & Belgium: measures to be taken on invasion by Germany, X.D. (D) – Orders for Officer-in-charge of party proceeding to Antwerp, 10 May 1940
4 Ibid, Instructions for Operation XD (Revised), Appendix II (Party D), 27 Jan 1940
5 TNA, ADM 196/47/149, Admiralty – Service Records – Arthur Henniker-Heaton
6 TNA, ADM 199/667, Admiralty – Operations off the French, Belgian & Dutch Coasts 1940 – Report on Operation "XD", HMS *Brilliant*
7 Ibid.
8 TNA, PREM 3/324/4, Prime Minister's Office – Report on Operation XD – Commander A.C. Stanford R.N., Party D (Antwerp), 20 May 1940
9 Ibid.
10 IWM, Documents.1676 - Private Papers of Major B Buxton DSO TD, Appendix 9 – Antwerp, Cpl. Jack Mitten's Diary
11 TNA, ADM 199/667, Ibid.
12 IWM, Documents.1676, Ibid.
13 TNA, ADM 199/667, Ibid.
14 TNA, PREM 3/324/4, Ibid.
15 IWM, Documents.1676, Ibid.
16 TNA, PREM 3/324/4, Ibid.
17 Ibid.
18 IWM, Documents. 1676, Ibid.
19 Gale Primary Sources (GALE | CS84752050) - *The Times* Digital Archive, 18 May 1940
20 IWM, Documents.1676, Ibid.
21 TNA, PREM 3/324/4, Ibid.
22 Ibid.
23 IWM, Documents.1676, Ibid.

24 Keyes, Roger – *Outrageous Fortune – The Tragedy of Leopold III of the Belgians*, p. 215
25 TNA, PREM 3/324/4, Ibid.
26 IWM. Documents.1676, Ibid.
27 TNA, PREM 3/324/4, Ibid.
28 Ibid.
29 IWM, Documents.1676, Ibid.
30 Roskill, Stephen – *Hankey, Man of Secrets* p. 469
31 TNA, CAB 63/132, War Cabinet and Cabinet Office – Lord Hankey Papers – 1939-45 War, Fall of Holland, Belgium and France – Reports of Demolition Parties - Destruction of Belgian Oil Supplies, 17 May 1940
32 Ibid.
33 TNA, PREM 3/324/4, Ibid.
34 Ibid.
35 Ibid.
36 TNA, CAB 63/132, Ibid, 18 May 1940

Chapter 16

1 TNA, WO 106/1733, War Office – Directorate of Military Operations and Military Intelligence – Special Operations: demolitions in Holland and Belgium, (7A) Report to M.O.4. from O.C. Kent (Fortress) R.E., 15 May 1940
2 TNA, CAB 65/7, War Cabinet – Conclusions, WM 123(40), Minute 4, The Netherlands, 15 May 1940
3 TNA, CAB 63/132, War Cabinet and Cabinet Office – Lord Hankey Papers – 1939-45 War, Fall of Holland, Belgium and France – Reports of Demolition Parties – Note by First Lord of the Admiralty, W.P. (G) (40) 135 – Demolitions in Holland, 25 May 1940
4 TNA, PREM 3/324/4, Prime Minister's Office – Report on Operation XD – Commander A.C. Stanford R.N., Party D (Antwerp), 20 May 1940
5 TNA, WO 106/1733, Ibid, Note: Brazier to Pritchard, 15 May 1940

Chapter 17

1 CRE Library, A231.53, Buxton, Bernard, *XD Operations – 1940*, pp. 29-30

Appendix I

1 TNA, CAB 63/129 War Cabinet and Cabinet – Lord Hankey Papers - Contingency plans for action in the eventuality of a German invasion of Holland and Belgium (ps. 34-44), Sir A Cadogan to Sir R. Clive, 12 Oct 1939
2 Ibid, (ps. 46-58), Sir A. Cadogan to Sir N. Bland, 12 Oct 1939

Appendix II

1 TNA, CAB 66/37/38, War Cabinet and Cabinet – Memoranda – WP (40) 158, Chiefs of Staff Committee, Weekly Resume (No. 37) of the Naval, Military and Air Situation from 12 noon May 9th to 12 noon May 16th, 1940

2 IWM, 007287 – Madden, Colin Duncan (Oral history), British officer served with Royal Navy Demolition Party A during Operation XD to Ijmuiden Harbour, Netherlands, 5/1940 [Transcription], 8 Dec 1983
3 Commander M.G. Goodenough R.N, Report on Operation XD.A (Ijmuiden), 17 May 1940 (http://www.holywellhousepublishing.co.uk/PDF/XDA-Ijmuidencompressed)
4 CAC, MISC 117 - Admiralty diary of Commander Michael G. Goodenough, 1939-1941 (https://archivesearch.lib.cam.ac.uk/repositories/9/archival_objects/1724425)
5 IWM. 007287, Ibid.
6 Martin, Roy. V. - *Ebb and Flow, Evacuations and Landings by Merchant Ships in WW2*, Aerial Edition (Independently published 26 Jan. 2020)
7 Wadey, Darron (alias 'Diamonds from Amsterdam'), Ships Nostalgia – Dotterel, post #10, 7 Mar 2021 (https://www.shipsnostalgia.com/threads/dotterel.16797/?post_id=3077029&nested_view=1&sortby=oldest#post-30770290
8 Walker, David E. – *Adventure in Diamonds* (Evans Brothers Limited, London, 1955)
9 Ibid.
10 Royal Navy – Historical Branch – War Diary, Naval, 1940-05 (https://cd.royalnavy.mod.uk/-/media/rnweb/locations-and-operations/navy-historical-branch/pdfs/1940/war_diary_naval_1940_05.pdf?rev=064e8736a5d241b0a2328ece0b8cef5b)
11 TNA, ADM 199/375, Admiralty – War History Cases and Papers – Second World War – Nore Command – War Diaries, 1st – 15th May 1940
12 IMBd – *Operation Amsterdam* (www.imdb.com/title/tt0053140/)
13 Jeffery, Keith - *MI6 – the History of the Secret Intelligence Service 1909-1949*, (Bloomsbury Publishing, London, 2010)
14 TNA, HS 9/306/7, Records of Special Operations Executive – Personnel Files - Montagu Reany CHIDSON
15 Ibid.
16 TNA, WO 373/16/272, War Office – Recommendations for Hours and Awards for Gallant and Distinguished Service - Recommendation for Award for Chidson, Montague Reaney Rank: Lieutenant Colonel
17 *Supplement to the London Gazette of Friday 20th December 1940* (https://www.thegazette.co.uk/London/issue/35020/supplement/7173/data.pdf)

Appendix III

1 TNA, ADM 1/11397, Admiralty – Foreign Countries - Awards to personnel carrying out demolitions in France and Holland
2 *Supplement to The London Gazette*, 26 July 1940, p. 4654 (https://www.thegazette.co.uk/London/issue/34907/supplement/4654/data.pdf).
3 TNA, WO 373/146/54, War Office and Ministry of Defence – Military Secretary's Department – Recommendations for Honours and Awards for Gallant and Distinguished Service (Army) - Kent Fortress Royal Engineers Territorial Army, Brazier to Gale, 17 Oct 1940

4 Ibid, Gale to D.M.O. & P. 5 July 1940
5 Ibid, V.C.I.G.S. to M.S., 22 Oct 1940
6 Ibid, Floyer-Acland to V.C.I.G.S., 23 Oct 1940
7 Ibid, V.C.I.G.S. to M.S. 24 Oct 1940
8 Brazier, C.C.H.& P.H. (ed) – *XD Operations*, (Pen & Sword Books, 2004), p. 157
9 TNA, WO 373/146/54, Ibid, Floyer-Acland (M.S.) to M.S.3 (Maj Illingworth), 31 Oct 1940
10 Ibid, War Office to H.M., 5 Nov 1940
11 Ibid.
12 Ibid, V.C.I.G.S. to M.S, 19 Aug 1940
13 Ibid, War Office to I.M., 5 Nov 1940
14 Ibid.
15 Ibid.
16 Ibid, *The London Gazette*, No. 35003, Friday, 29 November 1940